PRAISE FOR *THE POWER OF PLAYING OFFENSE*

"In both hockey and in business, establishing a winning culture takes commitment and the right plan. In *The Power of Playing Offense*, Paul Epstein shares one of the most detailed and easy-to-follow leadership playbooks ever developed. I recommend working hard to establish those core values and putting Epstein's plan to work for your organization. He and his book will help lead to something we all like to be a part of—a championship culture."

LUC ROBITAILLE

Hockey Hall of Fame Player; three-time Stanley Cup Champion; President, Los Angeles Kings

"Paul Epstein lives with meaning, mission, and motion. His energy is infectious, and his positivity radiates through the pages of this transformational playbook; a playbook to inspire a culture of leadership and get your entire team on the bus toward success—and significance."

JON GORDON

eight-time *Wall Street Journal* bestselling author, including, *The Energy Bus*

"I have seen firsthand the grit, passion, and perseverance that Paul Epstein leads with. It's one thing to achieve success with these qualities, but it's another to coach these leadership principles to others. In comes *The Power of Playing Offense*, a playbook to implement in our business and our lives."

BRIAN LAFEMINA

Chief Business Officer, LA 2028 Olympics; former NFL Executive

"In *The Power of Playing Offense*, Paul imparts practical and action-oriented lessons from the trenches of leadership. His people-first approach will resonate with leaders at every level, inspiring both teams and individuals who are determined and driven enough to take on the challenge."

RICH DIVINEY
retired Navy SEAL Officer, author, speaker

"Talent is the ultimate differentiator—but successful leadership is more than raw talent; it's the ability to unleash the full potential of that talent in yourself and others. *The Power of Playing Offense* delivers a tactical blueprint for how to do just that, detailing where the performance of people can be maximized, allowing our superpowers to be on full display."

GAIL STOLTZE
Executive Vice President, Human Resources, AEG

"In *The Power of Playing Offense*, Paul places the power of purpose at the forefront of your business model. Leading with purpose—with your 'why' and core commitments at the center all you do—does not mean managing without discipline. On the contrary, Paul shares the tactics and exercises to help leaders and coaches across the business ecosystem build a playbook for development and driven by results. He changes the long-held belief that motivating your executive team can only be fueled by competition with peers or opponents. Rather, our greatest advantage is understanding how our efforts and accomplishments fulfill our most meaningful personal goals—those far richer than those on a leaderboard. Lead with purpose. Lead with passion. Lead with a playbook that fosters a culture of teamwork, harnesses the power of passion and drives results."

SCOTT O'NEIL
Chief Executive Officer, Harris Blitzer Sports & Entertainment

"Paul Epstein is the master at playing offense to drive better outcomes in business and in life. In *The Power of Playing Offense*, he shares a proven system to inspire breakthrough levels of performance. The book is inspiring, actionable, and shows leaders how to unlock the full capacity of their teams and themselves. Your business will never be the same . . . highly recommend!"

JOSH LINKNER,
New York Times bestselling author; tech entrepreneur; venture capitalist

"In *The Power of Playing Offense*, Paul Epstein lays the foundation to propel teams from complacent to legendary. A seasoned business leader, Paul has quite literally written the playbook to success for teams and leaders alike."

CHAD ESTIS
Executive Vice President, Business Operations, Dallas Cowboys;
Executive Vice President, Legends

"In football, the most successful teams develop a plan and take deliberate and consistent steps toward achievement their goals every single day. Your leadership plan should be no different. Paul Epstein has provided the ultimate playbook for leaders that are driven to achieve their vision of success for themselves and their teams."

MERRIL HOGE
former NFL Player, former ESPN commentator, bestselling author

"Paul and I share a similar mission in life: empower others with tools to live with happiness and purpose so they can make a greater impact in the world. That might sound like a tall order, but that is exactly what *The Power of Playing Offense* delivers."

DAVID MELTZER
Co-Founder, Sports 1 Marketing; bestselling author; top business coach

"For anyone looking to level-up their leadership practice, *The Power of Playing Offense* should be an essential reference. Paul's playbook established a purposeful, actionable game plan that is designed to grow players into coaches and managers into leaders. It's time to level up."

TOM PENN

former President and Co-Owner, Los Angeles Football Club; ESPN analyst; NBA Executive

"Working in the NFL, there is no bigger believer in the value of a 'go-to' playbook than me. If you are a leader who is inspired to build the leaders of tomorrow, build high-performance teams, and build gold jacket culture, you've found your 'go-to' playbook in *The Power of Playing Offense.*"

ROBERT GALLO

Senior Vice President, Club Business Development, NFL

"Experiencing Paul's expertise around the organizational building blocks of mission, vision, and values was eye opening. He made the abstract concrete. The conceptual actionable. I'm excited for his playbook to now be shared with the world in *The Power of Playing Offense.*"

MARLA MESSING

Chief Executive Officer, United States Tennis Association, Southern California

"It's time to shift our mindsets from paycheck-driven to purpose-driven by applying the principles in *The Power of Playing Offense.* Whether personal, professional, or organizational, anybody looking to live and lead with purpose, this is your go-to guide."

AARON HURST

author, *The Purpose Economy*; Chief Executive Officer and Co-Founder, Imperative

"Constructing the right team, both on and off the field, is only the first step. True leadership is all about developing a plan that aligns personal and organizational success and doing the hard work necessary to create an environment that's conducive to both employee fulfillment and corporate achievement. In *The Power of Playing Offense*, Paul Epstein provides invaluable insights and a thorough plan on how to do just that."

JAMEY ROOTES
President, Houston Texans

"*The Power of Playing Offense* was written with one goal in mind: *Impact.* It is undoubtedly one of the most tangible and actionable playbooks on how to lead that we have ever seen. Every activity, exercise, framework, and tool has infinite value. Thanks to Paul Epstein, this is the game-changing book that will impact millions of lives."

GREG KISH
Head of Ticketed Revenue, SoFi Stadium

"With a shifting landscape in business, there has never been a more critical time to upskill our workforce. It starts by upskilling ourselves. *The Power of Playing Offense* is the guidebook packed with the skills, strategies, and tools we need to successfully lead the workforce of tomorrow."

SAM CAUCCI
Founder and Chief Executive Officer, 1Huddle

"*The Power of Playing Offense* challenges us all to lead with purpose, authenticity, and courage—characteristics that make Paul the ideal coach for this transformational journey to know who we are and why we serve."

MICHELE KAJIWARA
Senior Vice President, Premium Seating Sales and Service at Staples Center, AEG

"Paul Epstein's expertise is to maximize vision, purpose, and impact inside of an organization in order to create even greater impact outside an organization. *The Power of Playing Offense* provides a playbook for how to bring this to life, and it's accessible to us all."

DAVID SIEGEL

President and Chief Executive Officer, Los Angeles Sports Council

"According to an often-used sports cliché, 'defense wins championships.' In *The Power of Playing Offense*, Paul Epstein respectfully disagrees and shows why leaders in all walks of life must develop and execute a potent offensive game plan to help their teams achieve their goals."

TIM RYAN

radio color analyst, San Francisco 49ers; former NFL Player;
former NFL analyst, Fox Television

"Paul Epstein knows that teamwork is critical to winning championships—in sports and in business. In *The Power of Playing Offense*, he provides the ultimate playbook to achieve a winning culture and offers innovative tools to help organizations optimize their full potential."

BRAD SIMS

President and Chief Executive Officer, New York City Football Club

"A critical mass of our workforce are partially present and are just trying to survive. *The Power of Playing Offense* provides us with a cultural framework where all people thrive and know they matter. This empowering playbook exposes the reality that when all people have a seat at the table, organizations become optimized."

TORIAN RICHARDSON

investor, culture scientist, global executive coach

"Great athletes and teams recognize the importance of leading from the front and the strategy of going on the offensive. The same can be said of any front office, boardroom, factory, or classroom. *The Power of Playing Offense* is a great reminder of what it takes to be successful as a leader and as a teammate."

JARROD DILLON
Chief Marketing and Revenue Officer, Vinik Sports Group and Tampa Bay Lightning

"While many of us are after professional growth, what *The Power of Playing Offense* teaches us is that all growth starts from within. To achieve this personal transformation toward greater impact and fulfillment, you'll need a coach to guide the way. One who has already achieved their own transformation and is inspired to bring us along. Paul Epstein is one of the best coaches I know."

SUE ANN GONIS
EMBA Executive Coach and career consultant, University of Michigan, Ross School of Business; Executive and Leadership Coach, Sue Ann Gonis Coaching & Consulting

"Leading up to Super Bowl 50, both Paul and I found ourselves looking to achieve unprecedented industry feats from our unique perspectives. None of it would have happened without authentic partnerships, a quality that Paul exudes and this playbook will highlight. Meet Paul at the 50, as I once did. You won't regret it."

KEITH BRUCE
President, QuintEvents International; former Chief Executive Officer and President, Super Bowl 50 Host Committee

"Finally, a playbook that has answered the question, who's coaching the coaches? Many of us have been promoted from player to coach and were never provided a playbook on how to lead. *The Power of Playing Offense* was curated to solve this problem. Leave no page unturned. The impact it will create for your team, career, culture, and life, is infinite."

SANTOR NISHIZAKI
award-winning Chief Executive Officer; formerly with NASA and Disney Imagineering

"If you are looking for *the* book to transform your business and life, look no further. Having known Paul for years, I have watched all his expertise and leadership culminate into *The Power of Playing Offense*. Finally, here's a book filled with coaching tips and tools that feels as if it were written just for me."

ROB SINE
Chief Revenue Officer, AXS

"As the athletic director at UCLA for nearly two decades, I was fortunate to meet and build relationships with leaders across countless sports, entertainment, and business enterprises. What always stood out in those who were the most successful and respected by their peers was a set of clearly defined personal values by which that individual led. In *The Power of Playing Offense*, Paul Epstein provides a road map to success built upon a foundation of culture backed by salient leadership principles. Finding my 'why' and making decisions guided by my own set of personal values were the keys to my longevity as an athletic director. When you have that North Star, you can weather the storms and bear the criticism that comes with any high-profile role. The playbook that Paul provides takes the guesswork out of defining who you want to be as a leader, which then sets the stage for transformational personal and organizational growth."

DAN GUERRERO
former Athletic Director, UCLA

THE POWER OF PLAYING OFFENSE

www.amplifypublishing.com

The Power of Playing Offense:
A Leader's Playbook for Personal and Team Transformation

For more information, please contact:
Amplify Publishing
620 Herndon Parkway, Suite 320
Herndon, VA 20170
info@amplifypublishing.com

Library of Congress Control Number: 2020919925

CPSIA Code: PRV1120A

ISBN-13: 978-1-64543-624-9

Printed in the United States

To my future leader, PJ.

May you live and lead with purpose, happiness, and a spirit of playing offense.

This one's for you.

A LEADER'S PLAYBOOK FOR PERSONAL AND TEAM TRANSFORMATION

PAUL EPSTEIN
FORMER NFL AND NBA BUSINESS EXECUTIVE
FOUNDER OF PURPOSE LABS

CONTENTS

FOREWORD

Leaders set the tone for culture, and culture sets the tone for people. As each day passes, we increasingly need courageous leadership. So now the question becomes, what makes a great leader?

Mountains of books and research have been written on the traits, skills, and qualities that provide this answer. In my mind, one book easily rises to the top:

The Power of Playing Offense.

Paul Epstein is one of those great leaders. He inspired our leadership and sales team with a message of "playing offense" to expand our lens of impact on how we deliver happiness—which is our mission and core measure of success at Zoom.

Paul provides the map to this strategy in these key, game-changing principles in *The Power of Playing Offense*:

- Your company culture is the #1 most important thing to get right.
- The value of care is at the heart of winning teams and cultures.
- Putting people first is not a mantra; it is the foundation of leadership.

- Leadership is the engine that drives your organizational growth and potential.
- Before you lead others, you must first lead yourself.

The Power of Playing Offense emphasizes personal transformation, which is a key toward unlocking your team and organizational performance.

In that spirit, this book will help you discover what you stand for, what inspires you, and why you serve. It will provide clarity on your purpose to persevere so that you're armed with the grit and resilience needed to take on the inevitable challenges ahead.

Once you conquer your inside game, fulfillment and impact come in abundance, and the outside game of success takes care of itself. Even better, you'll have a team and organization to enjoy the journey with you because you created a culture of care together. And the best part is, you'll pave your path toward significance and legacy in the process.

In order to maximize your ability to do this, you'll need a courageous coach to serve as your guide, and a caring and vulnerable leader to share a playbook of their best days and worst days. *The Power of Playing Offense* is that playbook, and Paul Epstein is that coach—a coach who can inspire your team and organization going forward. This is an ultracandid look at the depths of leadership—both what it takes to thrive and the pitfalls to avoid.

At Zoom, we pride ourselves on a culture of care and are fully intentional in how we bring our culture to life. This ensures our mission endures.

While our culture is fueled by every employee on the inside, we ask for support from outside leaders along the way—specifically, leaders who care and align with our culture.

Paul's authenticity and purpose shined immediately, and his approach meshed perfectly with our philosophy at Zoom: *What makes people sense makes business sense.* In other words, it's the inside game of leadership and culture that will ultimately define winning the outside game in the marketplace.

While this book is designed for business and organizational leaders, I believe you will find the lessons, tools, activities, and insights universally applicable.

Because leadership starts with self, it can help you as much at home, in school, on the playing field, and in the community as it does in the boardroom.

I'm excited to see you play offense in your lives.

ERIC YUAN

FOUNDER AND CEO, ZOOM VIDEO COMMUNICATIONS

PREFACE

Trillion Dollar Coach author Bill Campbell once said, "Your title makes you a manager; your people will decide if you are a leader." *The Power of Playing Offense* was written to transform managers into leaders, so that every reader can and will inspire a followership to level up their lives, both personally and professionally.

So now I ask you—without title, influence, or authority, would anybody follow?

Think of the leader you would follow to no end. Likely none of those external factors caused you to choose whom you did. Odds are she or he inspired you to be your best, coached you to your full potential, and believed in you from day one.

Now, how are you showing up? Are you inspiring a team that would follow you to no end? Are you acting as the leader you wish you had?

Are you a leader who puts people first when it matters most?

The challenge is, many of us work and lead in organizations that preach from the mountain tops that they put people first. Until they don't. This short-term, results-obsessed mindset has a ripple effect where we lose trust, connection, and the loyalty of those who are closest to the work.

What if there was a playbook to spark the exact opposite?

To transform our teams from paycheck-driven to purpose-driven, from adversity to achievement, from disengaged to inspired, from controlled to connected, from success to success *and* significance.

If you want to show up as a leader who inspires people to follow, builds thriving teams, and cultivates championship culture, all while delivering best-in-class results—this is the playbook to show you the way.

PLAYING DEFENSE VERSUS PLAYING OFFENSE

Over a fifteen-year run in the business of professional sports, I became immersed in the world of high-performance teams and the impact of leadership on people and culture. As I began to understand the mindsets, habits, and practices required to show up and perform at your best, I was fascinated by what separated the elite from the pack—and how those elites led others to do the same. Over time, I recognized how these all-too-rare leadership skills could materialize into transformations. I seized the opportunity to implement and refine these practices. I've now curated these lessons and insights into an innovative framework of five pillars—which you'll soon learn in great detail.

I call it *playing offense.*

Playing offense is an all-gas-no-brakes methodology for personal and team transformation. It is a mindset that will inspire action and empower you to lead in business and across all aspects of life.

There are two types of people around us. Those who play defense—and those who play offense.

- Playing defense is playing from your heels. Playing offense is playing on your toes.
- Playing defense is playing not to lose. Playing offense is playing to win.
- Playing defense is letting the market dictate the terms. Playing offense is operating on your terms.

Playing offense is where leadership starts—with an inward look, competing with yourself, and taking full ownership of your actions, inspired by the possibilities and opportunities in front of you. After coaching this methodology within the sports business and other industries, I have seen the optimized performance and heightened levels of impact that result.

This is playing offense—and I wouldn't want to live or lead any other way. By the end of this book, I trust you'll feel the same.

THE FIVE PILLARS OF PLAYING OFFENSE

Let's briefly introduce the five pillars and transformations of playing offense—followed by the impact for you and your collective team.

1. **LIVE WITH CHAMPIONSHIP PURPOSE** – *Transform from paycheck-driven to purpose-driven.*

   INDIVIDUALLY, purpose is the fuel for your daily quest for meaning.
   COLLECTIVELY, purpose connects your team to something bigger than themselves.

2. **BE THE STORM CHASER** – *Transform from adversity to achievement.*

   INDIVIDUALLY, grit and courage are needed to endure the storms of business and life.
   COLLECTIVELY, resilience will form as your team bounces back from the inevitable adversities ahead—both internal and external.

3. **SALUTE THE LONG SNAPPER** – *Transform from disengaged to inspired.*

   INDIVIDUALLY, this is your opportunity to let people know they belong and matter.
   COLLECTIVELY, this recognition is what elevates the potential of every member on your team, when their superpowers are unleashed.

4. **EMBODY GOLD JACKET CULTURE** – *Transform from command and control to camaraderie and connection.*

   INDIVIDUALLY, earn your hall-of-fame worthy jacket and inspire others to do the same.
   COLLECTIVELY, culture is THE competitive advantage—inside your four walls and in the marketplace.

5. **LEAVE IT BETTER THAN YOU FOUND IT** – *Transform from success to success AND significance.*

   INDIVIDUALLY, welcome to a life of legacy, and continue to pay it forward.
   COLLECTIVELY, an environment of abundance, contribution, and impact will soon galvanize your team—the leaders of tomorrow.

We'll revisit these pillars throughout the book, and you'll see the following visual representation at the start of each of the five pillars. As we work our way down the field, I'll provide guidance so you can make the most out of your journey. There is even a printable copy of this graphic at **WWW.POWEROFPLAYINGOFFENSE.COM** so you can take some notes and keep them handy as you progress through the book to then share the experience with your team.

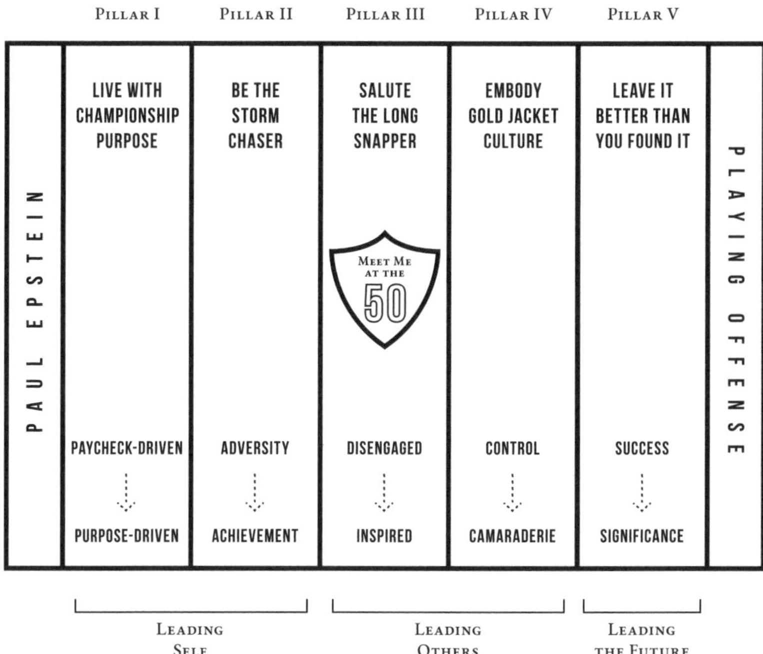

WHAT TO EXPECT FROM THIS BOOK

The Power of Playing Offense progresses through five pillars. Each pillar consists of three chapters filled with anecdotes, topical business principles, interactive exercises, and engaging case studies.

Within each chapter, you'll see "**TIME-OUTS**" intended to be quick-burst activities that you can activate, plan, or implement within minutes of reading. Think of it as a time-out while watching the big game, but instead of running to get a snack, you're leveling up your leadership.

To close each chapter, you will have the opportunity to "**APPLY THE PLAYBOOK.**" This will cover a broad range of high-utility trainings and exercises for you and your team—all designed to make you better on Monday.

A complete list of Time-Outs, Applying the Playbook activities, and other ready-to-use tools can be found in the appendix.

Many of these lessons will have supporting resources at **WWW.POWEROFPLAYINGOFFENSE.COM** to ensure the learning continues well beyond the last page. Consider the book and complementary online resources your leadership coaching manual for years to come. As proven with others who have *played offense*, when these lessons are applied, you will:

- **BUILD** leaders, teams, and culture.
- **GROW** yourself, followers, and careers.
- **INSPIRE** vision, action, and performance.
- **LEAD** with purpose, authenticity, and courage.
- **LIVE** a life of fulfillment, impact, and legacy.

The Power of Playing Offense is chock-full of front-row insights I've gained from leading in NFL and NBA boardrooms, advising Fortune 100 organizations, and coaching leaders across industry. You won't get lost in educational theory or consulting fluff. On the contrary, this book is written and backed by real experience from the trenches of leadership. You will learn as much from the losses as you do from the wins. Most importantly you will level up your leadership game to transform your career and life.

Meet me at the 50, and consider me your coach for the journey.

It's time to play offense!

Photo courtesy of San Francisco 49ers

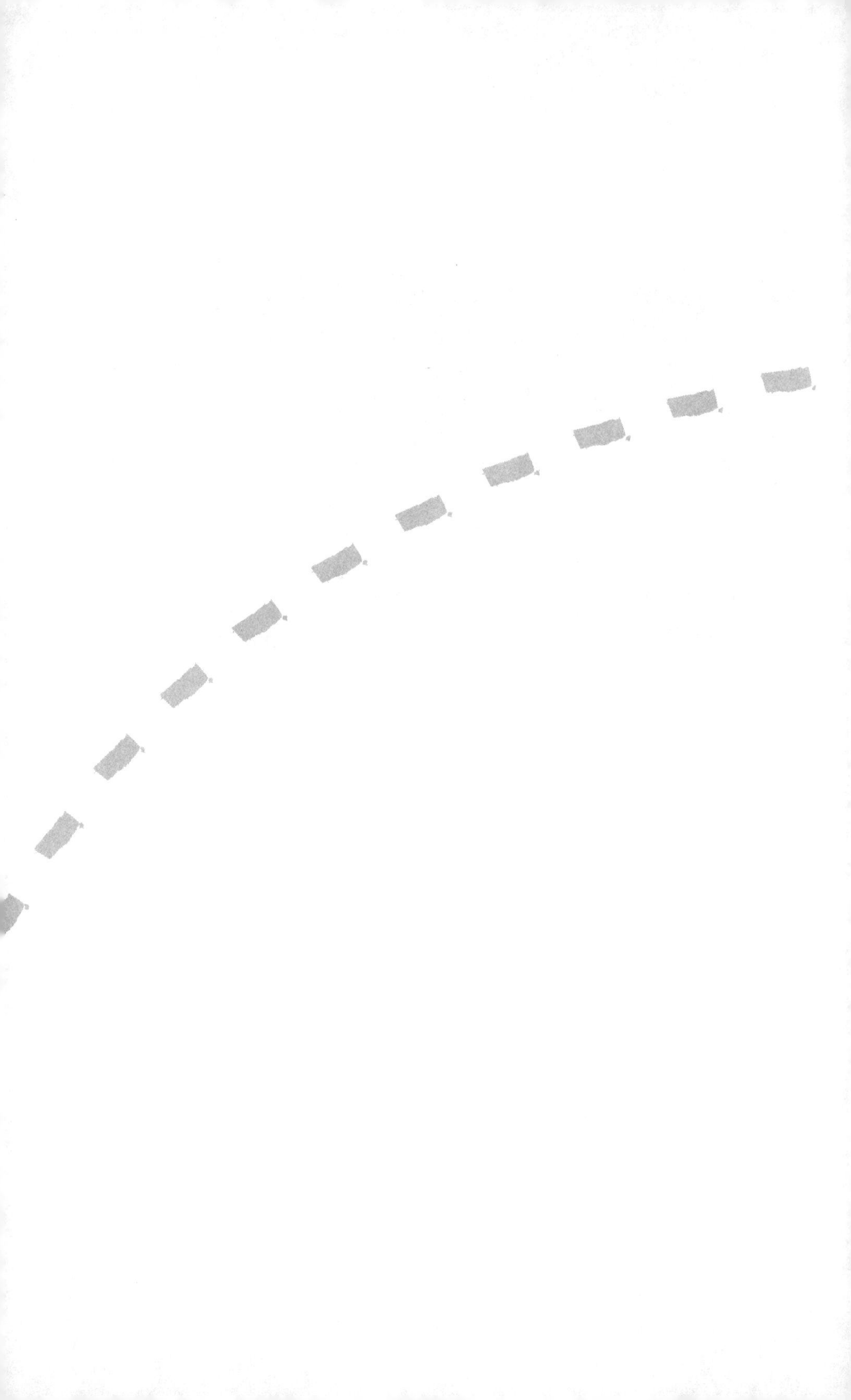

PROLOGUE

Welcome to the professional sports business. You may not be a star quarterback, but you are a star in the boardroom—working in your dream industry.

The intensity of the playing side sparks the energy of the business side, and you get to feel a priceless sense of passion every day of the week.

As you drive into the office, you see a palatial stadium appear from a distance. Minutes later, you approach then pull past the security gates. Players' cars on the right, management on the left.

Today there's a special vibe in the air. As you step out of the car, you see a red carpet leading up to the grand lobby entrance. Set-up is underway for tonight's premium client event. Celebrity guests and hall of fame alumni are expected. You'll be at the podium to make the opening remarks.

As you enter the lobby, the organization's most prestigious trophies, championship rings, and memorabilia are on proud display. Your team owner walks by and greets you, asking how your weekend was, then acknowledging he'll see you tonight.

Welcome to a Monday morning. Now, imagine what gameday is like.

This is not a fairy tale. This is reality, as you are immersed in the high-profile and high stakes world of professional sports.

You know you're one of the lucky ones.

But don't get too comfortable. There's a line of thousands waiting for you to slip. Waiting for you to take your foot off the gas. Aspiring to fill your coveted seat.

Game on.

THE DAY I LEFT SPORTS

I was heading up sales and business development for the San Francisco 49ers, loving my coworkers, loving my team, and loving life—in and out of Levi's Stadium. With a vision to prepare myself for the C-suite, I knew I had some holes, some of which could come back to haunt me. To date, all of my functional experience was in sales and marketing. With aspirations to lead a sports organization, I needed to gain the knowledge of how business unit heads across all verticals think, operate, and make decisions. So, I made a bold decision of my own—one that was not the norm in my industry. My decision led me to an environment I never anticipated returning to. After a thirteen-year gap, I was going back to school.

With a concentration in leadership development, I entered the Executive MBA program at the University of Michigan. I joined the cohort based in Los Angeles, where we would spend about 80 percent of our time over the twenty-one-month journey; the other 20 percent was back at the mothership in Ann Arbor, strategically timed in the nonwinter months. We Angelinos aren't a very pleasant people when it dips below a brisk fifty degrees!

This was my opportunity to level up as a leader and surround myself with some of the best and brightest across industries and roles so I could return with an elevated career trajectory and a broadened perspective.

In the sports business, I always had mentors. Within my MBA program, for the first time in a business setting, I had an executive coach. Little did I know that our first coaching call would open my previously fixed mindset. That mindset was set to continue the climb within my dream industry—an industry you don't leave on your terms when things are going well.

I still remember my former boss in the NFL League Office saying the easiest thing to do is stay on the treadmill you're on. My executive coach challenged that notion. By the time we hung up the call, I started to believe there could be other treadmills to run on.

You want the details?

Let's do it.

My coach got a feel for my role, then asked a series of questions: "What do you love about it? What do you hate about it? What's in between?"

After I answered, she asked me to go deeper on what I loved about my job.

I said, "I love the people side. I love being a coach, just like you. I love molding, growing, and developing talent. I love motivating with the hope of inspiring. I love when people max out on their potential because of the belief I poured into them. When they break through, it literally lights me up."

She excitedly responded, "That's fantastic! Now, on a good day, what percentage of your time are you doing that?"

Ugh. I started to slouch down in my seat, knowing the reality was far from ideal. Purely to save face in the moment, I padded the truth and said 20 percent.

She then probed, "If I were to wave a wand and you became your boss tomorrow, would that number, 20 percent, go up, down, or sideways?"

In my head, I thought, *More strategy, less people*. So I said, "Down."

Then came the question that changed everything. It turns out, it would go on to alter my entire career and life plan.

My coach asked, "So, what are you after?"

It was a simple yet profound question that I had never thought of, but was ready to hear. I had been fixated on this linear path. This treadmill where A led to B then to C. It was predictable. I could see each step. I knew others that had already taken the path. I too was capable of continuing on the treadmill. It was just a matter of time until the next opportunity tapped me on the shoulder. I felt fully in control of my destiny.

Processing my thoughts around "what I was after" left me with a feeling I had not sensed in over a decade. One of freedom. One of possibility. One of opportunity. One of "What if . . .?"

I was excited to not know all the answers. Excited about the blank canvas. And excited for the ability to pave my path and author my story.

But how could I?

I had invested nearly a decade and a half of sweat equity in the sports business. I loved the industry more than words could describe, and I loved the 49ers organization to no end. They were first class through and through—treating my family like gold. I loved our leadership. I believed in our culture. I adored my team. My career was on a fast track. I was running away from absolutely nothing.

And yet, prompted by my coach's question, there was an undeniable tug in my mind. I was now thinking about what I was running toward versus what I could be leaving behind.

This unanticipated feeling was building momentum. It was not optional; I was going to get off the treadmill.

But when? To do what?

The Power of Playing Offense will fill in the holes of my story—and I hope encourage you to write yours with renewed passion and purpose.

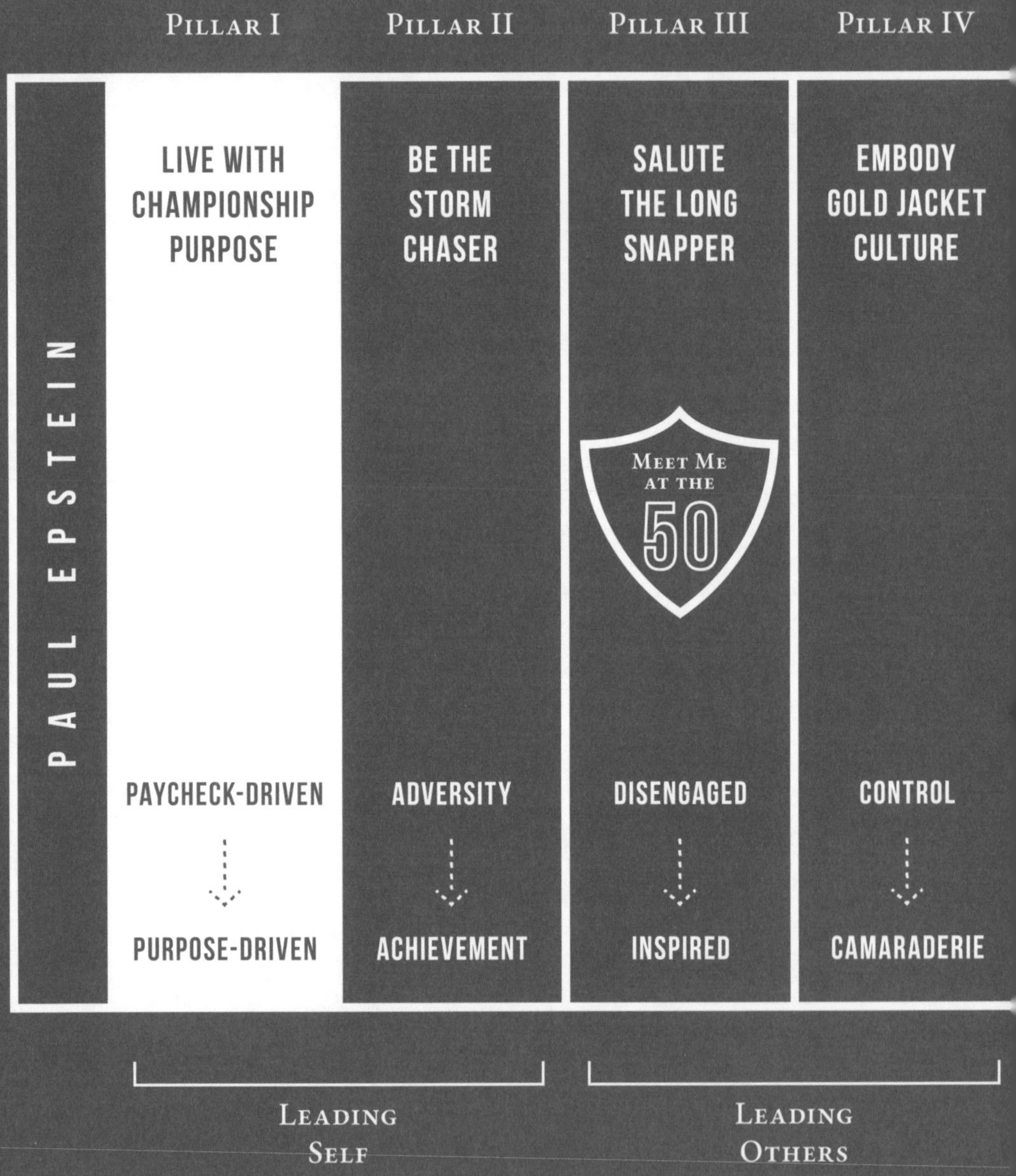

PAUL EPSTEIN

Pillar I	Pillar II	Pillar III	Pillar IV
LIVE WITH CHAMPIONSHIP PURPOSE	BE THE STORM CHASER	SALUTE THE LONG SNAPPER	EMBODY GOLD JACKET CULTURE
PAYCHECK-DRIVEN	ADVERSITY	DISENGAGED	CONTROL
↓	↓	↓	↓
PURPOSE-DRIVEN	ACHIEVEMENT	INSPIRED	CAMARADERIE

Meet Me at the 50

Leading Self (Pillars I–II)

Leading Others (Pillars III–IV)

Pillar V

LEAVE IT BETTER THAN YOU FOUND IT

PLAYING OFFENSE

SUCCESS

↓

SIGNIFICANCE

Leading the Future

LIVE WITH CHAMPIONSHIP PURPOSE

It is much easier to win the game when we care deeply about the game, and that level of care is only possible when it is rooted in purpose. Purpose establishes *why* we do what we do. It solidifies who we are at our truest inner core of identity. Purpose lights up as our North Star, to give us clarity and intention when we get out of bed. It is our personal mission. Purpose is the glue that keeps our values aligned, informs our beliefs, guides our decisions, and influences how we show up in the world, personally and professionally.

"When you're inspired with purpose, it's all gas, no brakes, and it never stops."

PAUL EPSTEIN

Within our profession, we will work more than 100,000 hours over the course of our lives. That number will either give us fuel or deplete us of it. The gap is purpose. Purpose can add fuel to the journey we're already on or give us the spark toward a new and more inspiring quest.

It's often said that when your 'Why' is strong enough, the 'How' takes care of itself. That is the power of purpose. It gets us to take the first step with passion and belief. Purpose keeps us on the treadmill, especially on the days we want to get off.

To unearth your mission, purpose will give you the courage needed to start the journey. The good news is you are not in this alone. I was ignited by going through my own transformation of purpose years ago. Now I am your guide, and I've made the pursuit of helping others discover their own purpose my life calling—from professional sports executives to Fortune 100 leaders, MBAs, Founders and CEOs, to professional athletes. You are about to embark on the same expedition that I have coached them through.

The Power of Playing Offense will reveal the blueprint for how to discover, activate, and align your purpose to something bigger than yourself, to then amplify your purpose so you can create greater impact within your team, organization, community, and beyond.

CHAPTER 1 *will help you reflect on your 'Why,' from a playbook learned at the 49ers.*

CHAPTER 2 *will reveal your authenticity, which can hide under the many masks we wear.*

CHAPTER 3 *will lead you to your tribe by discovering your true identity.*

With that, let's dive in.

1

FROM CAREER TO CALLING

Thirty days out, a calendar hold came from the president of the San Francisco 49ers. Executive Leadership Retreat. CordeValle Golf Resort. August 2–3, 2016. No details on the agenda.

The afternoon of August 3, just as the retreat was about to close, we were each asked to share two words or less in reflection. As we went down the line, I heard "inspired," "encouraged," "motivated." Then came my turn, and I answered, "Life-changing."

Immediately, heads snapped up in shock. Even the facilitators did double-takes. I didn't know how my life would change, but I was convinced something special had just happened.

"The two most important days in your life are the day you are born, and the day you find out why."

MARK TWAIN

humorist, known as the father of American literature

FINDING MY 'WHY'

It was at this retreat that I found my 'Why.' Through an immersive two-day experience, we each explored our individual life journeys. We revealed life's biggest moments to ourselves and to each other, triumph and tragedy, our most significant peaks and valleys, where we knew life would never be the same. This emotional arc was the backdrop, and every participant got out what they put in.

In my case, I was ALL IN, turning over every significant stone of life. I left transformed and inspired.

From the drive home through the coming weeks, I shared what I'd experienced with my inner circle. As you would expect, they were excited to hear my passion, and they could sense the curiosity and bullish eagerness for what would lie ahead. Some even asked what they had spiked the punch with.

That following Monday, I secretly was hoping to feel something magical on the inside, expecting the transformation I had just experienced to infuse each day with my newly found purpose. Instead, it was more of the same. Back to the firefighting. Back to business planning. Back to the grind, as we always used to say. This repetitive reality started to bother me, significantly. I began to feel an uneasy tension I had never sensed.

Why the tension? Life was good. Nothing was broke, so why fix it?

But now my life lens had a different shade. I sought purpose. I became fixated on my 'Why,' which was "to inspire purpose in others so they can play offense in life." I started to imagine a world where I could bring this to life each day—inspired to get out of bed and make a difference, all to be fulfilled at the end of the day, then equally excited to do it again the next.

As I snapped back into reality, I fell back in line, laboring and drifting one day at a time. Over the coming weeks, the only constant was the continued internal tension.

It became apparent that my 'What' was not aligned with my 'Why.' Pre–Why, I would have let this feeling sit and linger, and my daily actions would simply get done as they got done; I'd have had no resolve to shape them into something with meaning. Post–Why, this uneasiness became unacceptable. I was on a mission to play offense and live my purpose—and not a damn thing could get in the way.

I knew what I had to do.

WITH PURPOSE COMES OPPORTUNITY

In January 2020 I became the proud founder of Purpose Labs. I was graced with a Rolodex of relationships I wouldn't trade for the world, and my first client was a rising NFL executive whom I had met while training his leadership team years after my fateful retreat. He later admitted there was something that struck him as I introduced myself to his group that day. As he recalls, I shared how "finding my Why" had changed my life and that I'd never "felt more alive." My enthusiasm prompted him to call me. "That's exactly what I'm after," he said—and with those words, a partnership toward purpose kicked off.

As we developed a relationship, his performance and potential were unquestioned. What was missing was his deeper meaning, his North Star, his 'Why.' Without that sense of purpose, his contributions felt limited, his impact unclear. This led to a lack of fulfillment and inspiration within the work he was doing. While he was grateful for the opportunity to be a leader in the NFL, the initial feeling of being a kid in a candy store was waning, and he wanted to reignite the spark he knew was inside. But it had to be tied to something bigger than himself. It had to be fused to purpose.

I asked him to meet me at the 50, which is my philosophy for all partnerships. It takes two equally invested individuals or parties to come together, lock arms, and run through the wall together.

Our partnership was off to the races. Personal and professional vision exercises. Understanding who he was on his best day. A deep dive on strengths, gifts, talents, and passions . . . all intertwined with life reflection. We then shifted our energies from personal to professional development, including executive branding, job and career crafting, goal and impact alignment, coupled with clarity around legacy.

Over months, we accomplished what we had set out to do. We unearthed his 'Why' and core values, and he left empowered with a lens on how to push forward on life's most significant actions and decisions. As a cherry on top, he was promoted months later to an opportunity significantly more aligned with his purpose.

"Paul walked me through a life-discovery process, delivering a true aha' moment in which I uncovered my 'Why,' and I have never felt more alive," he said in his assessment of our time together.

This is *why* I do what I do. Purpose can deliver opportunity for us all—and we all deserve to feel alive.

"Don't ask yourself what the world needs. Ask yourself what makes you come alive, and then go do it. Because what the world needs is people who have come alive."

HOWARD THURMAN

author, educator, and civil rights leader

BECOMING THE WHY COACH OF THE 49ERS

Purpose Labs would have never formed had it not been for my experience at the 49ers. Post–Why, I had to tackle my tension head on.

I called a team meeting and revealed the transformation I had experienced at the retreat weeks earlier. Seeing the intrigue in the room, I then asked if anybody would like to find their 'Why.' Some hands went up; others emailed me later in the day. Bring it on.

Over the coming months, we individually found a private space in Levi's Stadium where I could help my committed teammates find their respective 'Whys.'

It immediately rekindled the sensation I'd felt leaving the retreat earlier in the month. I FELT ALIVE. I could see it in the eyes of others as they lit up with purpose and meaning. Our time together unearthed numerous North Stars and personal missions. I sensed the energy that sparked from them to gain clarity on *why* they do what they do and what gets them out of bed each morning—which, in turn, became the spark for me to invest myself even further as a Why Coach.

In the hours invested together during each Why Discovery Process, our relationships and connections surpassed what we had built over the course of working together for years.

Titles were out the window. There was no longer a boss–subordinate relationship. It was a partnership. It was an opportunity to meet at the 50, where I could serve as a coach rather than a manager. Interestingly, the closer our connections became, the less I had to "manage." This authentic trust brought out a side of others' gifts, talents, and passions that I had not seen. It also exposed to me a flaw in many people's leadership styles, including my own to that point. When we don't know our people from the inside out, our relationships are thin, are only built for the good times, and will crumble in the bad. This surface-based approach will typically lead to disappointing results and dispiriting work lives if we let it spiral out of control.

In this case, post–Why discoveries, purpose became embedded in our team DNA, and the tangible impact became evident. Engagement and productivity skyrocketed, and performance followed. We simultaneously experienced significant growth in revenues. While I would never suggest that it was wholly based on these transformations, it became evident that personal growth can be a catalyst for fiscal growth, and that became difficult to ignore.

I started to obsess about scaling this impact beyond my team. How could we infuse the power of purpose throughout the 49ers organization?

With that, the business plan that led to the foundation of the 49ers Academy was authored around the ethos of *People-Purpose-Performance*. Weeks later, we were approved to start the venture!

Beyond it getting approved, it ignited my own sense of purpose where I finally felt I could live my 'Why' each and every day. The most liberating part was I no longer felt like it was the "next step" on a career escalator. I was no longer focused on the treadmill I had been on for over a decade. I now felt like I was contributing to “a calling”—to serve as Why Coach for the 49ers.

This calling led me to facilitate ‘Why’ discoveries for every member of the 49ers Academy. Once others in the organization caught wind, I was approached by dozens of individuals. The momentum only grew from there. Though I'll keep names confidential, I was able to coach people throughout the 49ers front office, both from the business and the football side of the organization. Each ‘Why’ experience felt like a dream come true. While others thanked me after our time together, I felt even more thankful to them—for allowing me to live my ‘Why’ and step into my calling.

“Finding my ‘Why’ fundamentally changed my life. It’s the greatest gift I’ve ever received, and now I’ve dedicated the rest of my life to share this gift of purpose with others.”

PAUL EPSTEIN

THE ROI OF PURPOSE

While many view purpose as a "nice to have," the evidence of its connection to the bottom line is more transparent by the day; the business case for purpose is quite clear. At a high level, purpose-driven companies outperform the S&P by 400 percent, purpose-driven employees are 225 percent more productive, and consumers would prefer to spend their money with a company nine out of ten times.[1]

Still not convinced?

Here's more on the ROI of Purpose. In the following two graphics, you'll see some examples of research about the monumental impact when purpose is taken seriously—for internal and external stakeholders. Internal stakeholders include you, your team, and all employees. External stakeholders include shareholders, the marketplace, and consumers.

> *"If you aren't fully embracing the Purpose Economy by now and transforming your entire organization, you are going to join the likes of Blockbuster, RadioShack, Sears, Kodak, and Tower Records."*
>
> **AARON HURST**
>
> author of *The Purpose Economy*

THE ROI OF PURPOSE FOR INTERNAL STAKEHOLDERS

30%	50%	64%
of purpose-driven professionals are **MORE LIKELY TO BE HIGH PERFORMERS**[2]	of purpose-driven professionals are **MORE LIKELY TO BE IN LEADERSHIP POSITIONS**[3]	of purpose-driven professionals have **HIGHER LEVELS OF FULFILLMENT AT WORK**[4]

More than

9 out of 10

employees are **WILLING TO TRADE A PERCENTAGE OF THEIR LIFETIME EARNINGS** for greater meaning at work.[5]

HIGHEST-PERFORMING EMPLOYEES ARE

3x

MORE LIKELY TO WORK FOR A COMPANY WITH A STRONG SENSE OF PURPOSE.

Yet only 13% said their organization is differentiated by a "purpose-driven mission."[6]

For more on the most comprehensive research on purpose, visit **SCIENCEOFPURPOSE.ORG**

THE ROI OF PURPOSE FOR EXTERNAL STAKEHOLDERS

15:1

Purpose-driven company **STOCK PRICES OUTPERFORM THE MARKET**[7]

202%

HIGHER LIKELIHOOD REVENUE GROWTH for purpose-driven companies[8]

73%

of global consumers will **SWITCH TO HIGHER-PURPOSE BRANDS**[9]

Purpose-led brands saw their **VALUATION SURGE BY**

175%

over the past 12 years, versus a growth rate of just

70%

for listless brands uncertain of their role.[10]

Purpose-driven enterprises **GREW BY**

1,681%

COMPARED TO THE S&P 500 AVERAGE OF

118%.[11]

For more on the most comprehensive research on purpose, visit SCIENCEOFPURPOSE.ORG

PAYCHECK-DRIVEN TO PURPOSE-DRIVEN

If money were no object, what would you do? Would your career path, industry, and organization stay the course? Call a slight audible? Or do a complete 180?

The Japanese model of *ikigai* (reason for being) provides an illustration of this pickle we often find ourselves in—is it about the paycheck or the purpose? Frankly, the majority of the world finds itself in the paycheck bucket. We do what we do not because we love it, but because we have to. It puts food on the table. Others rely on us.

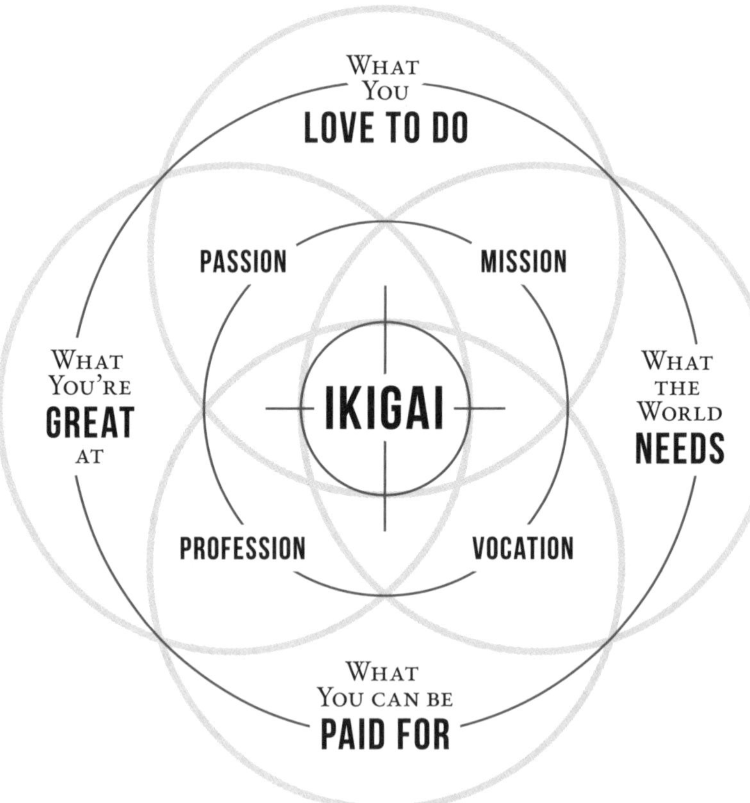

Consequently, using the *ikigai* model, we largely fall in the "profession" space. Some of us sneak into a "vocation." Rarely do we feel "passion," and "mission" seems like a pipe dream. Until we find our reason for being, our *ikigai*—that bullseye that we discover is our calling—we will live in a world that feels scarce instead of abundant. We will lose sight of what authentically matters, hollow from purpose, with a lack of vitality and enthusiasm to launch into each day. Ultimately, we all want to make a difference and feel part of something bigger than ourselves. The challenge is that our profession can only take us so far unless we believe in *why* we do it.

SIX FIGURES TO SEVEN DOLLARS

Straight from undergrad at USC, I found myself working for a Fortune 10 company as a territory sales manager with six-figure earning potential. Part of that experience had me riding around in a sporty Dodge Caravan from retail to wholesale accounts anywhere they sold our products. On the drive between accounts, I would keep myself entertained with ESPN Radio, never missing a beat of the action. Whoever said radio ads don't work, I'd beg to differ.

NFL Draft guru Mel Kiper's loud, energetic voice came through my speakers: "Have you ever wanted to work in sports? Have you ever dreamed of working for your favorite NFL, MLB, NBA, NHL team?"

I flew down the road yelling, "YES, YES, YES!" at the top of my lungs.

Mel said, "Call 1-877-SMWW-NOW."

I pulled over immediately while catching a glimpse of the speedometer, driving 70 in a 35mph zone. Safe and sound, juices flowing, I made the call.

SMWW stood for Sports Management Worldwide. I got the intel: an eight-week online course on how to learn the business of sports revenue management. If you turned some heads, SMWW would introduce you to their network of sports industry contacts.

I didn't even know this was possible. You can actually work in sports?!

Eight weeks later, they made true to their word and called the LA Clippers on my behalf. It was for an inside sales position, making seven dollars an hour, starting at a four-hour shift to earn your way up to an eight-hour shift, with minimal commissions, no benefits, and less than a 25 percent success rate to get promoted into the full-time ranks. I felt blessed and grateful to even be considered.

Back to *ikigai*—I'm doing what I love, I'm doing what I'm good at; of course the world needs sports, and they're actually paying me for it. Dream come true!

Until it wasn't.

A year later and multiple promotions in, I decided to leave sports (the first time) for a very clear and simple reason. I felt drawn to something that was evading me: money.

In sports, as great as it is, you sacrifice two things compared to other industries: time and money. The first I could live with, but the second became bothersome for a young sports pro at the top of the sales board feeling like he was making pennies on the dollar. At the time, my friends were killing it in commercial real estate. After a late night at Staples Center, we would always meet and hit the downtown LA scene. I wanted the lifestyle. So, I decided to jump ship.

I joined a top commercial brokerage in LA and got through the onboarding gauntlet. Within my first year, I held the largest single paycheck that I've seen in my life (to this day), and I expected to feel like I had "made it." The feeling never came. The zeros at the end of the check felt worthless. I knew I had made a mistake. The realization shaped what I have valued ever since and has helped me make decisions that reflect those values.

PURPOSE IS THE FUEL OF COURAGE

It takes courage to stand tallest when fear and risk are highest. Courage is not the absence of these elements; it is acting in spite of them. Easier said than done. The first step is the hardest one of all. When faced with major decisions in life, we often fall back to a place of psychological safety. Our brains are wired to prevent pain, danger, and suffering; thus, we avoid risk at all costs. Our default is to gravitate toward comfort, stability, and security above all else. While this may have been useful for a caveman looking for dinner, for a young person in a world of opportunities, it can hinder your attempt to find what will fill your days with purpose.

So, how do you burst through this barrier to action when your mind tells you to be content with what you have, but your gut and heart tell you to go for it?

This is where we can bank on the power of purpose. Purpose gives us the motive behind the curtain. It's the meaning beneath the surface. It's *why* we are urged and moved to do it.

Purpose gives us the courage to start the journey. To empower a growth mindset. To seek a more inspiring vision. To expand our potential. To take massive action when we're *called* to. Purpose shifts our mindset from hurdles, obstacles, and why we canNOT do something to possibilities, opportunities, and why we CAN do something.

MY JERRY MAGUIRE MOMENT

In the spring of 2017, I was riding a natural high coming off of the prior year's 'Why' discovery, now well into my chapter of serving as the Why Coach within the 49ers. This passion project provided the jolts of purpose and passion that I needed while I continued to serve as head of sales and business development for the team.

My ultimate aspiration was to one day run the entire business operation for a professional sports franchise, and I knew I'd have some holes to plug if I wanted to earn respect from every seat in the boardroom. So, I decided to accelerate this process by pursuing my Executive MBA at the University of Michigan, to surround myself with a tribe of leaders across industries and engulf myself in a two-year crash course in leadership development and a top MBA curriculum, all while juggling my responsibilities at the 49ers.

Little did I know that two months into the program, I would have a conversation with my new executive coach that would alter the trajectory of my career and life as a whole.

As I shared in the prologue, my coach asked me the simple, yet profound question, "So, what are you after?" It kept me up at night for weeks.

Professionally, I had everything I could dream of. Dream industry, dream career path, dream organization, dream team—what could be better?

Turns out I had an answer. I wanted to *feel alive*.

This life-altering conversation with my coach enlightened me that I need to feel energized by living with purpose and passion every day. Life is too short to not play offense.

Even though I was perfectly happy doing what I did—I felt great about where I worked and who I was doing it for—I only *loved* 20 percent of my day-to-day. The other 80 percent was filled with meetings, administrative duties, closed-door strategy, and putting out fires. What I *really* wanted to do was be a coach for my team, in the trenches of the locker room right by my players' sides, to develop their full potential and build an inspiring culture of purpose and impact.

Realizing that every daily activity either gives you fuel or depletes it was game-changing. Now, I analyze what I do in those two buckets; there's no in-between. We're all likely to work more than 100,000 hours over the course of our lives (more hours than we sleep or spend with our family). Why would we go through that journey without purpose?

"In the end, it is impossible to have a great life unless it is a meaningful life. And it is very difficult to have a meaningful life without meaningful work."

JIM COLLINS

author of *Good to Great*

Jerry Maguire infamously made his bold decision to leave his agency and asked, "Who wants to come with me?" In my case, I just had to be true to the mirror. Purpose gave me the courage to take the first step toward my calling, and I haven't looked back since. I decided to join the Chapman & Co. Leadership Institute, the same group that facilitated my Why Discovery with the 49ers. Fascinating how it all came back full circle.

PURPOSE-DRIVEN LEADERSHIP

Bob Chapman, CEO of Barry-Wehmiller (the $3 billion parent organization of the Leadership Institute), wrote *Everybody Matters: The Extraordinary Power of Caring for Your People Like Family*. I had the pleasure of getting to know Bob over the years, and this describes his philosophy to a T. He didn't call his ten thousand-plus global employees "reports." He referred to them as his "span of care." He viewed every person in his organization not as a faceless worker but as somebody's son or daughter. Bob is one of the pioneers in the quickly accelerating purpose movement and believes that purpose is not in opposition to profit. Rather, people, purpose, and performance exist in harmony.

The way Bob treated people and let everybody know they mattered reminded me of my former boss at the NFL League Office. I once referred to my former boss as a "father figure" because he treated me like a second son behind closed doors. With the intensity of a Super Bowl record-breaking campaign upon us, it was the private, late-night conversations I'll always remember. He took an interest in my life in ways other leaders hadn't. I wasn't a producer. I was just Paul, the whole person—and I felt like I mattered.

WHO HAS ACCESS TO PURPOSE?

To feel like we matter, our contributions must have meaning. Once we have meaning, our purpose comes to life, and the impact we create can be even greater. A life of purpose is a life of making a difference—isn't that what we're after?

The great news is purpose is accessible to us all. Unfortunately, not everybody feels this way.

There are barriers to purpose for some. In my opinion, these are solely barriers in the mind. In reality, we all have access to purpose. It's at our fingertips right now.

Below are the top perceived barriers to purpose. I'll call them "myths." I'll then counter each myth with a "truth" to ease our minds, with a hope to activate purpose for us all.

MYTH #1

Purpose is only for "high society" or people that are "well-to-do."

TRUTH #1

Purpose has no correlation to external riches or status in life. Authentic purpose is tied to your intrinsic sense of meaning. If you feel that your daily contributions and impact matter, you have already taken the initial steps of living with purpose. Purpose doesn't cost a cent.

MYTH #2

I'm in a junior role and don't have the opportunity to build purpose into my job.

TRUTH #2

Look no further than the global pandemic of 2020 and ask yourself, did every employee in our hospitals matter? Did the front lines of our first responders make a difference? Did the back-of-house staff at restaurants serve a purpose? How about the brave delivery women and men that risked their own health for all of us? Purpose does not discriminate based on role. It's the mindset with which we approach our roles.

MYTH #3

Purpose has to be around a major cause.

TRUTH #3

While this is a common belief, major causes are only a small fraction of the purposeful work done in the world. Perhaps major humanitarian or social impact causes are the most publicized aspects of purpose, but there are countless options and ways for us to contribute in other service and purpose-oriented ways. Take what I do as an example. I help people, teams, and organizations find their purpose. My clients and partners then integrate purpose in their daily work. We largely serve in the business space. Major cause or not, there is purpose in the work we do.

MYTH #4

I want to follow my purpose but can't take a financial step back.

TRUTH #4

I hear this all the time, from my inner circle to my business network at large. Purpose-related opportunities have minimal correlation with income. Purpose is less about the opportunity itself and more about why you want the opportunity and what the opportunity means to you. If anything, purpose will have a positive impact on income because you'll believe in the meaning of the work and be more fulfilled by the work. When you love what you do, you won't feel like you are working a day in your life. You tend to do well for yourself (financially and beyond) when you're living and working with purpose.

KNOWING YOUR TEAM INSIDE OUT

How well do you REALLY know each person on your team?

- Do you know their personal motivations?
- What gets them out of bed?
- Their biggest life moments and memories?
- Why they do what they do?
- Whether they love what they do?
- What they REALLY want to do?
- Greatest mentor in life?
- What inspires them?
- What impact they want to make?
- What would bring them true joy?
- What fulfillment looks like?

These are some heady questions, no doubt. Did I know this about every player in my business locker room? Absolutely not. Until I did. That's when the game changed.

The beauty of the questions above is you can ask them immediately.

You can engage over lunch, on a walk during a one-on-one outside of your office, or over an off-site coffee before you start your day. Knowing who somebody is on the inside will build trust, holistic connection, and authentic relationships. With this foundation in place, a formal Purpose Discovery to follow (see Purpose Discovery FAQ at WWW.POWEROFPLAYINGOFFENSE.COM) will have even more impact. Here's a quick time out to prime the conversations.

TIME-OUT: Schedule an impromptu team huddle for an upcoming Friday morning. Bring in some coffee and bagels. Title the meeting "Who's in Our Locker Room?" Ask each person to come prepared to share three things NOT on their LinkedIn profile. Guess who's going first? You are. The deeper you share, the higher you will raise the bar and set the tone for the entire group. By the end of the session, be prepared to see the side of people they always wanted you to see.

APPLYING THE PLAYBOOK

CHAPTER 1: KNOW WHAT INSPIRES YOU

Welcome to Applying the Playbook. Consider each application of the playbook an opportunity to activate *The Power of Playing Offense* so you can implement each exercise and practice inside your team and in your daily culture, immediately.

NOTE: *My suggestion is to read through each playbook activity as you naturally navigate through the book, dog-ear the ones that you would like to activate in the next thirty days, then come back to it so you can fully process the details of the process and instructions.*

Batting leadoff is one of my personal favorites. The exercise is called "Know What Inspires You."

I've used this exercise to start workshop engagements with senior leaders in Fortune 500 companies, kick off team meetings in the NFL, as well as set the table for an inspiring off-site retreat.

It is anchored on this foundational thought: **IN ORDER TO INSPIRE OTHERS, YOU MUST FIRST KNOW WHAT INSPIRES YOU.**

With that I challenge you to maximize your proficiency and brand as an inspirational leader.

Many of us have focused on how to inspire others, but do we know what inspires us? This exercise is a start to that introspective journey.

If we're going to talk about inspiration, let's at least define it.

In Latin: to breathe life into.

So now the question becomes, what breathes life into you?

Once you identify this inspirational link and share the experience with others, it can have tremendous impact toward knowing what breathes life into the people that you lock arms with each and every day.

It's time to play offense and get to work.

FIRST ACTION

Set a thirty-minute meeting with your team (no up-front agenda shared—this activity should be a surprise to maximize the impact).

RECOMMENDED TIME

Thirty minutes (five-minute introduction, fifteen-minute activity, five-minute debrief discussion, and five-minute buffer).

SUPPLIES NEEDED/SETUP

One sticky-back name tag and Sharpie marker (or pen) per person—you provide the supplies versus asking the team to bring them (keeps the surprise element). Lay the supplies out (one tag and marker per person) in advance of the meeting.

PRE-MEETING PROCESS

STEP ONE: Think of a word that inspires you.

STEP TWO: Think of a story or memory that made you think of the word that inspires you.

A quick time-out to share a personal example. My word is "impact." Impact is meaningful to me because I saw the way my dad impacted countless lives as an educator, mentor, and coach to students that had largely been given up on in a continuation high school. When his former students approached me years after my dad passed, I heard firsthand how he impacted their lives, and it gave me a glimpse into understanding the impact that's possible when you believe in people wholeheartedly. That is why impact is so important to me.

Now it's your turn.

IN-MEETING PROCESS

STEP ONE: Kick off the meeting with an introduction message on why you're gathered (center around the theme of inspiration). Proceed to share your "inspire word" and accompanying story/memory.

STEP TWO: Once done, ask each team member to think of their "inspire word" and the story/memory behind it. Once their word is identified, have them write it on their sticky name tag and place the tag high on their person (i.e., over the heart). Give them one minute for this step.

STEP THREE: Once everybody has their tag on, explain these quick introduction steps.

- Connect with as many people in the room as possible over the next ten minutes (leaving a few-minute buffer). The goal is three to five conversations at minimum.
- Walk them through the process. One person will share their word and story, then the other person will share (in the same pair).
- Once the second person has shared, move on to another person versus continuing the conversation with the first. Remember, the goal is to connect with three to five people versus connecting deeply with one.
- Ask if anybody has questions. If not, it's game time.

- Start the stopwatch or timer on your phone. Participate through at least a few conversations, then step aside to keep an eye on time, call a one-minute warning at the ten-minute mark, and call it a wrap at the twelve-minute mark (warning—it will be difficult to corral people based on the high energy in the room). Happens *every* time.

POST-ACTIVITY / DEBRIEFING DISCUSSION

After the group takes their seats, ask these questions:

- How was that? You'll get one-word answers such as "good." Then push. "Tell me more." After a handful of open-ended responses, then ask:
    - » What themes or similarities did you notice during the exercise?
    - » While some people may say they wrote similar words down, like "family," keep probing beyond the specific words chosen, and focus more on the meaning behind the words. The response you'll eventually get is that all inspire words tie back to "people."

That's the anchor of the whole exercise. People are inspired by people. Even when I've seen a client write the word "cash" down as his word of inspiration (which was a first), on the side I asked him why. He immediately shared a story about his three daughters and wanting to provide a better childhood for them than he had. It always comes back to people.

Now that you know what inspires you and each member of your team, think of where else and with whom else you can share this same experience. Your leadership team? Customer gathering? Personal reunion?

Hope you enjoyed the first round of Applying the Playbook. Onward.

2

AUTHENTICITY IS UNDER THE MASK

Malcolm Gladwell once enlightened us with the thought that in order to become an expert in any field, you must invest 10,000 hours. Well, how about 30,000 hours?

That is how many hours (conservatively) I spent in formal leadership positions over the course of my career in the professional sports industry. When reflecting back on this battle from the leadership trenches, I can now see clear themes materialize across four quarters.

FOUR QUARTERS OF LEADERSHIP

The first quarter started rocky as I was a newly promoted "player" into the "coaching" space. I had no formal leadership playbook like this to learn from. After much-needed mentorship from those who paved the path before me, the first quarter became about relationships, camaraderie, partnership, tribal bonds, and truly putting people first.

In the second quarter, themes of success and achievement began to emerge. Goals were surpassed year after year. Leaders above me were ecstatic with the results, leading to one promotion after another. More money, more title, more responsibilities—that became the play pattern, and it felt good. Actually, it felt great.

My leadership career had officially taken off. My brand had been established. It was only a matter of time before I would get the seat I ultimately wanted. Put in the work; hit the numbers. The rest will take care of itself.

Enter the third quarter. It was the biggest seat I had ever held. I was finally driving all revenues versus being the #2 guy, as I had been for most of the journey to date. Externally, things were rolling. Internally, I started to feel the pressure. I was no longer driven to hit the result; I was now obsessed. It was endzone or bust—and we continued to reach the endzone, so why fix it?

Then came my performance review. I heard the usual, "Great work, Paulie, keep it up." Normally, this pat to the ego was enough, and the meeting was adjourned. In this case, before walking out of the team president's office, something prompted me to turn around and ask for "one thing"—one thing to work on, one thing to improve. I could immediately see the pleasure in his eyes, like he had been waiting and wanting to give me this constructive feedback, but for some reason didn't until I asked for it.

Many of us have been here before. *Do I ask? Do I not ask? I know things aren't ideal, but do we really want the feedback? Are we ready to hear it?* These were the questions I wrestled with for years and typically wouldn't want the bad news. In this case, I went for it. There was an uneasiness inside of me, where I knew things weren't perfect, and I was about to find out why.

He asked me to have a seat and reaffirmed my performance and competence, and then shared a quote from Teddy Roosevelt: "People don't care how much you know until they know how much you care." After finishing the quote, he said, "That's what you can work on."

Immediately, I went numb. He kept talking, but I don't remember a word. He basically told me my team didn't think I cared about them. I felt hollow instantly because I knew he was right. I had sold out for the results, often at the expense of people. My heart cared, but my actions didn't back it up—and those were all that mattered to my team. Without this feedback, I may still be wearing a mask. I may have never entered the fourth quarter, where I permanently rededicated myself to being the leader I knew I was on my best day. The one who truly puts people first. The Paul from the first quarter, before he knew there was a game to be played.

THE GAME WE'RE ALL IN

When talking business, we often hear clichés referencing the working world as a "rat race," "running in the hamster wheel," or a "daily grind"—the last of which serves as a feather in the cap. A nod to the daily pledge of putting in the work. It becomes a mindset of "survival of the fittest," and we feel like we're on a never-ending treadmill, always striving for what's next.

Was the game always played this way?

We can actually trace it back to the 1970s, when Milton Friedman, who is thought of as the most influential economist of his time, shared a view that has permeated corporate mindsets ever since. A business exists solely to maximize shareholder value over all other stakeholders. This would be the equivalent of a coach prioritizing the fans (i.e., external shareholders) over the players (i.e., employees/internal stakeholders). This thesis of shareholder supremacy has largely led to bottom line–driven, results-obsessed practices that have flooded the world of work. If this is your corporate reality, consider it the outside game—a game that we can influence but never fully control.

What if there was a game that you could control? A game that, when conquered, would propel you to new levels of impact and significance within your career and life.

I call it *mastering the inside game*. The world calls it *emotional intelligence*.

EMOTIONAL INTELLIGENCE OF LEADERSHIP

Reflecting back on my four quarters of leadership, I now view it through a lens of emotional intelligence (EQ). The foundation of EQ is awareness. Awareness of self, awareness of others, and awareness of situation. Let's layer this EQ model over the chapters in my leadership journey, so you can gain the perspective and awareness in your own careers and not fall into the same traps and blind spots that I did.

FIRST AND FOURTH QUARTERS

AWARENESS OF SELF: I authentically knew who I was at my best and put it on full display. No mask required. I was values-based and centered around living with championship purpose. I smelled the roses and loved the journey more than the destination. I felt genuine happiness each day. I was inspired and excited on the drive in, then fulfilled on the drive home. Without question, I was playing offense.

AWARENESS OF OTHERS: I knew my team inside and out. I knew their life stories, understood their personal and professional motivations, and knew that they were the secret sauce of our success. Relationships were at the foundation of it all, and I wasn't afraid to build them outside of the office. My daily actions and behaviors backed up everything I said and felt on the inside. This was the foundation of "meet me at the 50."

AWARENESS OF SITUATION: Team success over individual wins 100 percent of the time. The players (my team) were more important than the coach. They deserved and received all the credit. I was their fullback; they were the star running backs. Their success would lead to my success, not the other way around.

SECOND AND THIRD QUARTERS

AWARENESS OF SELF: I created a second persona. There was "work Paul," and that guy had to be on top of things at all times. Hard charging. Always felt a need to have the answers, with a deep desire to impress others through a relentless, borderline unhealthy work ethic. No doubt, I had a playing defense mentality.

AWARENESS OF OTHERS: I was more aware of the people above me than anybody else. I wanted to please them so I could continue to climb. I rarely invested the time to build relationships to my left and right, and while I cared for my team on the inside, my obsession with results brought out the worst version of me as a manager (I wouldn't call myself a leader at that time).

AWARENESS OF SITUATION: In the moment I thought I was playing my cards right. The promotions and growth opportunities kept coming. I didn't realize I was overlooking people along the way. I regret going through phases of my journey without letting my team know that I saw them, they mattered, and their contributions made the difference between winning and losing. Most of all, I regret not building deeper relationships with them as people. I'll never get those days back.

I didn't realize I had a mask on. This reflection and awareness changed my life. I write these words to you as a leader on my best day, fully transitioned from playing defense to playing offense, permanently in the fourth quarter of my journey.

> *"We cannot change what we are not aware of, and once we are aware, we cannot help but change."*
>
> **SHERYL SANDBERG**
> COO, Facebook

LIVING ON YOUR TERMS

From a young age, we're raised with expectations. First our parents, then peer pressures of adolescence, and eventually decisions around school and work brand us, all while society has these looming messages about success and achievement.

As we navigate the earlier parts of life, we're largely living on other people's terms. But as we grow older, gaining perspective, experience, and insight along the way, do we ever break free from others' expectations? Or do we finally get to play the game of life on our terms?

This fork in the road is an opportunity for authenticity. An opportunity to break out from our mask. An opportunity to establish purpose.

Pre-purpose, I let others drive as I rode in the passenger seat. Post-purpose, I have embraced my own path. Authentic to who I am. Genuinely believing in each step with more clarity and conviction than ever before.

This is the path I'd like to explore with you. But first, let's take a look inside the world of somebody who had it all (or so he thought) until his fork in the road presented itself.

"To be yourself in a world that is constantly trying to make you something else is the greatest accomplishment."

RALPH WALDO EMERSON

American essayist, lecturer, philosopher

PURPOSE LEAVES CLUES

Imagine a life with all the riches in the world, literally not a single toy you couldn't buy. The most lavish experiences at your disposal. The world is your oyster. Ready to wine, ready to dine, ready to open its doors for you to indulge. All outsiders look into your world of abundance and imagine how "full" it must feel.

And yet, when looking in the mirror of life, you can't help but feel *emotionally bankrupt*—living without purpose. Constantly fighting through a mindset of "not enough," chasing the next win, only to get there unfulfilled while realizing the goal posts keep moving further away. You start to face the reality that with a mindset of playing defense, success is eternally fleeting and your mask continues to thicken.

This was the life of Ken Behring. A real estate mogul in the 1970s, acclaimed as one of the wealthiest Americans by *Forbes*, Behring lived a plush life filled with elaborate car collections and extravagant yachts. He even bought the Seattle Seahawks for show. Each experience more exciting and more filled with the material treasures of life, yet hollow on the inside, wondering if any of it even mattered.

One day, Ken's friend asked him to join on a service initiative as they embarked on a philanthropic journey to Mexico. Ken took part in the week of service, and just as they were about to leave, he suddenly felt a tug on the back of his leg. He looked down and saw a young boy speaking in Spanish, so Ken flagged over a translator, who shared that the little boy wanted Ken to stay. When Ken asked why, the translator responded, "Because he wants to remember your face. He knows the next time he sees you, it will be in heaven."

Ken was overwhelmed with a feeling that had been foreign in his life to that point. Deeply filled—but not with adrenaline or ego. Rather, with purpose.

From this day forward, Ken became fanatical about the sensation of having a deeper meaning. This moment became a catalyst for Ken's transformation from a life of self to a life of purpose.

Ken and his wife went on to become proud founders of the Wheelchair Foundation with a mission to mobilize the immobile. They have since impacted tens of thousands of lives in underdeveloped countries. Ken provided purpose to others through physical chairs and wheels, allowing them to access parts of their lives they otherwise would never be able to see.

The cars, the yacht, and owning an NFL team could only do so much. They all had a shelf life.

Then, Ken found the gift of service and contribution. Ken finally played offense and stood for something bigger than himself. In exchange, Ken received a priceless gift of living life on his terms. Ultimately, he had the opportunity to unleash his purpose. It was under his mask the entire time.

Purpose leaves clues. Just as Ken found his, we have to be ready to answer the call.

BET ON YOURSELF

It's the greatest investment you can make. The moment we focus on what we truly want is the moment that life's clues start to present themselves. Not because something radically changed in the environment. We just happened to take our masks off and show our authentic character.

You'll know when your mask is fully off. It's when actions happen swiftly, behaviors are bold, and massive decisions become simple. It's when you start to bet on yourself and never look back.

TIME-OUT: Think of the boldest example from your life of when you bet on yourself. Your chips were in the middle of the table. It made perfect sense to you, even if others thought you were crazy. Here are some questions to process; jot down your gut responses:

- What led you to bet on yourself?
- What did you learn from the experience?
- What can you activate or implement in your life right now using what you learned from betting on yourself?

Sidenote—for notetaking, there is complete flexibility on how you do it (written, phone notes, email to self, or voice recording on phone). The key is to take notes in the same way throughout the book so you can easily trace back and have them in one central location for future use, reflection, and to share.

As I reflect on when I've made that bet, I mentioned leaving a six-figure opportunity to make seven dollars an hour. What I didn't reveal is that I moved out of my mom's house (rent-free) to an apartment blocks away from Staples Center so I could burn the candle on both ends. That was the easy part. The real motivation behind it was that, at seven dollars an hour and 3 percent commission, I'd have to finish at the top of the sales board to pay rent.

Years later came my leap of faith from sports to pursue my vision of living with greater purpose. Then going ALL IN to start my own business, Purpose Labs. These were my bold decisions, and none of them gave me pause because I knew they *almost* never happened.

A NEAR-DEATH EXPERIENCE

I finally got my first car at sixteen—an old school VW Jetta. I was stoked. One night after dropping a friend off, I was on my way back home. It was a rare cold, rainy night in LA, so I had the heater on full blast. I started to get tired from the hot air and first realized it when my head nodded, as I almost fell asleep at the wheel. I shook it off and focused, less than ten miles from home. Within minutes, I heard a loud smack. My car had hit the far-left wall of the freeway. I was spinning on the slick, wet road across all five lanes. The steering wheel and pedals had locked. Suddenly, the car stopped spinning and started falling downhill off the right side of the freeway.

My car tumbled end over end. Within seconds (that felt like minutes), the car was caught, but I didn't know how. What I did know was I was upside down. My car was piping hot, and I was surrounded by smoke. My seatbelt held me in place upside down. I knew I had to get out. I unbuckled myself, hit the ceiling, and tried to climb my way out. As my hands reached above, I grabbed onto the first thing possible. It was a scorching hot pipe under the car, now burning deep into my flesh. Ignoring the scalding pain, I climbed out through the broken window and pulled myself up to stand on top of my upside-down car. There was nothing more than tree branches holding the car up. It looked like it was about to blow, so I scuttled across the pipes and made a jump for it. Just in time. The tree gave way.

The car tumbled to the bottom of the downslope, moments later smashing into a concrete wall. In shock, I climbed back up toward the freeway, now on the side of the road. Several drivers who'd seen this from behind had pulled over to help. We made the immediate calls to my parents and the cops as I started to calm down, knowing there was physical and mental pain to deal with on the other side. At that moment, the cops pulled up. We went through our questions, and they walked away telling me to hang tight.

The cops circled back after inspecting the entire scene and asked if I knew how lucky I was. They said my entire car was caved in from every direction, except one. The hood and trunk smashed in. Back seats crushed. Passenger side shredded. Only one quadrant of the car wasn't damaged: the three-by-three-foot driver's box. Thank God I was alone.

I'd thought *life is short* was a slogan. It almost became reality. Without a chance to experience adulthood, bet on myself, or ever share this story.

This experience taught me to cherish each day and max out on what matters. I still sometimes took life for granted in the years that followed, but this traumatic experience has always given me a perspective to return to—one of gratitude, intention, and purpose.

> *"If today were the last day of my life, would I want to do what I am about to do today? And whenever the answer has been 'no' for too many days in a row, I know I need to change something."*
>
> **STEVE JOBS**
>
> former CEO and Co-Founder, Apple

KNOW WHERE YOU COME FROM

We all start our lives where there is no *work* you and *personal* you; there is only *one* you. Then, at some point, it splits. To understand who we truly are, we often need to take a hard look in the rear-view mirror of life.

Until I was eleven years old (when playing sports required us to stay home), we visited my grandparents in Ensenada, Mexico, every other weekend. Those were the gold stars on the calendar. Every trip seemed like an adventure: fiestas, laughter, hugs, dancing, tacos, and tequila (for the adults, of course).

My favorite memories were from the holidays. I'll never forget my fourth Christmas, when Santa knocked on the front door then whisked away. I picked up the box and felt a shake, then saw a wet nose peek through. What I unwrapped became my first puppy. I still light up thinking about her.

When my family asked what I wanted for my fifth Christmas, I asked for a baby pig based on my obsession with bacon. I never got the pig.

Disappointment aside, I love my family dearly and will always stay true to where I come from. I also now know why Santa was a different shade of brown every year. Apparently, my uncles took turns!

TIME-OUT: Think of your favorite childhood-through-teenage-years memories.

- Who were they with?
- What moments or experiences have molded you to this day?
- What was a milestone or memory you're still proud of?

Over the next few minutes, take some notes on your immediate thoughts. Don't overthink; go with your gut. Keep these notes handy. These foundational answers often have clues in them about your purpose—more details will follow as we go along.

SPORTS ARE A UNIFIER

In 2014, I hosted my wife and mom for Super Bowl XLVIII. While I barely remember a play of the game as I was in the background entertaining clients, I'll never forget seeing them bond for the first time. My wife and I started our relationship over three years of long distance when she was in law school, so we didn't have significant occasions to get to know each other's families.

This trip to New York had a lot riding on it. When wife and mom get along, life is gravy. If they don't—well, I'm glad I never had to figure that out. They not only were having the time of their lives, it was as if the game was secondary. They were locked in on each other. Laughing and hugging like best friends do. I was grinning with joy as if I were the proud parent. Grateful to have created this opportunity for precious connection.

You are about to dive into an artifact exercise that I was introduced to years ago. The artifact should be accompanied by a story that shares something meaningful to you. My artifact was this Super Bowl XLVIII credential because of how it brought together the two most important people in my life. It was so meaningful; we were fortunate enough to do it again.

Most see this as a Super Bowl credential. I see it as a ticket that sparked a lifelong bond between my wife and mom.

APPLYING THE PLAYBOOK

CHAPTER 2: A LIFE ARTIFACT

Now that I've shown you my artifact, it's time to find and present yours.

Your artifact should tell us a story of who you are. It should have a special meaning to you and provide others with an insight about your life. As others hear about your artifact, they should have a sense of what's important to you, what motivates you, or perhaps what excites you. As long as your artifact (and what it says about you) is deeply meaningful, you're on the right track.

I have now experienced this exercise countless times; perhaps the most impactful time was with my cohort during orientation in our Executive MBA experience at the University of Michigan. The reason the impact was sustained was because our relationships and time together continued versus being a one-off experience with a group I might have never seen again. Doing this with your team can be equally transformational.

Others' artifacts included their favorite childhood memento, a college keepsake, a souvenir from the big game they attended as a youngster, or something a late grandparent left them—and these are just a few. Most important were the stories, learnings, and lessons behind each artifact. That's the true connector.

With that, let's play offense and bring this to life.

IDEAL SETTING

Team off-site or social gathering (avoid the typical boardroom/meeting room if possible).

PRIOR TO THE OFF-SITE GATHERING

Send out a note to all attendees with the following:

- Purpose and spirit of the artifact exercise (feel free to mirror some of my introduction language above)
- Examples of past artifacts used (again, feel free to mirror the above)
- Guidelines for artifact selection
    - Ideally not a photograph
    - Should be a physical and tangible item that they can easily transport
- In preparation for the gathering:
    - Think of the story that is tied to the artifact; however, do not write a script to present it. This should be a natural and informal share with the group.
    - Artifact presentations should range from one to three minutes in length.
    - What each presenter shares with the group should highlight what the artifact means to them and why they chose to bring this particular artifact.

AT THE OFF-SITE GATHERING

You, as the leader, go first. This will allow you to introduce the activity to the group while more importantly setting the tone for the level of vulnerability, courage, emotion, and authenticity that is possible when you choose to "go there."

No debriefing is needed. Simply provide everybody the opportunity to share, and then continue with the remainder of your off-site gathering, meeting, or event. Trust me, the organic side conversations will come—especially when two people have a similar story (that they likely just learned about one another).

BONUS ROUND

After you share this experience with the team, this can be an amazing addition to your onboarding process. As new hires are welcomed into your team and organization, look for ways to incorporate a presentation of their artifact to their new tribe.

3

During my undergrad studies at USC, I began a sales and marketing internship for Philip Morris USA, the parent company of Marlboro. At the time, I solely viewed it as an amazing opportunity to work for a Fortune 10 organization at such a young age, navigating my way through strategic networking channels to even be considered for the sought-after role. As I built my personal brand over multiple summers as a territory sales manager in training, I was extended the opportunity to serve as a recruiting ambassador during my senior year at USC.

I was the guy representing Philip Morris at the university career fairs, and again, solely viewed it as a platform for professional growth and experience. The first career fair took place at USC: home run. The next, I knocked it out of the park. In fact, it went so well that the company asked me to "take the show on the road" and go represent the organization at other campuses. No-brainer—I was in.

TAKE A STAND

This took me to the Bay Area, on campus at the University of California, Berkeley. Knowing what we know about the Berkeley brand, you can already imagine the ride I was in for. I arrived hours early at the strip where the career fair would be hosted. It all looked calm until I noticed a gathering of people down the road. As I approached, the now visibly rowdy congregation was right next to the Philip Morris booth. As I was setting up my materials, several security guards arrived to flank me; the crowd was growing by the minute.

At 10:00 a.m. sharp, the career fair began. Signs emerged and chants erupted. I was doing my best to maintain a professional look, do my job, and manage recruiting conversations with prospective employees. The chants grew louder and louder—impossible to ignore. Candidates were distressed, stepping out of line one by one. I became numb to the noise—but I'll never be able to erase what I saw. One person held up a bright sign that read, "YOU SELL CANCER." Another: "YOU WORK FOR THE DEVIL."

At that moment, my world stopped. This was bigger than doing my job. Bigger than building a career. Certainly bigger than landing a prized recruit. I had strongly violated others' values, even if only by representation. This was a lot to take in as a twenty-year-old.

It did teach me about the power of tribes, both the group that verbally ripped me apart, and the group I stood for. It taught me the power of brand and the power of identity. I wasn't the one selling the cigarettes, but that didn't matter. I was guilty by association. All of a sudden, working for a Fortune 10 didn't hold as much value. I began to develop a lens for what I stood for, to not only be a part of something bigger but also something that I believed in. As important as it is to know who your tribe is, it's equally important to know who your tribe is not.

BE A PART OF SOMETHING BIGGER THAN YOURSELF

People often ask me what "my cause" is. I've been blessed to be around wonderful humanitarians and philanthropists. Leaders in education and medicine. First responders and US Special Forces. The list of service-driven people in my life could easily continue.

My cause is unique. My cause is to inspire purpose in others so that they can go create the impact they were destined to have. I'm the front-end guy. The guy that catches people pre-mission.

I care more about you finding a cause that you believe in. A cause bigger than you that you are inspired to embrace each day and contribute to in meaningful ways. I want to help you make a difference and spark impact that matters—then be fulfilled knowing that you left everybody, every place, and everything that you touched better than you found it.

This vision came from my first dose of professional purpose. It was the first time I knew I was a part of something bigger—and this story contributed significantly to my eventual cause, and my understanding of tribes.

> *"Putting in long hours for a corporation is hard. Putting in long hours for a cause is easy."*
>
> **ELON MUSK**
>
> Founder and CEO, Tesla and Space X

HOW PURPOSE SAVED AN NBA FRANCHISE

In 2005, Hurricane Katrina devastated New Orleans. Over eight hundred thousand evacuated. Damage over $80 billion. Just as the city was nearly back on its feet years later, the BP oil spill hit. Over 200 million gallons of oil spread through the Gulf of Mexico in what is known to be one of the most impactful environmental disasters to date. Lethal to marine life, Katrina and BP clobbered seafood and tourism—two of the top three industries that kept New Orleans afloat.

I learned of this not through the news, but through firsthand stories and experience after moving to New Orleans in 2010 to lead the sales efforts for the NBA's New Orleans Hornets (now Pelicans). I personally saw what transpired in the New Orleans community and instantly became immersed in it all.

I was welcomed in by countless families and fans proudly sharing stories of the community's grit, resilience, pride, and passion. Just as I was getting acclimated, the unimaginable happened. Yet another body blow to the city. This time it hit closer to home, potentially derailing a career move I had been so excited about only months before.

The former owner of the Hornets was diagnosed with prostate cancer, which removed him from day-to-day operations, causing the NBA to step in as stewards of the franchise. Upon further examination of the business, we learned that the books weren't healthy. We were the least viable franchise by all economic measures in the league. The late NBA commissioner David Stern gave us an ultimatum: Improve the business to the top five in league revenues, or the league will be forced to permanently relocate the team.

We had one year to play offense, defy the odds, and make history. The light bulb ideas started to flicker. With hope. With potential. With purpose.

We recognized football was king in the South and basketball was a mere afterthought. We also knew we lived in an impassioned community, with a soul unlike any other. What sparked this passion? After all the disasters that had ravished New Orleans, what kept everybody here? How could we tap into their pride, identity, and energy?

With that came the launch of the "I'M IN" campaign. It was bigger than basketball. It was about civic pride and standing up for YOUR city.

All the stops were pulled out. The governor, mayor, and celebrities from the music, culinary, and entertainment industries that called New Orleans home opened their living rooms to host one hundred influencer events in one hundred days and share the dire situation and story with their inner circle—ending with an ask for support.

Digital billboards throughout the city showed a live look at where we stood on the march toward ten thousand season tickets. "I'm In. Are You?" was heard in every corner of the community. Pledge after pledge was made to save the Hornets. Private citizens committing to one seat. Families committing to four. Businesses committing to fifty. Tireless days and nights invested in a citywide effort.

After a dogged year, the dust settled. Our marching orders had been for ten thousand season tickets. Final count? Over eleven thousand . . . leading the NBA in new season ticket sales! The unimaginable had happened.

We saved the franchise by inspiring the community to stand for something bigger than themselves and bigger than basketball. This was every New Orleanian's opportunity to live with championship purpose—and stand tall for *their* city.

AUDIT THE WORDS ON THE WALL

Mission, vision, and values can make or break an organization, sending a strong signal to their current and prospective tribes. Often, these elements that should symbolize the most inspirational aspects of a company are painted on the organizational walls—with one of two effects.

The words on a wall can be fuel for the day-to-day culture. A mission as the North Star. A vision as the magnetic compass. Values as the lens on actions, behaviors, and decisions that color the culture.

Alternatively, the words on a wall can show hollow if they're not backed by the actions, behaviors, and decisions of the organization and all its team members. I would argue it's better to not have words on the wall than to put them up for show. Everybody knows. You're not fooling anybody. Tribes talk, for better or worse.

Perhaps you're already in the tribe you always envisioned. Perhaps you're not. Take the mission, vision, and values as table stakes to get a glimpse of what an organization stands for. Read their online Glassdoor reviews. Do a job shadow or talk to employees to get authentic insights into their daily work life there. None of this intel is perfect, but doing your homework to find out what a place is really like can help you find where you want to be.

Let's take a look at mission, vision, and values on their best day.

MISSION

"MEET HAPPY." These were the words I saw as soon as I stepped off the elevator at Zoom Video Communications HQ in San Jose. In 2018, I had the privilege of coaching and consulting the leadership team at Zoom. Their culture had, by far, one of the most inspiring, energized, and authentic vibes I've ever experienced. As soon as I walked in, I sensed everybody wanted to be there and felt invested in something bigger than themselves. The mantra "Meet Happy" was brought to life by every employee I encountered. A tribe of happy people bringing the world together through a video platform so we can all experience human connection in a more authentic way.

I caught Zoom on their upward rise within the highly competitive tech space of Silicon Valley. Little did I know then that two years later during the global pandemic, Zoom would shine as bright as any organization. The pandemic brought about a necessity for virtual and global connectivity in ways we had never seen. Beyond business and social communications, Zoom played offense and lived their mission one step further by providing countless schools with free access to their platform so that education for our youth could continue. It's no surprise that the same amazing culture I'd experienced years before many were familiar with Zoom was now bringing *happiness* to the world when we needed it most.

> *"A mission statement is not something you write overnight, but fundamentally, your mission statement becomes your constitution, the solid expression of your vision and values. It becomes the criterion by which you measure everything else in your life."*
>
> **STEPHEN COVEY**
> author of *The 7 Habits of Highly Effective People*

VISION

LITTLE JOHNNY: MLS Commissioner Don Garber approached the podium at a New York Red Bulls sales event we were hosting. He shared his vision for the up-and-coming soccer league:

> *Little Johnny is a ten-year-old boy coming to games with his dad, having the time of his life. A decade later, Johnny is in college and is social chair for his fraternity. Remembering the great times, he organizes a fraternity–sorority outing at the stadium. A decade later, John is a young professional with*

a young family of his own, buying a ticket package to enjoy quality time with his daughter. A decade later, John is a senior executive and cuts the check to buy a corporate suite at the stadium. This journey took decades. We are still a growing league, and we all want it to happen sooner and faster. Let's take care of Little Johnny today so we earn a fan for life. The rest will take care of itself.

Every attendee joined the Red Bulls tribe that evening. This is the power of vision.

TIME-OUT: What is the vision you have for your career one year from now? What is one action you can take to best position yourself? Jot these notes down.

This is an example of a personal vision exercise. Now, let's take it beyond a quick-burst time-out; let's include your team. Here's an example of how you can set your collective vision, together.

Set a sixty-minute meeting for the next two weeks with your team; call it **"OUR Future."** The agenda is simple. Open by sharing the Little Johnny story to illustrate the power and impact of vision. Now, hand the ownership to your team and ask two questions, giving everybody a chance to participate. It's important to let them share their thoughts before you share yours.

- **Q1:** What is your vision for our team one year from now?

After everybody has answered the first question, then ask:

- **Q2:** What is one action you can take to bring us closer to that reality?

Set monthly or quarterly check-ins to create a series of meetings around the theme of **"OUR Future."**

VALUES

IMPACT WAS MY TICKET: Post–Jerry Maguire moment, I immediately felt at home with my new tribe at the Leadership Institute. I believed in our impact. I was ALL IN on the mission. I felt like a life-long student of the leadership and culture space, destined to be there. My first crash course: learn how to inspire leaders through a foundation of knowing who they are, cemented by purpose.

During my orientation, I absorbed the nuances of the purpose discovery process. Rather than being solely focused on the 'Why,' the process also unearthed a discovery of values. Our values are lenses for how we make meaning out of our experiences and what informs our attitudes and decisions, which ultimately drives our actions and behaviors.

Without knowing it at the time, this was the formula that led to my leap of faith from sports. My value of impact became the driver as I evaluated the fork in the road to stay in sports or join the Leadership Institute. Create impact inside of four walls *or* create impact around the world?

Before pulling the trigger, I asked the Leadership Institute what my primary role would be; without knowing it was my core value, they said "create impact." The decision became easy, and now I know why.

Aligning your values with your tribe can be extremely empowering. I would argue it's essential if you want to play offense and "feel alive" throughout your journey.

THE PURPOSE MOVEMENT

In early 2019, the world's largest investment manager (over $6.5 trillion dollars) took a bold stance on purpose. Larry Fink, head of Blackrock, shared a note with all clients and partners that stated that purpose and profit are inextricably linked—going further to share his stance that purpose is, in fact, the animating force for achieving profits. These words inspired a business roundtable of two hundred CEOs, including Jeff Bezos from Amazon and Tim Cook from Apple, later in 2019. There, more momentum built around the idea that shareholder value is no longer the main objective, which has pretty much been gospel since highly influential economist Milton Friedman proposed it in the 1970s. At long last, this new idea is evolving into action. The two hundred CEOs signed a letter to focus on purpose and invest as many resources in internal employees and their communities as they do on outside shareholders. The purpose movement has taken form, and more purposeful times should be ahead. Let's look at the research.

When executive leaders were asked which were the most critical factors when integrating purpose throughout their business:

93% said **"OUR CULTURE AND BEHAVIORS, ESPECIALLY OUR LEADERS"**

93% said **"CLEARLY EMBEDDED INTO OUR GOALS, STRATEGIES AND OBJECTIVES"**

92% said **"OUR GOVERNANCE AND DECISION-MAKING PROCESSES AND SYSTEMS"**[12]

89%

of executives believe that a clear **PURPOSE IS A GOOD GUIDE/INSPIRATION TO FUTURE INNOVATION OF PRODUCTS AND SERVICES.**[13]

84%

of executives believe that **BUSINESS TRANSFORMATIONS WILL HAVE GREATER SUCCESS IF INTEGRATED WITH PURPOSE.**[14]

75%

of executives tell us that the integration of **PURPOSE CREATES VALUE IN THE SHORT TERM, AS WELL AS OVER THE LONG RUN.**[15]

73%

of business leaders say that having a well-integrated **PURPOSE HELPS THEIR COMPANY NAVIGATE DISRUPTION.**[16]

While it is inspiring to see the purpose movement gaining momentum, the actions still need to follow, as there is evidence that shows potential masks being worn by executives and organizations. Here's a glimpse into these areas of authentic concern.

79% of business leaders believe that an organization's purpose is central to business success, *yet* **68%** shared that purpose is not used as a guidepost in leadership decision-making processes within their organization.[17]

65% of CEOs think the main role of purpose is to connect with employees or customers *but only* **46%** of executives think their organization has a strong sense of purpose.[18]

76% of marketing heads were of the belief that their own organization had a defined sense of purpose, *yet only* **10%** could produce a corporate purpose statement and plan to back-up these beliefs.[19]

86% of B2B companies recognize purpose as important to growth, but they are still working out how to implement their purpose so that it influences business and social outcomes, *but only* **24%** said purpose is embedded into their business to the point of influencing innovation, operations and their engagement with society.[20]

"People want to do well and do good. They want to understand how they're making a difference in the world. Things change all the time, but your organization's purpose transcends any individual product or service."

MARK WEINBERGER
former CEO, Ernst & Young

That said, there is hope.

WHICH TRIBES ARE DOING IT RIGHT

We should start by acknowledging that no organization is perfect. That said, there are organizations that are living and leading with purpose better than most. LinkedIn conducted the largest research study of purpose at work and found these organizations to be leading examples of purpose-driven cultures we can aspire toward. The cultural measure of purpose is how consistent their daily actions, behaviors, and decisions are with their greater purpose. Here are fifteen of the shining stars, and I'm proud to say there are countless others beyond that I look forward to highlighting in the future.

- Airbnb
- Apple
- Cisco
- CLIF
- EY
- Fitbit
- IDEO
- LinkedIn
- Nike
- Patagonia
- SolarCity
- Southwest Airlines
- TOMS Shoes
- Virgin Galactic
- Whole Foods

THIS IS MY TRIBE

Some of my favorite memories of the Michigan Executive MBA experience involved hosting recruits. Every month, there was a new group of prospective students that would come in, experience a class, and socialize with the cohort.

Sitting around the table at lunch was where the deepest conversations were possible. I remembered being on the candidate side and gaining so much value from the students' insights and candor, so I was inspired to pay it forward, now sitting on the other side.

One day, there was a recruit at the table, and their engagement was off the charts. We were finishing each other's sentences. Connection was sky high. It just felt right. When lunch ended that day, I'll never forget what he said: "This is my tribe."

That has stuck with me ever since. On behalf of everybody in my cohort that made an inclusive impression on him that day, that's what life is all about. He felt the power of belonging.

You won't ever know your tribe until you experience it. If you're curious, check them out. If you're convinced there's another tribe out there with your name on it, what are you waiting for?

TIME-OUT: Pick one tribe you'd like to build or enhance your relationship with. It can be personal, professional, social, philanthropic, academic, tied to your kids, and so on. Pick one.

Put a commitment on your calendar for how you will take your relationship with this tribe to the next level. After the first commitment is fulfilled, plan the next three months' commitments out. Consistency will be key in order to build momentum.

In the example we just read, the recruit clearly was exploring MBA tribes. His commitment would have been to attend a preview day. What's your commitment?

PURPOSE STORYTELLING

Oftentimes we're stuck in the weeds of "what we do" and lose sight of "why we do it." In 2015, KPMG found themselves in a similar spot. They knew there had to be a newly found sense of purpose, but it couldn't be a top-down push that would lead to empty words on the wall. Instead, they took a crowd-sourced approach.

Through extensive qualitative research and hundreds of interviews, a new organizational purpose statement emerged: *Inspire Confidence, Empower Change*. To create a stronger emotional connection to the statement, they needed employees to experience it for themselves, so they encouraged everyone, from interns to the chairman, to share their own stories about how their work is making a difference. An app was developed to create and share digital posters on what it meant to work at KPMG called the 10,000 Stories Challenge. They asked twenty-seven thousand partners and employees to develop posters as individuals or teams, leading to over forty-two thousand stories.

The cultural results were astounding, with scores on employee engagement surveys rising to record levels. Ninety percent of employees now considered KPMG a great place to work, resulting in KPMG surging seventeen spots on *Fortune's* 100 Best Companies to Work For list, making them the #1 ranked Big Four firm for the first time in their history.

To double down on the impact and ensure this wouldn't be a flash in the pan or flavor of the month initiative, KPMG incorporated purpose storytelling training into their leadership development programs, helping leaders speak to their teams by touching their hearts as well as their minds.

One graduate of this training spoke to a group of fifteen hundred interns about her own higher purpose then concluded by recounting the parable of three bricklayers who were rebuilding a church after it had been damaged by fire. The construction architect observed three workers on a scaffold and asked, "What are you doing?" The first bricklayer replied, "I'm laying bricks." The second responded, "I'm repairing a wall." The third declared, "I'm building a cathedral to the Almighty."

So, she asked her audience, "Do you want to be bricklayers or cathedral builders?" Over one hundred emails followed shortly after: "I want to be a cathedral builder." They realized it's not about what they do, it's about 'Why' they do it.

Purpose does not require title, influence, or authority. It requires a mindset where you are ready to step in and make a difference into something bigger than yourself, for a tribe that you take pride in going to battle with.

Storytelling can be an amazing catalyst to inspire your tribe.

KNOWING YOUR TRIBE MEMBERS' IDENTITIES

Imagine you have a superpower to see the world through the lenses of each and every person in your locker room—knowing what drives them and what they deem most important in life. That is exactly what happens when you know the identities of each member in your team. It's as if you're playing a game of cards where they're all open face and the color and suit are the core values of each player around you. You now understand their strategy. Where they're coming from. Why and how they make decisions. Even what's behind their actions and behaviors. The connection, empathy, and relationships that result can be astounding.

At the 49ers, we went through a 1.0 version of the identity process that you're about to learn. We then posted our values on the wall so they were visible to the entire team. This transparency and vulnerability brought us closer together than ever. In good times, they became the fuel for laughter and banter. In tough times, they became a filter on how we analyzed why somebody showed up the way they did and gave us a construct to spark a productive and solution-oriented dialogue to get through the storm together.

MAKING YOUR VALUES ACTIONABLE

Professionally, this process led to my decisions around my career-to-calling transformation and starting my own company. Personally, this process led to me going back to school (something I said I'd never do) and becoming a professor (in the legacy of my late father, who was an educator). We'll unpack more of this over the course of the book to help you on your journey.

I have now internalized the playbook on values and untangled the formula. I have applied and audited life's most significant moments when critical and bold decisions needed to be made. Similar to how an NFL quarterback describes their second year in the league, the game around me has started to slow down, and I can now see things clearly. I'm able to call my future shots with more confidence and greater results. As empowering as this has been, my only regret is not learning it sooner! The cherry on top? I'm now able to transport this framework to cultures, teams, and leaders—just like we're about to do.

Meet me at the 50, and let's bring your values to life.

APPLYING THE PLAYBOOK

CHAPTER 3: OPERATING VALUES

The Identity Model below is an illustration of your identity. From the inside out, the goal is to have alignment and congruence between all levels if you want to show up and operate as your most authentic, consistent, and confident self. The objective is for you to have such a deep knowledge of the inner layers that they become the "go-to" source and lens for how you "show up" in the world (the outer layers). To do that we must have clarity on the inner workings of our identity, which is the focus of this playbook exercise.

THE IDENTITY MODEL

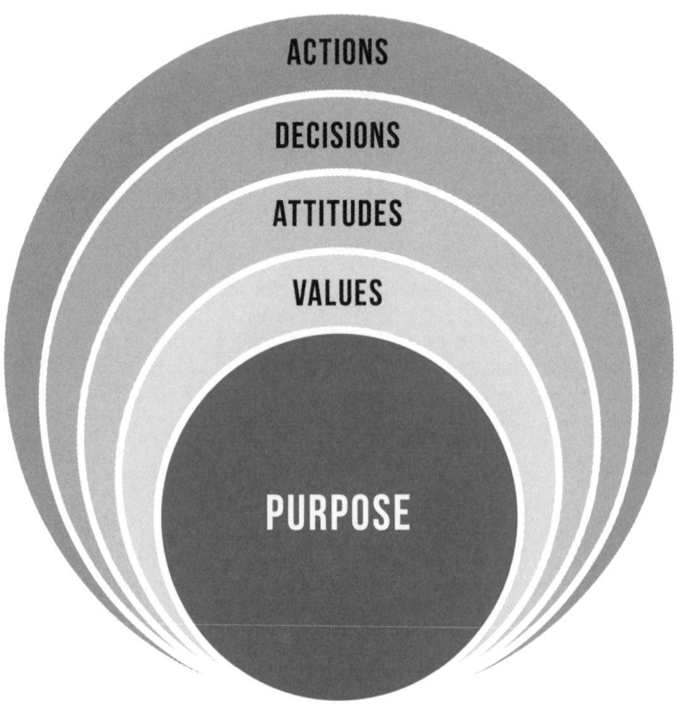

In Chapter 13 we will expand this model at an external, goal-defining, and legacy-building level. But first, let's examine the relationships among purpose, values, and attitudes and how they play out at a personal level. When we do the internal work well, inspiring results follow.

- Your **PURPOSE** is your 'Why,' which serves as your North Star.
- Your purpose is largely conceptual. Your **VALUES** bring it to life and make it more actionable.
- Your values inform your **ATTITUDES**, otherwise known as your belief system.
- Your attitudes influence your **DECISIONS**.
- Your decisions drive your **ACTIONS** (which are the sum of your behaviors).

The outside world, how we are perceived, and how we are understood are all a byproduct of our outer layers—how we "show up." We can have the best intentions, the most idealistic values, and the most inspiring purpose—it all leads to nothing if we don't show up with the right actions and behaviors each and every day. The key is, are you sourcing those actions and behaviors from a consistent place? That's the value of values.

With that, it's time to play offense and unearth yours.

There are two ways to discover your individual values (a third, which is more suited for members of your team, will be covered in Chapter 7 of Applying the Playbook).

1. The more robust route to discovering your values is a part of the full Purpose Discovery process. To learn more, see the Purpose Discovery FAQ at **WWW.POWEROFPLAYINGOFFENSE.COM.**
2. The most turnkey way of identifying your values is through the following process.

STEP ONE

Select three values from the following list that resonate most with you. If there is a value you strongly associate with that is not listed below, run with it.

ACHIEVEMENT	EXCELLENCE	LEARNING
AMBITION	FAIRNESS	MASTERY
AUTHENTICITY	FAITH	OPTIMISM
AUTONOMY	FUN	PASSION
CARE	GROWTH	PERFORMANCE
CHALLENGE	HAPPINESS	PERSEVERANCE
COMMUNITY	HOPE	POTENTIAL
COMPASSION	IMAGINATION	PURPOSE
CONNECTION	INFLUENCE	RECOGNITION
COURAGE	INSPIRATION	SERVICE
DISCOVERY	JOY	SIGNIFICANCE
DRIVE	KINDNESS	TEAMWORK
EMPOWER	LEADERSHIP	TRUST

STEP TWO

For each of your selected values, define them in your own words.

STEP THREE

For each of your selected values, create an "I Will" statement. Start by jotting some notes down to fill out this sentence for each value.

> "You'll know I'm living my value of ____(insert value)____ when I ____(insert applicable actions, behaviors, and decisions)____."

Capture your thoughts and create an "I Will" statement from them. Consider this your commitment to action—in other words, how you operate.

A final "I Will" statement will have this format.

I will ______________________________________.

Once the exercise is complete, keep your values visible each day, whether on paper at your desk or office, or as a daily tech reminder in your work calendar or cell phone. In any form the most important factor is to keep them top of mind and see them consistently.

To support you, I've created a form for you to fill out with your values and "I Will" statements. You can find it at WWW.POWEROFPLAYINGOFFENSE.COM.

Below are my values and "I Will" statements as examples.

When ready, head back to step one!

PAUL EPSTEIN

PERSONAL VALUES DEFINITIONS AND "I WILL" STATEMENTS

GROWTH: Growth is a mindset. We are here to grow, develop, and evolve—not live with a fixed and linear mentality. I *will* focus on possibilities and opportunities and why things *can* happen versus why they can't.

BELIEF: I believe in people because they have believed in me. Even when people let me down, I *will* hang on to the belief that people are well intentioned and always redeemable.

AUTHENTICITY: Never sell out and go against my values (I've done it, and it sucked the life out of me). Don't closely associate with superficial people. I *will* live with the character I was raised to have.

COURAGE: Life is too short. Live it to its fullest. Live it on your terms. Double down on your passions, and bet on yourself when life calls you to do it. I *will* stand tallest when fear and risk are highest.

IMPACT: How I measure success each and every day—something my late father inspired me with. I *will* use impact as the lens (over monetary and other means) on how I make significant decisions in life.

PARTNERSHIP: Meet me at the 50. I *will* invest myself in each relationship with this state of mind.

	Pillar I	Pillar II	Pillar III	Pillar IV
PAUL EPSTEIN	LIVE WITH CHAMPIONSHIP PURPOSE	BE THE STORM CHASER	SALUTE THE LONG SNAPPER	EMBODY GOLD JACKET CULTURE
			Meet Me at the 50	
	PAYCHECK-DRIVEN → PURPOSE-DRIVEN	ADVERSITY → ACHIEVEMENT	DISENGAGED → INSPIRED	CONTROL → CAMARADERIE
	Leading Self		Leading Others	

Pillar V

LEAVE IT BETTER THAN YOU FOUND IT

PLAYING OFFENSE

SUCCESS

↓

SIGNIFICANCE

Leading the Future

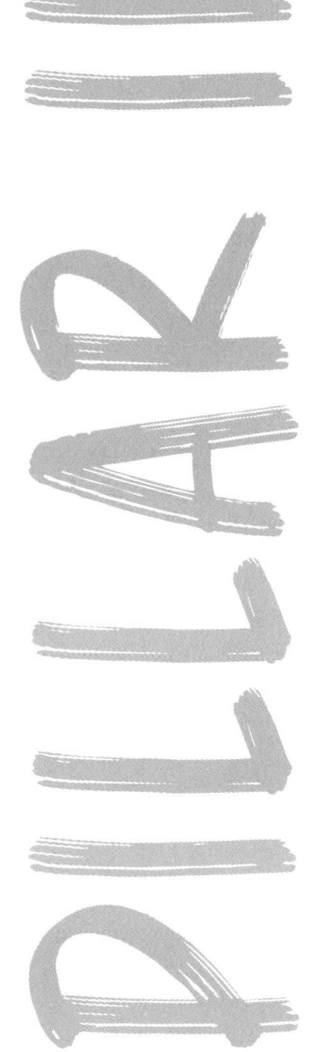

BE THE STORM CHASER

If purpose inspires us to take the first step, chasing the storm prepares us for the next one. As essential as that first step is, continuing the journey is no less so.

Whether personally or professionally, we will all experience countless storms in life. It is these storms that will mold us, that will help us grow, and that will challenge us to be the best version of ourselves.

As leaders, we have two choices. Run into the storm head on *or* run away and hide from the inevitable adversity that is in front of us. Too often I see leaders who believe adversity and challenges are the paths to failure and so spend all their energy avoiding those challenges however they can. As a result, they rarely fail spectacularly—but they never win big, stonewalling the possibility of transforming adversity into achievement.

I have been in the tense meetings and received the furious calls as team owners wonder why their franchise is losing revenue and fans night after night. I've experienced firsthand how it feels when an entire city or entire region turns against their disappointing team. I've walked through fire and in the process learned that victories are on the other side—that underneath our biggest problems lie our biggest opportunities. I've learned that truly impactful leaders and organizations don't try to hide from the things they can't control—they master the things they can control, until that mastery turns them into the champions they want to be.

This pillar in *The Power of Playing Offense* will arm us with the grit, the resilience, the adaptability, the agility, the bravery, the tenacity, and the courage to stand tallest when fear and risk is highest. We will explore how to conquer the many storms of life so that adversity does not derail us but rather serves as a catalyst to own the hardships and grow stronger from them.

CHAPTER 4 *will navigate the arc of adversity, from revealing true character to transformation.*

CHAPTER 5 *will empower your mindset to cultivate daily grit and master enduring resilience.*

CHAPTER 6 *will provide a playbook on what is required to lead through the storm and inspire followers during the toughest of times.*

With that, let's dive in.

4

ADVERSITY DOESN'T BUILD CHARACTER; IT REVEALS IT

It was a day unlike any the NFL had ever seen. On this Monday morning, I walked into Levi's Stadium with no idea what to expect. Over time, I'd been groomed and prepped on how to handle the wins and the losses—but for this one day in particular, there was no playbook to learn from.

I was at the 49ers when Colin Kaepernick kneeled.

This is *not* a political or social view, but rather what it was like to be on the inside, heading up sales for the 49ers, on the front lines facing our fans and clients the day after Colin took a knee.

THE DAY AFTER COLIN KAEPERNICK KNEELED

You could cut through the tension with a knife. The anxiety only rose as our inboxes and voicemail boxes filled overnight. Phones were still ringing off the hook from season-ticket holders, corporate partners, and every other stakeholder you can imagine—expressing their views as a backlash to Colin expressing his own views. Many were threatening to walk away and never invest another dollar in our organization until we cut him from the team. Tens of millions of dollars hung in the balance.

At 8:00 a.m., we got the word. Our owner and president wanted to meet with the entire sales and service team, from department heads to front lines.

In my mind I expected the reaction most would—one where the universally understood approach of CYA (cover your a**) and damage control would script our responses and reactions to the outside world.

What transpired in that meeting left us in shock. We couldn't believe what we were told. It seemed unreal.

While we anticipated a PR-laden message, we got the opposite. No direct opinions of right or wrong were discussed. It was purely our executives saying that we support every employee of our organization in expressing their views—whether an entry-level accountant or our star quarterback. *We at the 49ers will forever support that human right.*

No script was given to us. We were told to chase the storm—return all calls, openly listen to differing views, take any meeting requested, and allow the access to our executives that we felt appropriate. We stood united to support Colin in his efforts to express himself while also respecting how everybody internal and external to our organization needed to process it. That was it. Meeting adjourned.

With those marching orders, we set out to play some offense of our own. As expected, many on the outside walked away from their bills and invoices as they said they would, but few questioned our approach and values. By not voicing right or wrong, listening with empathy, and standing firm on the right to freely express oneself (as Colin did), we braved the storm and came out stronger as a team, as a unit, and as a tribe—with a newfound respect for our owner and president to proudly wear the red and gold. I was honored to be a 49er. And I think many of my colleagues were, too.

The decision may have cost us millions on the books, but it gained us priceless commitment, dedication, and accountable service by our most valuable internal gifts—our people.

What this rare experience taught me is that our internal values and character have the opportunity to shine brightest in the most trying times. Better said—adversity does not build character; it reveals it.

Thank you, Jed York and Al Guido, for revealing your character—we're all better and stronger for it.

"The ultimate measure of a man is not where he stands in moments of comfort and convenience, but where he stands at times of challenge and controversy."

MARTIN LUTHER KING JR.

minister, activist

ADVERSITY IS INEVITABLE

Life will continue to test us. Adversity will inevitably knock on each of our doors. The storms of life may vary by severity, but they don't vary by probability. It is not an *if* game; it is a *when* game.

They say death and taxes are the only two certainties in life. I'd argue adversity is a close third. It comes in many forms: tragedy, crisis, loss. And it enters our life in many ways: family, health, business, relationships, career.

Adversity does not discriminate. I know this to be true because I have been surrounded by it my entire life. I also acknowledge that everybody processes adversity in different ways. I don't wear overcoming adversity as a badge of honor; rather, I wear it because it has molded me into who I am today. I hope that I have already experienced the worst day of my life, but I'm not sure—and may never know.

What I do know is my life forever changed on December 8, 2001.

LOSING MY ROLE MODEL

I picked up the phone as a boy, and I hung up as a man.

During finals of my freshman year at USC, my mom's next-door neighbor called to tell me I needed to come home. I didn't know why, but I didn't question it. Halfway through the eight-mile drive from campus, I burst out in tears, sensing what was coming. I pulled up to the driveway. My neighbor walked right past me. No eye contact, like I was a ghost. I opened the door and saw my mom crying hysterically on the floor—pointing at my room.

I found my dad resting in my bed, looking as peaceful as I'd ever seen him. It felt like a dream. I didn't want to believe it, but I knew I would never have a conversation or watch another baseball game with him again. To this day, I can't explain it, but that was the first night he ever slept in my bed—as if he knew it might be his last. Ultimately, diabetes got the best of my dad at the age of fifty-five, something he had been battling since he was seventeen years young.

With our tragic loss, a silver lining did appear years later. My relationship with my mom, which had largely been one of traditional love and respect, took on a new light—especially since I am an only child. She went from mom to best friend. From parent to partner.

As for my dad, he has inspired me more since the day he passed then when he was did when he alive—and I feel like the luckiest person on earth to have enjoyed every second of nineteen years with him. We always watched baseball together. Our team was the Angels. The year after he passed, they won their first and only World Series to date. My mom and I watched each and every pitch—thinking of the Angel in our life.

"Turn your wounds into wisdom."

OPRAH WINFREY

media executive, philanthropist

Later in the book, I will share my thoughts on how my dad has impacted my life since his passing. For now, I'd just like to say, "I miss you every day, Dad—and I hope I'm making you proud."

My dad's gravestone: "Larry J. Epstein. Beloved Husband of Esthella. Father of Paul. Teacher and Friend to Many. An Inspiration to All. 1946–2001."

LIFE IS A SERIES OF TEMPORARY TESTS

"This, too, shall pass." We've all heard this ancient adage, and in the case of adversity, there couldn't be a truer statement. As much as adversity is guaranteed in life, the other side of the pendulum is that any given dose of adversity is temporary. I realize that sentence is hard to take, and I'm not saying the doses of adversity aren't devastating for a time. But the sun does come up the next day. And the one after that. We do keep living after adversity knocks—and if we understand this process by mastering the *inside game*, we can keep thriving.

Regardless of the severity of the storm, it always ends. Some linger. Some are tragic. Some we overblow. The only conclusion we can draw for all tests that come into our lives is that they are temporary. This doesn't lessen the setback or make it less impactful, it's just a reminder that every storm of life will pass. How we respond to those storms will define whether we come out stronger and more resilient than when we came in.

One of my favorite thought leaders, Tom Bilyeu, shared a similar thought: "Every human being decides how they are going to live their life because we all decide what meaning we give to each and every moment in our lives. We do not decide what shows up. But we do decide how we show up."

If life is like boxing, some adversities come in the form of a haymaker, while others are frequent body blows. What I have realized is that the more I'm hit, the more my body is calloused, the more my mind is toughened . . . and the more I'm ready to punch back.

STUDY YOUR LOSSES

"Every no gets you closer to a yes." Words of the sales gods.

Over the years, I took this message to heart when I was doing battle over the phone. As Ben Affleck, the lead trainer in the movie *Boiler Room* said, "A sale is made on every call. Either you sell the client some stock, or he sells you a reason he can't. Either way, a sale is made, the only question is who is gonna close? You or him?"

I fell in love with the game on every call. I loved a *yes* but got more fired up with a *no*—knowing that the next *yes* was that much closer. It was the fuel that I needed to go through each day. As I gained experience, my inner belief and confidence caught up to my natural sales ability, resulting in top performance within my team, followed by league-wide recognition.

Soon, confidence became cockiness. Ability became arrogance. But the scoreboard looked great, so I was well taken care of and looked after.

I stepped into an interview for the highest-selling role that Staples Center had to offer. I thought I was a shoo-in. My resume spoke for itself—and the interview, piece of cake. Or so I thought.

I walked out of the conference room feeling fantastic. Nailed every response. Finished the interviewers' sentences. Now it was just a waiting game. The call came quick.

After the initial pleasantries, the verdict hit. I heard a word I had become very comfortable and accustomed to, but this time it felt different. The word *no* didn't bother me one bit on a sales call. It was nothing personal. But this time, hearing that I didn't get the job, I took the *no* real personal.

I couldn't understand why they passed. I asked and didn't get much feedback. It crushed me because I felt destined for this role. It reminded me of the time LeBron James said, "I'm taking my talents to South Beach"—only I was going to take my talents from the Clippers to AEG, one of the largest players in the sports and entertainment landscape.

Life had a different plan. I needed to deflate myself back to reality.

"Success is a lousy teacher. It seduces smart people into thinking they can't lose."

BILL GATES

philanthropist, co-founder and former CEO, Microsoft

This *no* got me closer to the *yes* that really mattered. The *yes* of being myself. Humble, as I was raised to be. I don't know who that other Paul was, but I own it. I didn't deserve that opportunity at that time.

The process of overcoming this once-heartbreaking rejection taught me another invaluable lesson: *study your losses.* I now study every loss knowing that there has to be a deeper meaning. While the analysis is painful in the moment, it has unlocked countless truths in my life. I now know who I am and who I'm not. I'm certain that the learnings from the losses have paid greater dividends than the wins.

As for the manager that didn't hire me, she and I are now great friends and enjoy some laughs about "the old Paul." She's since hired me to train her team on leadership, culture, and purpose. Funny how it all worked out. I just took a long, humbling, and inspiring road to get there.

TIME-OUT: Think of the top professional loss you've endured. Then think of the key lessons learned and how you've applied them to create positive outcomes in your future. Write those notes down so you can share them out.

This is an example of how to transform a mindset of adversity into achievement, by displaying themes of grit, resilience, and perseverance. Beyond the time-out, let's take this impact to your team—with the flexibility of making it personal.

Set a meeting (off-site recommended) with your team in the next three weeks called "Study Your Losses." Here's an email template for you to use:

> **Subject: Study Your Losses**
>
> In life, there are moments we win, and moments we lose. Nobody is immune to these results. Think of a time you lost. It can be personal. It can be professional.
>
> - What is the key lesson you learned from it?
> - How have you applied that learning in your life?
> - What positive outcomes have resulted since?
>
> We'll all share our losses with the group; I'll go first.
>
> Looking forward to the conversation!

This can be an empowering conversation by showing up as a team with humility, vulnerability, transparency, and courage. The trust, bonds, and connection will follow, no doubt.

Wild card idea—once it has been experienced with your team, propose this for your next leadership retreat.

TRANSFORMING ADVERSITY TO COURAGEOUS ACHIEVEMENT

As we've acknowledged, adversity is inevitable—and it comes in many forms, for many purposes. It's often adversity that's needed to shine a light on our most significant growth opportunities. It can be more difficult to grow and develop when skies are blue and life is utopian—but with storm comes potential. Show me a storm that you come out of, and I'll show you an opportunity to achieve things you didn't think were possible.

Coming off the humbling experience I just shared, my career got on a roll. One promotion after another—there was nearly a decade spanning four organizations where growth opportunities came in abundance. Of course, I had to earn the climb—but I was in a groove and started to feel unlimited in my potential—so long as I kept putting in the work, building relationships, and hitting the marks.

THE POWER OF OWNERSHIP

I was already in the formal leadership ranks of the sports industry, and this decade-long run of career growth led to heights I had never imagined. I humbly served legendary leaders, and I learned from every experience. I absorbed the playbook on what fuels high-performance teams, what inspires intrinsic motivation, what cultivates grit and resilience, and how to build championship cultures. This journey consisted of multiple record-breaking revenue campaigns in the NFL and NBA, with the industry accolades to accompany them.

I felt ready for the big seat. I had built up experience and expertise across all sales and service disciplines. I thought I was as well positioned as I possibly could be.

Months after finding my 'Why,' I got called into the team president's office. I knew that he was evaluating who would take over the entire sales and service enterprise. I was ready for the announcement—already envisioning the aftermath of sharing the great news with my wife. I could barely contain myself.

What I got was something I didn't expect. I got a compliment sandwich—and I wasn't hungry. Paraphrasing what I heard—*We love ya. You didn't get the promotion. I know this sucks. Keep it up.* There was minimal explanation other than the leader who'd gotten the job had more experience.

Personally, I was demoralized. I felt like I had let everybody down. I dreaded the chat with my wife.

Professionally, I was disgusted. This would likely mean years in my current seat with little to no growth based on the domino effects of this decision. I was embarrassed to share the news with my team. I wanted no part in talking to my new boss, even though he had done nothing to me personally. I was mortified at the thought of sitting in the next leadership meeting, feeling like every peer leader would understand that my new boss's gain had become my loss—and I had to *wear it.*

I started to question whether this blemish would derail my career brand after being on such a hot streak. It was a massive hit to my ego and my self-worth. I'd thought I'd earned it, and then I didn't. Especially coming fresh off finding my 'Why,' I felt like this was my time. This was my shot—only no fairy tales here.

Full of dread, I went home to share the news with my wife. She was heated—and I'm being polite. It was beautiful to see the fury because there was love buried deep down in it. The silver lining was that calming her down significantly calmed me down. So much so that I woke up at peace.

After driving to the office, the water cooler buzz had already spread. I half-heartedly accepted the professional condolences and was shocked at how much of a gentleman I was being. My demeanor defied logic with the wound being so fresh—but it was my authentic feeling at that time. I still disagreed with the decision, but I *owned* the result—and I *owned* that my story wasn't fully written.

The next weekend, I coached myself through the ramifications of the decision—how it would impact my career, whether I still believed in staying where I was, if I could genuinely serve as a leader in this organization, and how my newly found purpose and values could serve me at a time like now, when I felt like I was in a professional gutter.

I began to think about my experience with the organization holistically, from start to finish. This decision was merely a data point in the journey. Through that prism, the bigger picture still looked positive. From there, I shifted my energies to my 'Why' and core values. I vowed to make them actionable and provide positive momentum to this otherwise undesirable situation. Here's what my notes looked like:

MY WHY:

To inspire purpose in others so they can play offense in life.

MY VALUES:

BELIEF: I believe in people because they have believed in me. Continue to believe in the people around me, especially at a time like now.

GROWTH: This is the mindset I can attack each day with. *How can I grow from this experience?*

AUTHENTICITY: This is who I am. Don't sell out or change because things got shitty on the outside. Be who I am on my best day, now more than ever.

COURAGE: Stand tallest when fear and risk are highest. It's easy to get small right now. Use this as an opportunity to take a bold action SOON.

IMPACT: This is how I will measure success in each day. My position shouldn't limit my potential for impact. Find a way to create impact from my current role, or find a role where I can.

By using my 'Why' and values as my lens, I gave myself an opportunity to brush myself off and transform adversity into professional achievement. Within weeks of writing these notes, I took action. I doubled down on my passion project of being a Why Coach inside the 49ers and put pen to paper on a professional vision I had of creating a department centered around purpose. This vision became the business plan for the 49ers Academy, to this day the crown jewel of my career—one that never would have happened without each step and decision along the way.

"Responsibility equals accountability equals ownership. And a sense of ownership is the most powerful weapon a team or organization can have."

PAT SUMMITT

former Tennessee Lady Vols college basketball coach, winner of eight NCAA championships

"UNDERNEATH OUR BIGGEST PROBLEMS LIE OUR BIGGEST OPPORTUNITIES"

I heard these words spoken by NFL Hall of Fame running back Curtis Martin, as our Leadership Institute hosted a TED Talk in 2019. Curtis shared heartfelt stories about his upbringing—stories that would easily lend themselves toward him being yet another statistic on the street. But that's not how Curtis looked at it. He saw light in the darkness. He saw opportunities under the adversity. These opportunities led him to become one of the greatest running backs of his time, now on a mission to create a philanthropic impact even greater—to leave this world better than he found it.

When Curtis said, "Underneath our biggest problems lie our biggest opportunities," it struck me as one of the greatest truths I'd heard. Reflecting back on life, I have found that there are two mindsets when we confront adversity: one that sees the hurdles, obstacles, and why we *cannot* do something, and one that sees possibilities, opportunities, and why we *can* do something.

YOU'VE BEEN HERE BEFORE

For many of us, the global pandemic of 2020 provided an opportunity to reflect on what matters most in our lives. It showed us how abruptly adversity can strike. It also offered an opportunity to transform into role models—to shift from *helpless* to *helpful* for those who needed us during these *unprecedented* times.

While we may not be able to personally prepare ourselves for a vast pandemic, I do believe we can show up with a grittier and more resilient mindset the next time a storm of this magnitude rolls around.

As mentioned in the prior pillar, our minds are wired to seek stability, security, comfort, and safety—none of which were available in abundance during the pandemic. The immediate reactions brought about tremendous fear, risk, and anxiety—driving uncertainty across all aspects of life.

My perspective is that one word amplified these negative feelings. It was a word that was on the news every second. You couldn't avoid it if you tried—and it got in our heads, especially early on.

The word is *unprecedented*.

This word struck fear in all of us because we felt as though we hadn't been here before.

My view is that a belief that *we have been here before* could have had a tremendously positive effect on our morale and mindsets throughout the pandemic. Perhaps the health-related aspect of the pandemic was *unprecedented*, but the ripple effect and the impact on our lives were *not* all *unprecedented*.

Based on our personal histories, we have felt the way elements of the pandemic made us feel before. Many of us have been afraid in our lives. Many of us have faced tremendous risk in our lives. Many of us battle with anxiety every day of our lives. These are the same feelings we had because of the pandemic. And yet, we said *we've never been here before*—yes, we have.

We've experienced these negative emotions, and we've battled through, in some cases to come out bigger, faster, and stronger.

You have made it out of the past storms in your life—and that can be an empowering playbook to learn from and apply when a storm strikes back.

So, the next time you hear the word *unprecedented*—stop. Process it and ask yourself if you've been there before. Then use that memory as motivation for how to take the next step.

Let's dive deeper and apply this exercise in our lives.

APPLYING THE PLAYBOOK

CHAPTER 4: YOU'VE BEEN HERE BEFORE

Let's take a trip back to memory lane and look at the adversity you've faced in life. Those times when s*** inevitably hits the fan, *but* you came out stronger for it. We've all experienced those moments where we had a feeling that things would never be the same.

How awesome would it have been if you had a playbook before those moments hit that would have empowered you to fight through with more grit, resilience, courage, and perseverance?

This is that playbook.

This process will not prevent the storms or remove them from your life, but it will guide you in navigating through them in a more confident fashion, feeling as if you've been there before. Our minds are wired for stability, security, comfort, and safety—but then when adversity hits, it derails our train of thought, and fear and risk avoidance creep in.

This exercise calls a time-out so that you're aware of these feelings and now have a process to acknowledge them, work through them, and come out of the other side with a gritty game plan—because it will connect your past examples of perseverance to the times in the future where you'll need it. Think of this as your tool belt of resilience.

With that, let's play offense and get to work.

STEP ONE

Identify three major storms in your life. Examples are losing a loved one, a medical condition impacting you or somebody close to you, financial hardships where you didn't know what life would look like in ninety days, or hitting rock bottom professionally—losing hope for your future career ambitions. These are merely a few examples of hundreds that are possible. Pick three that have been most impactful in your life.

Write them down on a piece of paper. As examples, "Lost father," "Fired from job," "Grandma became ill."

STEP TWO

For each example reflect back to the biggest lesson that you took away from the experience or person. Focus on the positive aspect of that discovery. Of course, this is not easy; it was a storm, after all. It may have come years later, but reflect back on a light at the end of that tunnel. This could be the redirection that forced your hand in changing companies when you didn't get the big promotion, and that's when your career started to flourish. In the case of losing a loved one, consider a significant lesson or wisdom they imparted to you and how you've now applied it to better yourself.

Write these notes down. Give yourself a few minutes to do so.

STEP THREE

In each example reflect back on what actions you took or decisions you made to advance the process, fight through the adversity, dust yourself off, get back up, or provide closure on the negative experience/storm in your life.

Write these notes down. Give yourself a few minutes to do so.

STEP FOUR

Keep these notes handy for the inevitable storms in life that are ahead. I hope that you are feeling pretty damn strong right about now. You endured the struggle and came out if it. It may not have been pretty (or easy) in the moment, but you persevered. You came out bigger, faster, and stronger—although you may not have seen it that way at the time, or even until now. At minimum, you learned and continued to move forward. These past experiences give you more armor for the battles of tomorrow. Use these notes as your shield when negative thoughts come into your mind. When you feel like "you haven't been here before," remind yourself that "you have been here before." The next moment adversity appears in your life, ask yourself these five questions:

1. What situation (storm) have I been through in the past that reminds me of this?
2. When did I feel a similar sense of fear, risk, anxiety, helplessness, ______ ________________ about a situation? Fill in the blank with a different negative feeling if it better describes your situation.
3. How did I emerge from that situation?
4. What did I learn from that situation?
5. How can I apply it to this current situation?

Simply put, go back to the playbook of how you conquered the storms of the past in order to conquer the storms in your future.

You got this.

5

CULTIVATING GRIT AND MASTERING RESILIENCE

"Young man, you have walked through fire."

Those were the words I heard from the HR director just after being hired by the New Orleans Hornets, coming from the Los Angeles Clippers. Based on the environmental turmoil I had experienced in LA, he explained why he believed in me and challenged me to approach the opportunity in New Orleans with the same levels of grit, tenacity, and resilience.

Little did he know that his advice would be tested within months, as the story you heard in Chapter 2 about saving the Hornets became reality—and the rest of the script started to unfold.

WALKING THROUGH FIRE

The HR director knew my career journey to that point, and, yeah, I certainly felt like I had walked through some flames. Here are the grittiest of highlights:

- sold what ESPN voted the worst brand in sports during an economic recession
- represented the red-headed stepchild in a two-team market where the other was clearly king
- salvaged an NBA franchise from permanent relocation
- was immersed in a community where fans have boycotted ownership
- endured an NBA lockout, stripped of the daily ability to contribute and make an impact, with daily threats of pay cuts and furloughs looming
- on the front lines facing clients the morning after Colin Kaepernick kneeled
- took sharp hits to the ego while hosting potential partners in half-empty stadiums
- sold hope to fans in the midst of decades of futility—all while being tasked to deliver business results for cellar-dwelling teams time and time again, only enjoying one playoff experience over a fifteen-year career in sports

Some might call that the luck of a black cat!

These were the market conditions our teams had to endure through my run in the NFL and NBA as a business leader and coach of sales organizations. It would have been easy to make excuses, point fingers, or play the victim, especially when team performance was 100 percent uncontrollable from our seats.

Many of us fall in love with the high-stakes, public facing side of sports—the reality TV of each game, intensity of the locker room, dramatic post-game press conference, agony of defeat, and the thrill of victory. I was attracted to the industry for many of the same reasons. But now, I faced a different reality and a different drama.

I was the guy behind the curtain responsible for filling the stadiums to watch the players play, and those challenges had no simple answers. There wasn't a draft pick or big free agent to alleviate our struggles. This was a world of brute daily force to grind it out and battle the market. We were tasked with successfully carrying out each campaign, then asked to take on the next, and on and on.

Given the high stakes, I ask myself: How did our sales teams navigate these difficult market conditions to get recognized with industry-wide accolades for top business performance?

That is the playbook we will continue to unpack through *The Power of Playing Offense*.

MARKET CONDITIONS ARE EXCUSES

At times in our careers, we'll work for the market leaders. Let me know how that feels.

At other times in our careers, we'll work for the underdog—where we have to scrap and claw our way through each day. Always swimming against the current, wind never at our back, no 50–50 balls bouncing our way.

I would argue this is the fun part—where the world knows you have to catch what you eat. No white-glove delivery service. No incoming calls with massive customer orders. It's the daily battle that many of us face in our careers as we work for the runner-up.

Ultimately, we have two choices in this scenario: complain that we're not the market leader, in envy, spending countless hours trying to chase who they are and what they do, then realize that when we're about to catch them, they've already made their next move. We're playing checkers while they're playing chess. That's the reason they're leading the pack.

Or, we can embrace the fact that there's only one direction to go. The market conditions only reflect the score of today, not tomorrow. We own where we are, and we're inspired by where we're headed. We choose to compete with ourselves and play the game by our rules.

I have learned that regardless of the market conditions or our position in it, somebody will always end up on top of the board. So, I ask you: How scrappy are you willing to get? And will you do the things that others won't?

When I hang up my cleats at the end of a career, I want them to be muddy. I want them to tell a story of the fight. I want others to know that nothing was given to me. I went out on my terms, known less for my talent and more for the courage and conviction in the journey.

> *"You can choose courage, or you can choose comfort. You cannot have both."*
>
> **BRENÉ BROWN**
> author of *Dare to Lead*

HIRE THE PHDS

When you only experience one playoff run over a fifteen-year journey, the losses become routine—dare I say expected? My job as a leader of customer-facing teams was to keep us insulated from the toxicity and noise. My aim was always to keep morale and engagement high, inspire the troops, and spread positivity every opportunity I could—while balancing the performance on the books.

There were two challenges that I faced in these scenarios. One internal, one external. While I expected to deal with the noise of the fan externally—after all, *fan* is short for fanatic—I was surprised at the impact of the water cooler buzz internally. With the losses stacking up on the playing surface, the negativity would start to penetrate the walls of our front office. Eventually, the voice of the market would break through.

Leading a team of sales and service executives who hear it from fans all day—venting about the team, canceling orders after buyer's remorse, one rejection after another, then repeat this cycle to make one hundred calls a day, year-round—you can imagine how taxing this could be for anybody, regardless of how gritty and resilient their demeanor was.

From my seat, the playbook of infusing daily positivity and inspiration was only partially working—my spiel became white noise if overdone.

It wasn't until I took a radical shift in my approach that everything changed. Knowing I couldn't control the negativity and noise of the market, I started to think about what I could control and could influence. I started to evaluate our business locker room, player by player—studying who was succeeding in these toxic times. A trend emerged.

Those who succeeded came in with a story beyond a chip on the shoulder. They had lived lives that some of us could never fathom—tragedy, crisis, significant loss, rough upbringing, given up on. And yet, here they were, wanting to work in professional sports—for a different reason. They weren't doing it for the flash of the business card. They were doing it to prove to themselves that they could.

They were doing it to escape the trials of their lives, which had led them to largely *play defense*—to have glimmers of hope so they could now *play offense*. In turn, they knew that they would also prove themselves to all the doubters who'd said they wouldn't make it. Similar to how the Hornets HR director described my path, they had already *walked through fire*. A losing team or screaming fan would be the least of their worries.

This persona became my target. To endure the losing cultures, we needed winning mentalities. Mentalities that only life experience could mold. Mentalities that don't need things to go right on the outside for them to feel great on the inside.

I started to seek out the scrappy. Proven grit was a must. Proven resilience was non-negotiable. The hungrier and more determined, the better. Resumes became secondary. Life story became primary.

We hired the PHDs. *Passionate—Hungry—Determined.*

Implementing this philosophy early in my leadership career is one of the foundational elements that led to success on the books. Trust me, there were some dark days—but it was the people around me that made it worthwhile. They inspired me to be even more grateful for the opportunity. In turn, I poured every ounce of belief back into them. Most were already on a mission. My job was to clear their path toward greatness, knowing that they would scrap their way toward success—and significance.

TIME-OUT: Time to create your own version of PHD. Make it specific by role; pick just one for now. Think of your top three performers in that role. What three characteristics do they have in common? That's your new PHD. Have some fun with it. Once I started to socialize the PHD mantra, I was constantly asked by others around the office, "Where's the next PHD?" Most importantly, make your PHD criteria nonnegotiable. It will pay major dividends for your internal culture and external recruiting efforts.

Set a meeting with your fellow leaders or head of HR to co-create. I'm always curious and excited to see what different leaders and teams come up with. Feel free to send me a message on LinkedIn with your version of the PHD.

FALL DOWN SEVEN, RISE EIGHT

Mike Tyson always said that "Everybody has a plan until they get punched in the mouth."

Knowing that adversity will inevitably knock on our door, our choice is not whether to accept it—it's how to embrace it and get up off the mat.

This is the spirit of resilience. Resilience is about the bounce back. Resilience doesn't care if you fall. It actually needs you to fall, so you have something to get up from.

There are two elements of mastering resilience.

One is mindset. Over time, there comes a belief and acknowledgment that you've been here before. Perhaps you fell for different reasons, but the muscle memory is built—knowing that this is simply the next time, and it likely won't be the last. Nelson Mandela, who endured years as a political prisoner before becoming president of South Africa, epitomized resilience: "Do not judge me by my success; judge me by how many times I fell down and got back up again."

The second is an essential prerequisite to achieve this resilient mindset—experience. No shortcuts. You have to go through the pain, go through the losses, and go through the rejection to fully realize this strength.

Unlike the boxing world of Tyson where the best fighters can virtually go undefeated over decades, business and life are much closer to the Ultimate Fighting Championship (UFC)—where the champion changes belts several times a year, and even the best fighters constantly lose fights.

There is no perfect record in business or in life. It's how you respond to the losses that will define you.

> *"To be gritty is to keep putting one foot in front of the other. To be gritty is to hold fast to an interesting and purposeful goal. To be gritty is to invest, day after week after year, in challenging practice. To be gritty is to fall down seven times, and rise eight."*
>
> **ANGELA LEE DUCKWORTH**
> author of *Grit*

RISING FROM REJECTION

How's this for a life?

You do stand-up comedy as a hobby and frequently get booed off stages—a reminder that this is far from your calling. Since you can't buy a laugh, might as well go to the Happiest Place on Earth. You get a gig at Disney World to audition as Goofy—only to find out that there is a 5'8" height requirement, so you end up as a freaking Chipmunk!

Determined to take a different path, you explore the white-collar world of business to follow in your family's footsteps. Your father is a successful attorney, so you prep for the LSAT—only to fail twice.

Broken but not defeated, you settle to get any role possible at this point. Set a low bar, get a low bar. You're now at a ground-level sales role, selling fax machines. Not only selling fax machines—you're doing it at a time where they're close to becoming obsolete.

These body blows and nonstop rejection were the reality for somebody who is now recognized by *Time* magazine as one of the one hundred most influential people in the world. *Forbes* has also recognized her as one of the most powerful women in the world—mentored by Richard Branson, running in business and philanthropic circles with Oprah, Bill Gates, and Warren Buffett, just to name a few.

Her company now generates north of $350 million in annual revenues. If you ask her what she attributes her success to, she openly admits that it wouldn't have happened without the daily rejection of selling fax machines. Knocking door to door, kicked out of countless buildings by security guards, hung up on one cold call after another, even having her business card ripped in front of her face on multiple occasions.

She calls it "great life training." I call it one hell of a storm chaser.

This is the story of Sara Blakely, founder of Spanx.

While selling fax machines by day, Sara dedicated her evenings and weekends for years to developing a prototype for what would one day become Spanx—all from a personal experience where she cut the feet off her pantyhose while getting ready to go to a party.

As Sara tried to socialize the concept, again, she ran into the same issues she faced in the fax machine game. One rejection after another, she continued to play offense, tenaciously persistent, displaying the grit necessary—all in an effort to stay optimistic enough to brave the storm and catch her much-needed break.

It finally came—ironically, from someone who had rejected her in the past.

The rest is history. Spanx is now a household name, and Blakely is one of the world's wealthiest self-made women. Sara proudly shares a great life lesson for us all: "One of my greatest weaknesses is also one of my greatest strengths," she said. "Being underestimated."

Sara rose from the trenches of rejection, as we all have the ability to do. Adversity did not build Sara's character; it revealed it.

To think, even Goofy rejected her at one point!

TIME-OUT: Rejection can be a powerful force in our lives. Hopefully, we are all learning and growing from it. Let's flip the script and also ask who has said YES to us.

Put thirty minutes of private reflection time on the calendar sometime in the next two weeks. During your reflection, on a two-column sheet of paper, write down the following:

- Top three to five professional rejections of your life (we've all had them). Write those in the left column
- Top three to five professional "yeses" of our life (it can be a job, an idea, a project, etc.). Write those in the right column.

Look for the themes and patterns in each column by asking yourself these questions:

- How did I show up leading up to these situations (your actions, behaviors, attitudes)?
- Is there any similarity or commonality of the types of people or groups that reject or are attracted to me?

As an example, more technical and analytical types have rejected me. Big thinkers, visionaries, and optimists have been attracted to me and said yes more often to me as a person and my ideas. They've given me opportunities.

Know whom you attract and whom you repel. This will tell you a lot about how you show up, and perhaps the type of people you want to be around in all aspects of life, while still acknowledging that you can do a better job of attracting those who traditionally have rejected you. It's a great exercise to process on your own, then potentially share with your team.

CONQUERING CHANGE

We live in a working world that has never been faster, more complex, or more disruptive. Competitive threats are around every corner. There's a fight for finite resources, rising consumer standards, and shifting expectations—all the wars for talent are becoming fiercer and more intense than we've ever seen.

If this is the game we're playing, I ask you one simple question: how can you possibly survive by *playing defense,* where you let the market dictate the terms?

- Are you feeling the pressure versus applying the pressure?
- Are you playing from your heels versus playing from your toes?
- Are you playing to survive versus playing to thrive?
- Are you playing not to lose versus playing to win?

In these highly disruptive times, I challenge you to *play offense*—now more than ever.

MASSIVE DISRUPTION LEADS TO MASSIVE OPPORTUNITY

In January of 2020, I launched my consultancy, Purpose Labs. Within our first two months, we had engaged an entire team of over one hundred business executives responsible for all revenue at SoFi Stadium (home of the Los Angeles Rams and Los Angeles Chargers). The experience was focused on finding their collective 'Why' and their personal 'Why'—then aligning the two so they could amplify their purpose through the stadium's mission.

What resulted was SoFi Stadium's 'Why': *to unite so that we inspire life's greatest moments.*

The scene was set at Banc of California Stadium (home of LAFC) for Purpose Labs to guide a team from Legends and SoFi Stadium to—as the scoreboard says—"Find Our Why."

In that same week, Purpose Labs held engagements with the USC Marshall School of Business Alumni Association and Pepperdine University MBAs. It was one of the most purposeful and impactful weeks of my professional life, and the next thirty days would be equally exciting and even more jam-packed.

Coupling the successful launch of Purpose Labs with my keynote-speaking trajectory, 2020 was booked and ready to take off. People around the world were about to *play offense.*

Then March of 2020 hit, and the global pandemic was suddenly upon us.

Individually—most in society became uncertain, anxious, fearful, and risk-averse, putting most aspects of life on hold.

In business—markets crashed, industries were ravished, unemployment was at record levels, and budgets for anything unessential were paused indefinitely.

As a result of the pandemic, my 2020 calendar was cleared. Live events—the lifeblood of my speaking and training business—were all canceled. Months after betting on myself and walking away from stability, security, and financial comfort, I found myself at a fork in the road that could have life-altering effects.

I was determined to see my business through. Failure was not an option. I had the necessary family conversations and decided to plow forward—but where? To do what? My entire industry was on hold with limited light at the end of the tunnel.

It turns out that this chapter of life had a valuable lesson baked into it.

In sales, we trained others to have no fear of loss. When thinking of prospects, we coached that some will; some won't. So what? That mindset empowers you to not get attached to outcomes, take it personally, or be afraid to lose something that wasn't there to begin with.

That's exactly what I felt in this moment. My business had been turned upside-down—but the good news was I had nothing to hold on to, so I wasn't afraid to lose it.

"Every adversity, every failure, every heartache carries with it the seed of an equal or greater benefit."

NAPOLEON HILL

author of *Think and Grow Rich*

After this light-bulb moment, I came back to my *ace in the hole*—my 'Why'—as I had in the past when major life decisions were in play. I asked myself how I could *play offense* at a time like now. I started to look at the key goals I had for my business pre-pandemic, did some visioning exercises, then attached my goals to the impact I wanted to create, and the legacy I wanted to leave behind.

My North Star became: *Impact one million lives by 2030.*

This led to a complete overhaul and reinvention of my business. The mission remained intact, but how I would get there would require some hard pivots. *Adaptability* and *agility* became the name of the game. I detached from what I had built and treated my life and business as a rebirth and relaunch.

The end result? You're reading it. This book would have never happened in 2020 without the pandemic. I got the gift of time back during the quarantine period and went *head-down* for months to pour my heart and soul into these pages—all to create impact for everybody who applies it.

The bigger reinvention goes beyond the book. I am a self-proclaimed technological caveman. Pre-pandemic me used that as a crutch. It was an excuse to do everything old school, in person. While that once worked, the times changed. Even more so, my vision of impacting one million people by 2030 would not be possible if I didn't learn to scale my reinvented business.

That is what led to the continuation of this book's training and application of the playbook online at **WWW.POWEROFPLAYINGOFFENSE.COM**, so the impact of *The Power of Playing Offense* doesn't stop when you flip the last page—you're just getting started.

As Curtis Martin once said, "Underneath our biggest problems are always our biggest opportunities." So true, especially when we chase the storm—and are transformed by it.

CONTROL THE CONTROLLABLES

A common saying in the sports industry, especially in the sales game, is to *control the controllables*. The message is intended to remind us to show up, do our jobs, and focus on what you can control—win, lose, or draw.

As the inside sales manager at the Clippers, I took this up a notch by creating a written pact with my team—I titled it the "Constitution." My intent was to have them focus on three core controllable elements. From my view, these were the essential traits of what made a successful inside sales executive. The catch? None of them were sales results. In a job where that was the sole driver, I looked at it differently. I believed that it was my job to hire the most talented people—and if they could deliver on these three controllables, the score would take care of itself. In exchange for the three controllables, I would take care of their next career moves, opening my Rolodex with no limits, as their biggest champion imaginable.

The three controllables were:

1. Work ethic
2. Positivity
3. Coachability

They were nonnegotiable. Put them in your lunch pail and bring them into work every day. If you didn't, we'd have a conversation the first time. There would be no second conversation. The rules were clear.

An inside sales program was designed to be a six- to nine-month developmental training ground to groom and train the future stars of the sports business landscape. With this backdrop, we wrote the Constitution commitments on a whiteboard in our office. Each sales executive signed it, as did I. I even wrote their six- to nine-month window next to their name, so it was a visible carrot each and every day that I was eager to deliver on.

This pact proved to be extremely powerful. It transformed our team by bonding us as partners to meet at the 50 and focus on what we could control. The Clippers were a perennial last-place team at the time. We certainly couldn't control that—but we could control the controllables, which served as the foundation to show up with a gritty mindset and be resilient enough to bounce back when all odds were stacked against us.

Later in *The Power of Playing Offense*, I'll share how our inside sales team went from #28 in league revenue to #2 during this time.

EXPAND YOUR INFLUENCE

While I was with the Chapman & Co. Leadership Institute, we were training the leadership team at a major airline when we heard a story about how lost baggage got solved at London's Heathrow Airport. Our eyes opened wide—our ears perked up. Many of us have unfortunately experienced this pain. The baggage carousel is slowing down, most on our flight have already left the airport, and we're left searching with no hope in sight. The inconveniences of life and business become reality. We then do what any sane person would do—storm into the lost baggage office!

The manager of Heathrow's baggage department described their team and role as the "face of failure for the organization." Sad, but true. Their jobs were designed to meet customers in their worst moment.

What they did differently at Heathrow was chase the storm before it could fully form. As the baggage carousel was slowing, they would send an agent from behind the desk to connect with the waiting customers. Nothing special or scripted, just small talk about whether it was their first visit to London or recommendations on where to visit.

By creating this human connection, it didn't change the outcome of the situation. The baggage was either lost or it wasn't—but it did diffuse the tension and anger of their customers, so they could now calmly walk over to the lost baggage office to troubleshoot the issue.

In the upcoming exercise of Applying the Playbook, we're about to explore the Control and Influence Model. Here's what this experience would look like from the lens of mindset and action.

OTHER AIRPORTS

CONTROL: Nothing—the baggage is lost.

INFLUENCE: Nothing—the baggage is lost.

CAN'T CONTROL: Everything—the baggage is lost—just pray!

HEATHROW

CONTROL: Our attitudes, our reactions, and how we show up—let's do what we can.

INFLUENCE: Let's play offense by sending a gate agent to the carousel, building connection, and diffusing the situation.

CAN'T CONTROL: We can't control whether the baggage is lost; let's do our best to not lose a customer for life.

Same situation, same dilemma—perhaps it leads to the same outcome, but yet it feels drastically different. Applying this model, you realize that your sphere of influence expands greatly when you troubleshoot what was previously perceived as uncontrollable to become something you can influence.

We all have our version of a "lost baggage problem" in business and in life—something we believe we have no control over. If we do nothing, we lack grit and throw our hands up, giving up hope. If we tackle the storm head on, we build resilience to know we can do more about this situation than we previously thought, and prepare ourselves for the next piece of baggage.

With that, let's dive in.

APPLYING THE PLAYBOOK

CHAPTER 5: CONTROL AND INFLUENCE MODEL

Here's what the control and influence model looks like visually, followed by a populated model filled with examples of things we control, influence, or can't control.

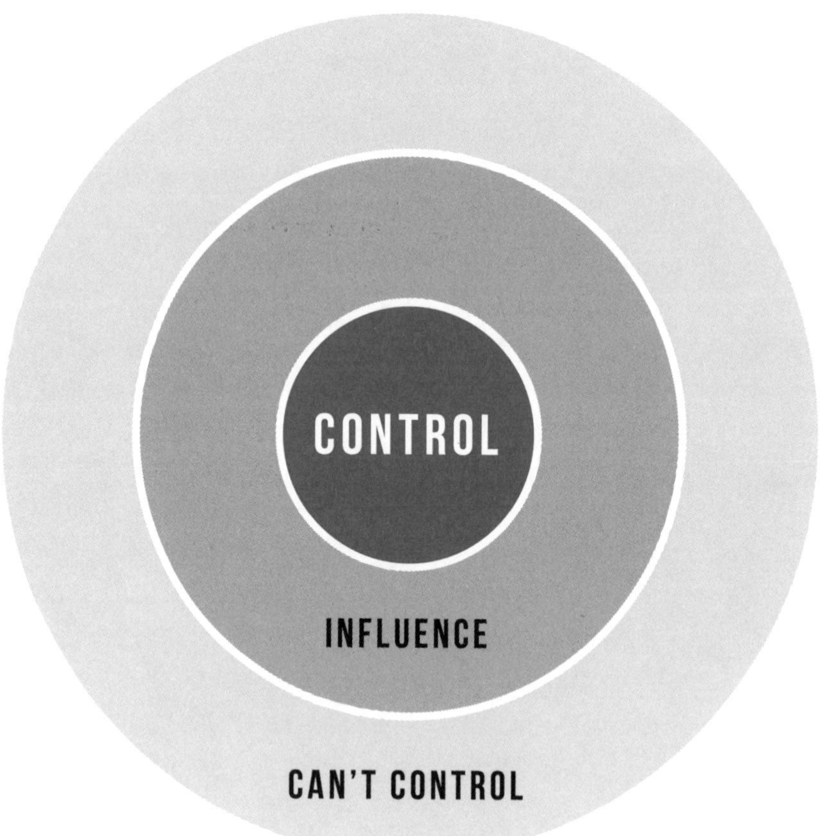

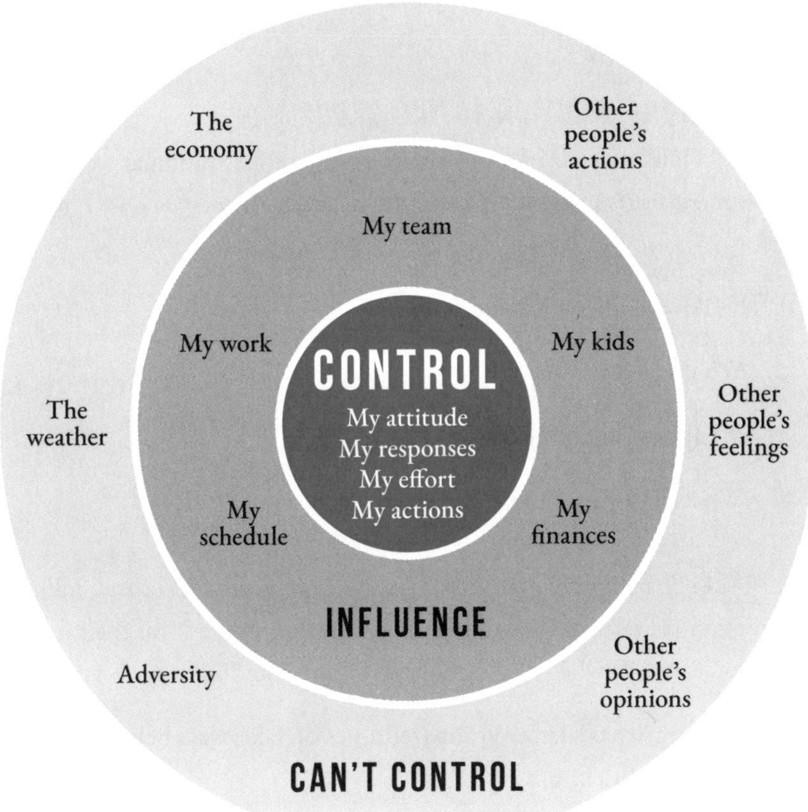

These models will anchor a conversation that you can have with your team, or better yet, your peer group of fellow positional leaders. Either way you slice it, it's time to play offense and maximize your influence.

PRE-MEETING

Set up a sixty-minute meeting to talk through "Process/System Improvements." Frame it as a candid conversation around what's working and what's not. This will excite the group to (a) share their thoughts and (b) increase the impact of the end takeaways when they come to realize that often the external challenges start in our mind and how we approach them. We'll continue to unpack this in the end takeaways of this exercise.

IN-MEETING INSTRUCTION TO THE GROUP

STEP ONE: Think of your biggest process or system frustration at work *(note—this is not a frustration with a person; rather, this is a frustration with a process or system).*

STEP TWO: Answer these three questions:

1. What can you control?
2. What can you influence?
3. What can't you control?

STEP THREE: Share with a partner to talk through what you control, influence, and can't control relative to your biggest frustration, and ask for their feedback on how you can shift what you "can't control" into the "influence" category.

STEP FOUR: Debrief as a larger group (see notes on takeaways below to help you guide the group debriefing).

SIGNIFICANT TAKEAWAY

What you'll uncover from this exercise is that there are very few things we can't control. The weather, economy, and adversity are a few examples, but the list isn't long. Similarly, there is very little we can *fully* control. Our attitude, responses, effort, and action are several examples. In reality, the majority of things we encounter or frustrations we face fall heavily in the influence bucket. View the following model as if it's drawn to scale, with "influence" owning the lion's share of the real estate.

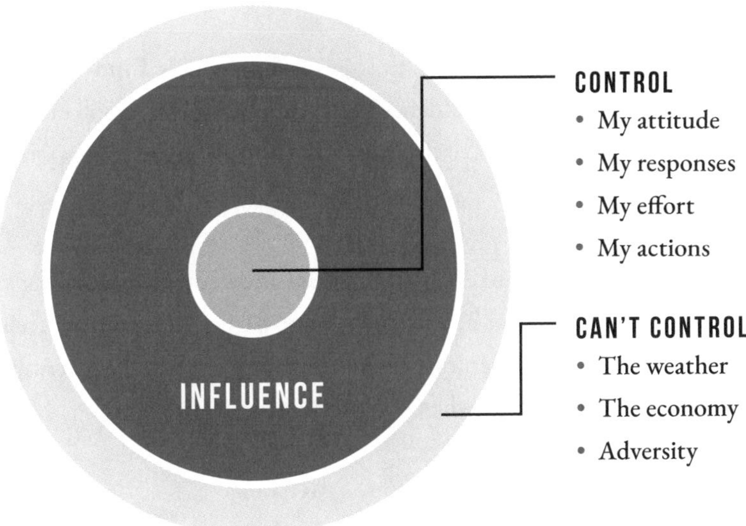

It is empowering to see how much influence we truly have. You as the facilitator will likely hear this "aha" realization from the group during the debriefing period. The key is that we had an opportunity to discuss it with a team member. If this exercise is done privately, we get stuck in feeling that we "can't control" something. When we talk it out with another person, we shift some of those uncontrollable elements into a space of influence—especially when they coach us to do so. This mindset shift of "can't control" to "influence" can be highly effective to train within your direct team and/or your peer team of leaders.

BONUS TAKEAWAY

In this case we're talking about a system or process frustration. The same can apply to any challenge or frustration in life, even people-related problems. The two lessons are:

1. Talk your frustrations out with another person. Ideally, this person is neutral and doesn't have skin in the game relative to your situation. For

example, if it's a boss or employee problem, talk through it with somebody outside of your company.

2. The outcome of the conversation is to shift details from the "can't control" bucket to the "influence" bucket. This question will help: "In which details of what you currently can't control do you see opportunities to create influence?"

When you apply this question to every aspect of business and life (with a person, a system, a process, a job), it can be extremely empowering. You go from feeling helpless to feeling that you can at least create some influence in the given situation. This can be a game changer when you put it into practice.

LEADERS THAT LAST

You've achieved success in your career. CONGRATS. I mean that. In case nobody has recognized you lately for all of the sweat equity that goes into building your career, let me take a moment to say, "I see you, you matter, and what you do makes a difference." Smell the roses, raise a glass, then keep leveling up.

INSIDE A LEADER'S WORLD

You go back into the office tomorrow. The majority of your focus is spent determined to get to the next goal or KPI (key performance indicator) of the month. You're constantly fighting fires, attending nonstop meetings (often meetings to talk about meetings), pulled in different directions between boss, peers, and team—expectations from all angles, just trying to juggle it all and stay afloat.

Every day feels like a dogfight. Time is stretched, and it's only getting worse. Competing priorities couple with internal tensions (if you even have the time to be aware of the tension), and you often question what it all even means.

Then you think of your team—and it snaps you right back into focus. You love your team (on their best days, for sure). If you're being honest, you likely don't spend enough time with them, coaching them and investing in their personal and professional motivations. Coaching sounds amazing, but who has the time?

If I surveyed your team, would they want more of you (as a coach) or less of you? As of today, they're hesitant to knock on your door. You say it's an open-door policy, but it's always closed as you're putting out fires and in yet another "mission critical" meeting. Your team sees how busy and overwhelmed you are—always sprinting, never sitting in place for long, certainly not taking a breath. Without even knowing it, a vicious cycle builds momentum. Less connection with your team has lowered morale, engagement, purpose, productivity, and performance.

You got into leadership because you wanted to be the coach that would inspire others to be their best, to achieve their full potentials, and to impact people much the way the most significant leaders in your life have you. While you've gained the title, money, and responsibilities, there's a gap between who you've become and who you want to be.

So, who are you? Really—at your core, who are you on your best day?

Just when you sit down to process it all, your boss comes around the corner—another fire, cape on, time to save the day.

This is a typical Monday. What I didn't mention is the impact this is having on your home life. The sixty-to-seventy-hour weeks are taking a toll on family and inner circles. Back in the office await intense, short-term pressures, politics, CYA emails, negative water cooler chatter and red tape—all packaged as a never-ending rat race—adding to the stress and anxiety of the day-to-day.

The treadmill you're climbing is only getting faster and steeper, with less support as the weeks and months go by.

You just want to be there for your team so you can be the coach you always envisioned. You want everybody in your locker room to grow personally and professionally. You want to invest in their careers so they can be the best versions of themselves, find purpose in everything they do, and feel like they're part of something bigger than themselves—knowing they make an impact each and every day, to be fulfilled when it's all said and done. You haven't said this out loud, but that's exactly what you want, too.

Leadership is a tremendous responsibility. It gets messy, and it's extremely hard work. The good news: there is a playbook for what great leaders do—to win and to last. You're reading it.

This chapter and the next three pillars will help, tremendously.

BEFORE YOU LEAD OTHERS, YOU MUST FIRST LEAD YOURSELF

As a leadership consultant, I frequently get brought into organizations to do a "people problem" audit. It's often a senior leader who calls on me to evaluate their team, fellow leaders, and individual contributors. They sense that something could be better but can't quite put their finger on it. If I had a nickel for every time I heard the words, "They just don't get it"—let's just say I'd be very well compensated.

While every organization and team has its own unique dynamics, there are a few constants. Culture is the dominant gap—and leaders are the tone setters of culture.

As much as the most senior leader believes that the problems all lie on their team or in the environment, the answer is often in the mirror. That doesn't make me the most popular consultant, but it makes me an honest one.

Leaders often neglect to lead themselves—which becomes a loss of focus and awareness on how their daily actions and behaviors are impacting their team and their organization. Their locker room is fractured by gaps in trust, camaraderie, and connection.

So, how do you solve this puzzle?

Elements of the solution will typically require a mix of vulnerability, humility, candor, trust, and acknowledgment that we as leaders may be the issue, or at least play a major role. The bright spot is, this opens the door for personal growth and transformation.

Before you lead others, you must first lead yourself. I'll start by pulling out a mirror of my own.

GROWTH FROM WITHIN

The day I stopped looking to my left and right, everything changed.

I once mentored an up-and-coming sales executive from another club, connected to me by a fellow mentor of ours. Our chats were always filled with support, generosity, insights, and gratitude. Over the years, we spoke less frequently. We both paved our independent paths as he joined me in the formal leadership ranks of the sports industry.

One day, I saw a LinkedIn profile update—my former mentee had gotten a massive promotion.

I would love to share that I felt substantial joy. But I didn't.

I felt envy as he had now climbed past me in the org charts of our industry. I felt like I'd done my small part in grooming him, and he got the lucky break before I did. The sports industry can be brutally competitive. In this case, it got the best of me.

I was so hyper-focused on looking to my left and right that I lost sight of being the best version of myself. I should have been ecstatic to see the news—but in the microseconds before that reaction, I pulled out a superficial measuring stick of my *perceived* success versus his.

Notice I say *perceived*. It was all in my own head. It was my own insecurity. Shame on me for not being a better leader in this moment. I'm not proud of how I showed up (or in this case, didn't), but I am proud of what transpired after.

I got away from all the career noise on LinkedIn—and decided to focus on my own growth and development. I started to compete with myself.

I no longer looked to my left and right. From that point on, I've looked solely in the mirror, fully in control of my actions, mindsets, and how I show up each day. No outside factors pollute my thoughts. I am purely focused on my own world, my team, my organization, my friends, and my family. You could say I went cold turkey on the rest of the world, but I had to. This was my way of tearing through the muscle and growing as a person. I started by leading myself, measuring success by who I am on my best day—and living to this standard every day.

With this mindset fully internalized and locked in, I re-entered the industry network feeling revitalized and rejuvenated. I was at peace—now able to enjoy and recognize everybody's success because I realized we weren't in competition with one another. We were in our own competition—within ourselves.

This perspective started to color my leadership lens beyond success. It became about significance. By no longer looking left and right, I was now prepared to lead (and mentor) others—because I took the time to lead myself.

"There is nothing noble in being superior to your fellow man; true nobility is being superior to your former self."

ERNEST HEMINGWAY

American novelist, Nobel Prize winner

LEADING IN THE STORM

Leadership is akin to character. Measure a leader during the storm—not in the blue skies. When we chase the storm, we inevitably face daring decisions.

In business, this often leads to a fork in the road—people or bottom line? In blue skies, you can have both. In storms, your morals, ethics, values, character, and compassion will all be tested to levels you may not be comfortable with—but are required for a leader.

Leadership is a responsibility—to provide support and safety for your span of care (i.e., team) to get through the storm. If you do, they'll never forget it on the other side.

There are leaders who I would follow to the end of the earth based on how they treated me and looked after me during a storm. They didn't have to—they wanted to. Thanks to these leaders, I was prepared for the many storms ahead—to pay it forward for the next leader in line.

PARTNERSHIP DURING AN NBA LOCKOUT

The media positions professional sports lockouts as billionaires fighting millionaires. When you put it in that context, it can be challenging to feel sympathy for the owners and players. However, I've been around long enough to know the human side behind these parties—and I do feel empathy for the battles between labor unions, leagues, and ownership.

I look at lockouts through a different lens. Having lived it on the inside of an NBA front office and having seen the domino effects of who is impacted, it can be one of the more disruptive chapters in our careers. Our business, our livelihood, our job security—all in doubt when games are not played.

As a leader at the Sacramento Kings during the 2011 NBA lockout, I experienced this firsthand. After the initial shock waves of the announcement, you hope for a quick resolution. Then you realize the complexity behind the core issues between both parties. Negotiations, strategy, bravado, stall tactics, posturing, salesmanship—all come into play.

On the business development side, things can be extremely problematic. With no games, there's no business to develop. You'd love to connect with fans, but many of those conversations become venting sessions around the billionaire versus millionaire media feud or crystal ball predictions around the *insider scoop* projecting when the lockout will be resolved—which we naturally have no answers for.

As I reflect back on the lockout experience, there was one shining star on our team: my boss. Somebody I would do anything for because of how he led during this storm. He stayed grounded, he was real, he was honest, and he was vulnerable—always providing the best information and support he could at that moment in time.

Personally, this was the tightest things ever got financially. Without games, pay cuts were reality and furloughs were looming. In the many heart-to-hearts with my boss, he listened and never gave a single sales pitch to stay. He respected the individuality of the decision and the circumstances that I and others had to face—even going to the extent of letting us all openly look for outside opportunities with his full blessing, free of repercussions, knowing it was the right thing to do given the uncertainty of the future. He wasn't afraid to lose his best people if there was something better for them. This gave us all peace of mind.

Months into the lockout, an opportunity presented itself. On paper it was a no-brainer: double the salary, huge brand, leadership second to none. There wasn't a reason to not take the job—and yet, I felt a tug to not immediately jump, out of loyalty to my boss.

I went into his office and openly shared the details of the opportunity. Out of care, he probed—as he should have—to make sure I really wanted it and it was right for me. The meeting ended with his full blessing, not wanting to hold me back, affirming that it sounded like a great growth opportunity.

I had had bosses give me "the blessing" before, and I've had bosses give me the blessing since—but this one was different. This one was during a storm. He could have reacted differently, thrown some shade, or questioned my loyalty—but he didn't.

I'll never forget that and am eternally grateful. He embodied leadership at its best, at a time we all needed it.

Thank you, Phil—for paving the path and showing me the way.

"Tough times never last, but tough people do."

ROBERT H. SCHULLER

minister, motivational speaker, author

BUILDING TRUST

Trust is the foundation of relationships, and relationships are the foundation of leadership. How we build trust is the secret sauce to becoming a leader who wins—and lasts.

For some, it takes years to give trust. For others—including me—we default to trust until somebody gives us a reason not to. Is there a price to pay for this approach? Absolutely. But what's the alternative in this fast-paced, up-tempo world where we need people and trusted partnerships now more than ever?

Through my lens, showing up with a positive intent toward partnership is non-negotiable. It is the foundational spirit of *meet me at the 50*. I have to trust that you will do your part and meet me there.

This foundation of trust can be the bedrock of all your relationships. Personally, it lays the groundwork for your authenticity, character, and compassion. For your team, it lays the groundwork so they know you're coming from a good place, and they can count on you when things get challenging.

Here's the test: Have you ever received constructive feedback from somebody you didn't trust? I have. What's our immediate reaction? *What an asshole.*

Receive the same feedback from somebody you trust. What's our immediate reaction? *It stings, but we're glad they told us what we needed to hear.*

That's the power of trust in leadership. It opens gateways for candid conversation, robust relationships, and genuine partnership—especially during a storm.

LESSONS LEARNED FROM A NAVY SEAL

While working for the Chapman & Co. Leadership Institute, I had many opportunities to collaborate and partner with Rich Diviney, who served in the military for over twenty years as a commander in the navy and as a Navy SEAL. What struck me immediately about Rich was his humility, authenticity, and compassion toward humanity.

As amazing as his accomplishments were and as fascinated as I was in hearing Rich's stories of service, he was equally curious to know the ins and outs of my path in the sports world. Both of us, while wearing different hats, had been immersed in high-performance spaces throughout our careers.

As we facilitated more often with one another, I noticed a special spark when Rich would work a leadership team through the topic of trust. Specifically, how to build trust. He would share how they did it in the SEALs.

Even as a member of the SEALs, where you would think high performance was the end-all, be-all for how you are measured and how you earn trust and respect from your peers, Rich took it a step further. He shared his background and research on the subject of trust, and I quickly learned that trust is about more than performance. Trust is also more than just a feeling—it is a belief in someone or something. Trust is a belief that another has developed about you, and it's based on the way you behave.

You can't make someone trust you; you can only behave in a way that allows somebody to develop a belief in whether they trust you.

With that spirit in mind, Rich and the Chapman & Co. Leadership Institute codified these thoughts and created a model of trust, which you are about to learn. In this model, there are four elements of trust, none more important than the others, that serve as a set of conditions that must exist for trust to be strongest, most resilient, and most durable.

TRUST MODEL

The four elements to build trust, with my quick descriptions of each, are:

- **COMPETENCE**: do something right
- **CONSISTENCY**: do something right over time
- **CHARACTER**: do the right thing
- **COMPASSION**: do the right thing for another because you care about them, even when it's hard

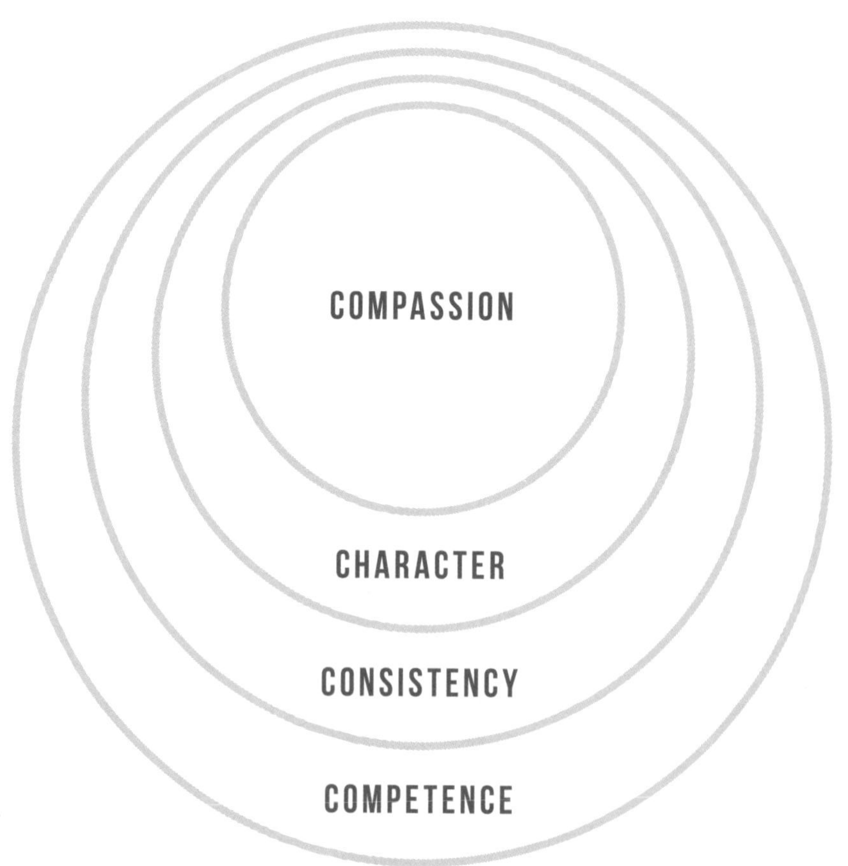

Credit: Chapman & Co. Leadership Institute

BEHAVIORS THAT BUILD TRUST

Using these four components of trust, let's take a look at how we can show up through our behaviors to build trust.

COMPASSION

- Listen
- Walk a mile in their shoes
- Look after people's well-being
- Be an advocate
- Recognize and celebrate people

CHARACTER

- Be honest
- Keep your word
- Behave in ways that are aligned with your values
- Give credit when and where it's due
- Speak truth to power

CONSISTENCY

- Be someone people can count on
- Display stable performance over time
- Show up in a way that is predictable
- Make equitable decisions
- Make decisions that are aligned with organizational vision and mission

COMPETENCE

- Know your job
- Do your job efficiently
- Become an expert
- Display initiative
- Coach another

Credit: Chapman & Co. Leadership Institute

HOW TRUST IS BUILT

Lastly, as you examine your team or organization, here is a look at the environmental factors where trust is limited versus where trust is built and can thrive. Which column best describes your team? Your organization?

TRUST IS LIMITED	TRUST IS BUILT
Fear of challenging organizational policy	People "speak truth to power"
A paycheck is the only thanks people get	Recognition is abundant
There is little or no risk-taking	Initiative is recognized and rewarded
Approval is required for all decisions	People are accountable for their decisions
Compliance is mandated	Excellence is inspired
Only formal leaders are listened to	Leadership is a behavior, not just a position
Leaders use the pronoun "I"	Leaders use "we"
People are copied on emails for protection	Communication is purposeful
People are nervous when a leader is near	People go about their business
People do not say "I don't know"	People feel safe to ask for help
People who are struggling are avoided	People who are struggling get help
Feedback is left unsaid	Feedback is part of normal discourse

Credit: Chapman & Co. Leadership Institute

Guiding leadership teams through this model of trust led to a lot of reflection. I started to think about whom I trust the most and *why*. What did they do to earn my trust?

Themes emerged, and it always came back to several core principles:

- They cared about me as a whole person
- Their character was even stronger behind closed doors
- I knew what *and who* I was going to get every day
- I knew I could count on them without hesitation, especially during a storm

TIME-OUT: Think of the person you trust the most, personally, professionally, in any walk of life. Then answer:

Who is the person you trust most in your life?

What is your short list of factors (see my list bulleted above) around what built that trust? Write those down.

What behaviors did they model to earn your trust? Write those down.

Keep these trust-building criteria and behaviors easily visible in your workspace or set a reminder in your phone where they pop up daily. This will ensure you keep trust top of mind for your greater character and leadership brand.

To become a leader who inspires trust in and from others, establish trust as the foundation of all relationships—knowing that relationships are the foundation of leadership.

BE THE LEADER YOU WISH YOU HAD

Bill Campbell was the business coach of choice for Jeff Bezos (Amazon), Steve Jobs (Apple), Sheryl Sandberg (Facebook), Eric Schmidt (Google), Larry Page and Sergey Brin (Google)—advising a collection of leaders who represented over one trillion dollars in organizational value.

Remember his quote that I opened the book with? "Your title makes you a manager; your people will decide if you are a leader."

The "Trillion Dollar Coach" constantly shared that message with the trailblazers you see listed above. What's fascinating is that he didn't coach these tech giants on technical business strategies as Bill felt their companies were too close in competition with one another. Advising Google on how to create a better mousetrap might negatively impact Apple, and so forth.

To avoid any negative competitive effects, Bill only advised them on the "people side" of business. Bill felt that his job was to coach the coaches on how to lead people. If you can lead people effectively, you will lead teams effectively. If you can lead teams effectively, you can lead organizations and cultures effectively. That was Bill's philosophy.

The best part is that Bill believed all these people-driven practices could be trained. All leaders needed was some awareness. In that same spirit, *The Power of Playing Offense* was written.

LEADERSHIP IS NOT A POSITION

I'm often asked, "Are leaders born or made?"

Perhaps there's a third option.

Leaders are developed.

Leadership is a set of trainable behaviors. It is not a position, and it is not a right. It is a responsibility.

I refuse to believe that we live in a world where less than 10 percent of us are leaders, as our org charts reflect.

I envision a world where we all have the opportunity to lead. It's up to each of us to *step into it*.

Leadership is trainable. It is behaviorally based—and it is founded on awareness. Until we know what great leaders do, how can we show up as that great leader?

As we apply the playbook in this upcoming exercise, we will examine what great leaders DO. The goal is that one day we come to mind as somebody else is asked to think of the greatest leader they've ever had. *Do you want to be thought of in that moment?* I do. Let's flip the page and get to work.

"If your actions inspire others to dream more, learn more, do more, and become more, you are a leader."

JOHN QUINCY ADAMS

sixth US president

APPLYING THE PLAYBOOK

CHAPTER 6: WHAT GREAT LEADERS *DO*

This is one of my favorite experiences to facilitate. From London to Los Angeles, I've personally seen jaws drop when the grand takeaway hits. It is worthy of a mic drop. You'll have a chance to learn the takeaway at the end of this exercise (I know it's tempting, but don't peek ahead!).

It's your time to play offense and drop the mic.

SETTING

Any meeting space will do, so long as your team is comfortable and has visibility to the front of the room.

SETUP

Flip chart on an easel board (sticky-back ideal) and marker

MEETING INVITE

Set for thirty minutes. Title the meeting: "What Great Leaders *DO.*"

MEETING KICKOFF

You will open by sharing a story of a leader (personal or professional) who has inspired you. A few minutes max. Make sure to include what the leader *did*—meaning their behaviors and actions, not simply how they made you feel.

MEETING FACILITATION

Now it's time to include the group; here is the script:

Each and every person in this room has been around a great leader in their lives. I want you to think of that person now. It can be personal; it can be professional. Once you have that person in your mind, think of what they *did*—meaning their actions and behaviors. I'm going to ask for your responses in a moment and capture them on this flip chart. These should be one-to-two-word quick-fire responses. As an example from my intro story, two behaviors were __________ and __________. I'll write those down to get us started [write them on flip chart]. Only shout out the behaviors and actions of this great leader in your life. Let's go.

Start to script the responses. Remember, they're not supposed to share a story like you did. That was simply a tone-setter to kick off the meeting.

You should get words like "listen, recognize, care, challenge, mentor, empower, engage, coach, vulnerable, sacrifice," as examples.

Here's a visual of a list I had in a past facilitation exercise as an example.

After the flip chart page is filled (usually thirty to fifty words or short phrases), ask the team this question: **"IF THIS IS WHAT GREAT LEADERS DO, DO YOU HAVE THE ABILITY TO DO THESE THINGS EVERY DAY?"**

You'll likely see some head nods. After a few seconds, reinforce this by selecting a handful of things you wrote down, and fill in the blank using those words as the filler for:

- "Do you have the ability to ____first item____?"

Wait for their positive affirmation (saying yes or nodding head).

- "Do you have the ability to ____second item____?"

Again, wait for their positive affirmation.

MIC DROP MOMENT

- Set the table by acknowledging that the group said they could do everything that great leaders *do*.
- Then ask, "If we were hosting this meeting a decade from now, and we asked a different group of people to think of the greatest leader they've ever had, would you want to be thought of as that leader?"
- You'll see *every* head nod and eyes burst open with passion and excitement—like they're about to run out of the tunnel before the big game.
- Then say, "Ladies and gentlemen, **YOU JUST WROTE YOUR JOB DESCRIPTION.** If you want to be thought of as that great leader, *do* this [pointing to board] every day."

Mic is dropped.

These words—which they came up with—are their job description. Of course you will continue to have your KPIs and goals; this list is the other 50 percent.

Stick this page up on the wall so that it is visible to your team. This list will set the tone for your daily culture going forward. From performance reviews to team huddles, recognition messages, or constructive feedback opportunities (when the list is not lived up to), this is the team's accountability tool for being a great leader, every day.

Go drop the mic and make this a reality.

BONUS LEARNING

This list reinforces that leadership is not a position. It is a trainable set of behaviors. You don't need a rank, role, or title to do these things. You likely didn't write "boss," "manage," or "supervise" under what great leaders do.

For those rising stars and ambitious high potential people around you that want to "get in the leadership seat" and are constantly asking you *how*, it starts by acting as a leader—every day.

This list is that training manual as everyone is now *aware* of what great leaders do and can hold themselves accountable to it.

When all else fails, remind yourself and everyone around you: Before you lead others, you must first lead yourself.

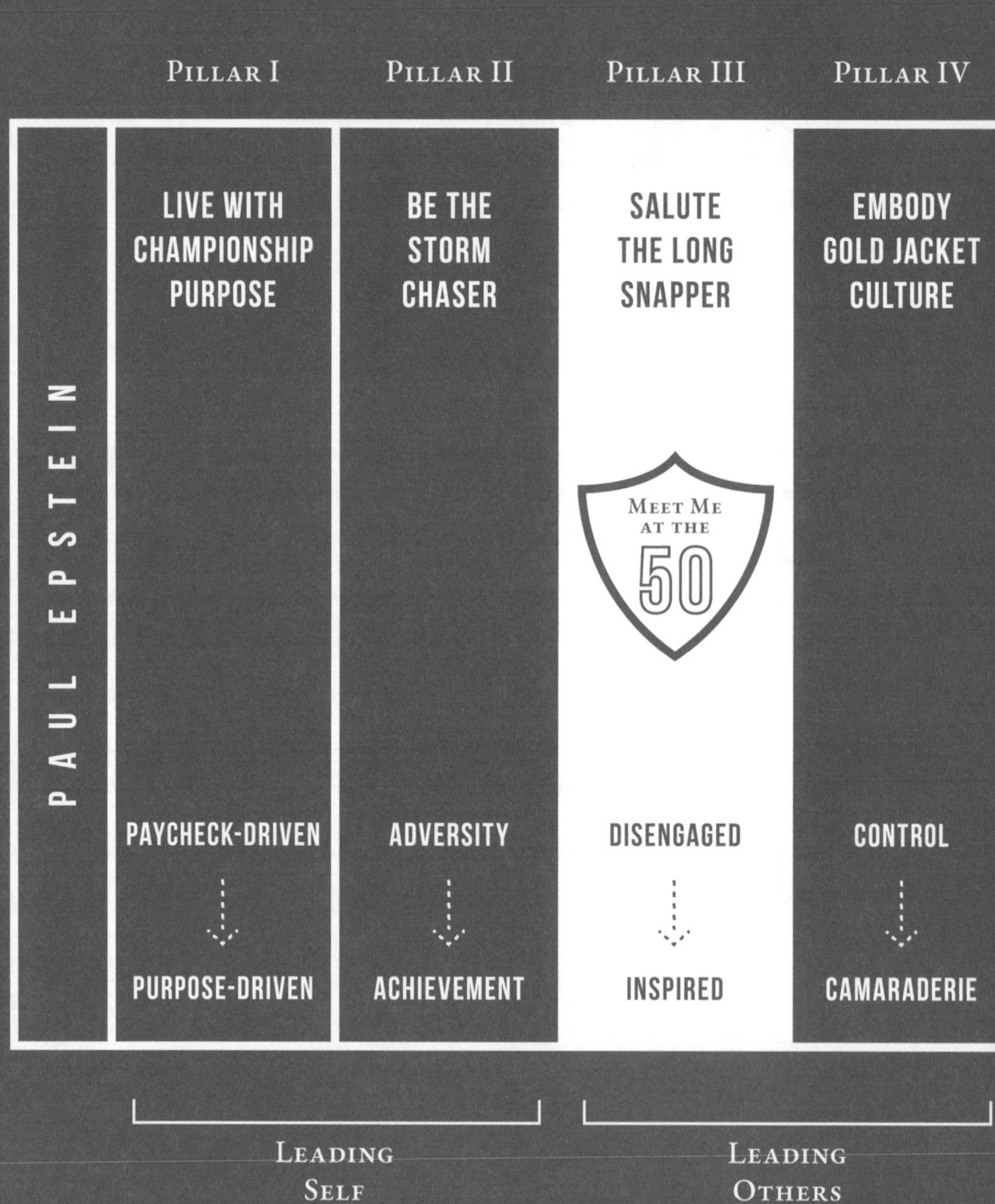

Pillar I
Pillar II
Pillar III
Pillar IV
PAUL EPSTEIN
LIVE WITH CHAMPIONSHIP PURPOSE
BE THE STORM CHASER
SALUTE THE LONG SNAPPER
EMBODY GOLD JACKET CULTURE
Meet Me at the 50
PAYCHECK-DRIVEN
PURPOSE-DRIVEN
ADVERSITY
ACHIEVEMENT
DISENGAGED
INSPIRED
CONTROL
CAMARADERIE
Leading Self
Leading Others

Pillar V

LEAVE IT BETTER THAN YOU FOUND IT

PLAYING OFFENSE

SUCCESS

↓

SIGNIFICANCE

Leading the Future

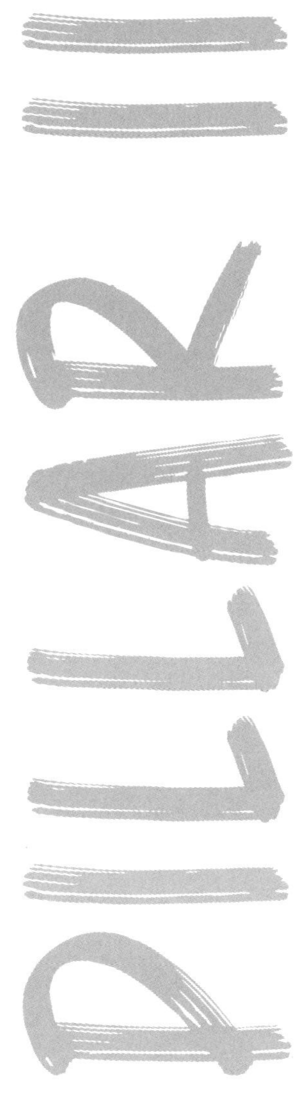

Even the most casual football fans are familiar with the most visible positions on the team. The flashy quarterback, directing motion on the field and making plays. The running back, twisting and turning his way through the defense. The wide receiver, diving for an impossible one-handed catch to the thunderous applause of the fans.

But teams are made up of more than these iconic roles. Enter the long snapper, a player who serves an incredibly specific role and who might appear on the field for just a few seconds per game. However, a good long snapper is worth their weight in gold in the NFL. Why? Because they do a difficult and essential job better than anyone else.

Now, imagine you're the long snapper. You enter the game in the fourth quarter; everything is on the line. Safe snap to the punter—you're on your way to victory. A snap over their head—the other team recovers and emerges victorious. Ninety-nine snaps right—you'll never hear a word. One snap wrong—you'll never hear the end of it. Sound familiar?

This pillar in *The Power of Playing Offense* will expose the reality of a long snapper. Just like the ones on the field, they're all around us—on our teams and in our organizations. Many of us have been a long snapper at some point in our lives. You—like I—may know what it's like to not feel seen or valued. Think of a time when you've felt a lack of appreciation and recognition for the contributions and impact you made. Together, we realize that the long snappers in our world can make the difference between winning and losing, and we wouldn't be where we are without them.

Now imagine the possibilities when we transform the infinite number of long snappers who are disengaged into being inspired and feeling like they matter—ready to make the difference needed for a team to succeed.

CHAPTER 7 *will highlight putting people first (long snappers included), so they can emerge as the secret sauce on your team.*

CHAPTER 8 *will establish how to maximize the gifts in your locker room, along with thought starters to discover your own superpowers.*

CHAPTER 9 *will provide a blueprint on talent and leadership development, jam-packed with fifteen portable practices for you to implement immediately.*

With that, let's dive in.

EVERYBODY MATTERS

Down the hall from his office, NFL Commissioner Roger Goodell approached me to ask what all the colors on the pin board represented.

Each pin reflected the remaining premium hospitality inventory for Super Bowl XLVIII in a sales campaign I was leading on behalf of my global agency—for the game that was now six months away.

Here's the breakdown of the pins:

- **GREEN** = sold
- **YELLOW** = in conversation (with a prospective client)
- **RED** = available (no action)

At this early stage in the campaign, there was a sea of red on the board. Recognizing my job was a once-in-a-lifetime opportunity, the last thing I wanted to do was disclose this harsh reality.

I answered, "Green is sold. Yellow is in conversation. Red is a red-hot prospect."

The commissioner responded, "Wow. Looks like we've got a hot market," as he walked away.

Phew. Still alive.

A SUPER BOWL DREAM TURNED NIGHTMARE

This conversation was a moment I'll never forget. To be working in the NFL League Office was a dream come true. Every day was a kid-in-a-candy-store experience. Each minute felt like paradise, coupled with the high intensity of the campaign for a game that was being touted as the highest grossing in Super Bowl history.

I still remember the daily strolls on Park Avenue. Coming up the elevators, NFL Films music as you exit. Turn a sharp left and see a pristine lobby with the glisten of all the Super Bowl rings to date on display, along with the Vince Lombardi trophies of Super Bowl winners to accompany them. This was an opportunity of a lifetime, one that I poured myself into. Realizing it was a career-catapulting platform—I was ALL IN.

Burning the candle on both ends, weekends didn't exist, holidays took a year off, meals became optional, and exercise was relegated to smiling and dialing—I was laser-focused like never before.

We had six months to reinvent the Super Bowl revenue model, break league records, and send shock waves through the industry. The reason behind the reinvention? It was the first ever Super Bowl in New York, the league's backyard, flush with cash, resources, and swagger. On the books, this represented 300 percent revenue growth in the premium hospitality category versus the prior year's game. For context, the norm was 10 to 20 percent.

Months into the campaign, we were well-positioned. Early bird corporate buyers were in. The rest of the world expectedly said, "Call me when you know who is in the game." All we could do at that point was continue to plant half-million-dollar seeds and pray for the right matchup.

January finally hit, and the playoffs were now underway. Each game had *MASSIVE* implications. The final four were set.

NFC Championship: 49ers versus Seahawks

AFC Championship: Patriots versus Broncos

Putting your business cap on—you want big brands, mega media markets, robust corporate base, star players, and a legacy fan base.

By those standards: Go Niners! Go Pats!

You can guess what happened. Super Bowl XLVIII: Seahawks versus Broncos.

Without discouragement, we welcomed this hurdle and felt up for the task—but a handful of days out, as bullish as we were, the market hit a grinding halt. Four suites and several million dollars from goal, reality started to set in that we *may* not get to the finish line. I started to think about news spreading of the disappointment. My massive career catapult might never launch, instead feeling like a potential scarlet letter.

But then, on the eve of our deadline, a fan named John from Seattle called me back and asked, "Still got those suites?"

Hell yes, we did! And with that, euphoria set in throughout the office. History had officially been made. After all the bear hugs, I picked up the phone and called my wife and mom to join me in New York for the big celebration. They were on the next flight out of LAX and made it in time for the red-carpet events; Super Bowl XLVIII, here we come.

One of the photo-worthy moments from Super Bowl XLVIII: From left, me with my wife, Mayra; my mom, Stella (smiling ear to ear); and 49ers legend, Steve Young.

Enjoying the game with my two favorite people in the world was a dream come true.

Life was perfect—until it wasn't.

As part of the festivities, the league awards were set to be announced, including our record-breaking campaign. Recognition began. Name after name revealed. Waiting—just wanting a small tip of the cap for what had undoubtedly been the most taxing chapter of my career.

My name never came. There was no salute for the *long snapper*.

To kick me even further while down, the individual who made the announcement walked over immediately after, patted me on the head, and said, "Nice work, Pauly. We know who did the real work."

Demoralized. Defeated. I couldn't leave fast enough. My dream night had turned into a nightmare.

That experience taught me so much about how to treat people and how to let others know they matter—*long snappers* especially. I'll never forget the feeling I had that night—a feeling I never want anybody to have on my watch.

I now look for the *long snappers* who rarely get saluted and rarely get the recognition—but certainly deserve it. I let them know that I see them, they're valued, and we wouldn't be where we are without them.

TIME-OUT: Take a moment to recognize a long snapper in your life, just to say thank you and let them know they matter.

A simple text will work wonders. Go for it.

PUTTING PEOPLE FIRST

Leaders in every team and organization say they put people first, but do they? When times are toughest, look no further than their actions, behaviors, and decisions in the moments of truth—when adversity reveals their character and values for the world to see.

In reality, putting people first is not as difficult as it appears—if it comes from your core beliefs. Do you authentically believe that people are the fuel to the engine? Do you sincerely believe that putting people first is the right thing to do, even when it's hard? If so, are you willing to take a bold stance to practice the daily behaviors and commitments of putting people first?

Putting people first isn't a bumper sticker. It isn't a flavor of the month campaign. It isn't always convenient. It isn't what we do when everybody is watching. Putting people first is how you show up behind closed doors.

If this is your belief, it likely comes from your past—as it has for me.

THE ROOTS OF PEOPLE FIRST

In elementary school, I had a friend named Vicente. He was the happiest and most enthusiastic person I knew, lighting up the room, always a joy to be around. We grew close in class, on the monkey bars, and creating mischief, like kids at that age do.

Come to find out, times were tough for his family. Something as simple for me as paying for a haircut would be a tough decision for Vicente. It was that or lunch. Learning of these disparities was a rude awakening as I had previously assumed everybody had the same access and opportunities.

This started to trigger thoughts going back even earlier in my childhood, enjoying time with my family in Ensenada, Mexico. While we never had a lot of money, I always felt we had what we needed. The innocence of my youth probably blinded me to the realities of why there were so many candles (to provide warmth) and why we had to take such quick showers (heated water was scarce).

These memories, among countless others, shaped my views at a young age. I saw the warmth in people, but I also saw the hardship. I felt the friendship and love, but I also saw the sacrifice. Most importantly, I saw how people could light up when you treated them well and made them feel like they belonged—to know that they mattered.

From these early days, I started to pay very close attention to how people treated each other. This impacted my mindset regarding whom I chose to be around and what tribes I would eventually associate with—which carried over into the schooling decisions of my life.

My parents always gave me the freedom of choice on where I would go to school *if* I stayed in line, got good grades, and stayed out of trouble. As an independently minded only child, I thought this was a deal worth taking.

I made the decision to attend public school through twelfth grade after vetting out multiple private schools along the way. During the tours, I would focus on the people around me: Were they laughing? Were they together? How did they talk to and treat one another? Too often I left these tours confused and disappointed. I especially didn't like how they spoke to "the workers," as they referred to them. It reminded me of how you often hear of people called "the help" in hospitality settings. It felt elitist. I imagined if the workers were my family. How would I feel if they were treated that way?

Our world is filled with people from all classes, I acknowledge that. But we need to treat others with respect. Everybody deserves to feel seen, *long snappers* included. Ultimately, there will be far more long snappers than star-studded quarterbacks in our world. We'll need each and every person in our locker room pulling the rope in the same direction if we want to accomplish special things.

Start by putting people first to bring their best selves out—then step back and watch them amaze you.

> *"People want to know they matter, and they want to be treated as people. That's the new talent contract."*
>
> **PAMELA STROKO**
>
> Human Capital Management Transformation, Oracle

THE TRANSFORMATION OF DISENGAGED TO INSPIRED

Look to your left. Look to your right. Seven out of ten people don't want to be here. They'd rather be working somewhere else for someone else.

If we were to helicopter into the average US company, this would be the cruel reality. As research by Gallup in 2019 shows, 65 percent of our US workforce is currently disengaged. This leads to a void in discretionary effort. People are doing just enough to get by (a.k.a. keep their jobs and not get fired), which places artificial ceilings on their performance and productivity, leading to an unnecessary ceiling on an organization's profit.

When you put it this way, especially knowing how bottom line– and results-obsessed organizations can be, why have we not solved this problem?

The equation is simple:

MORE ENGAGEMENT = MORE INSPIRED PEOPLE = MORE PERFORMANCE = MORE PROFITS

Yet the stats from Gallup around disengagement have been consistent for decades. It's why the term TGIF resonates so much. Yes, we all look forward to the fun of weekends, but we also enjoy closing the books on yet another uninspiring week at work. Fast-forward to Sunday late afternoon, and the "Sunday Scaries" (as I've heard it referred to) kick in.

The reason we continue to be in this dilemma is we haven't prioritized those who truly matter. The external business results we crave immediately take us to an obsession with our customers and putting them first.

In reality, we have it backward. If you want to achieve this external transformation in the marketplace, it's an *inside game*. A game where inspired employees lead to inspired customers, as the founder of Virgin, Richard Branson, and others have embodied in their cultural DNA—and it's a logical flow.

> *"Clients do not come first. Employees come first. If you take care of your employees, they will take care of the clients."*
>
> **RICHARD BRANSON**
>
> business magnate, investor, author, philanthropist

I have personally seen this transformation take place while at Levi's Stadium.

EVERY SEAT HAS A STORY

The organizational 'Why' of the 49ers is "to go one step further so everybody feels a part of the family."

While this statement provided a North Star, it was the "Hows" of the organization that became the catalysts for action—starting with a radical shift in mindset.

In the workshop where our "Hows" originated, I shared a story about one team member, Andrew, who always took the extra step for somebody to feel a part of the family. He invested the time to know the story behind each seat. For some, it was a birthday surprise for a lifelong 49ers fan. For others, it went deeper. A fan that had battled cancer and was now in remission, wanting to see their favorite team play for a much-needed escape. Or stories in the form of a written wish from the brave women and men who serve our country overseas; at the top of their bucket list upon return—attend a 49ers game.

These examples shone a light on the essence that *every seat has a story*—which became one of our organizational "Hows." We felt as if we had just uncovered a Super Bowl–worthy rallying cry—one that would inspire us for years to come.

Our facilitators were ecstatic that we'd unearthed this extremely powerful mantra. But then came a challenge from our lead facilitator. Whether or not we were ready to hear it, he let it rip.

"You're so focused on the seventy thousand red seats outside. When's the last time you gave a damn like that about the two hundred-fifty on the inside?"

The 70,000 referred to fans and customers, the two hundred-fifty referred to employees. While his point was abrupt, it made us take a deep, hard look in the mirror. It turned out to be exactly what we needed to hear.

We started to focus obsessively on our employee experience in a way we never had. It always came back to the same mantra we used for our fans: *Every seat has a story*.

What is the story of our entry-level marketer? Our analyst? Our communications intern? Our groundskeeper? What inspires them? Why are they here? Why do they love being 49ers?

With that, personal videos were filmed of what it means to be a 49er by everybody who felt moved to share. At our next all-hands meeting came the grand reveal. There wasn't a dry eye in the house.

While this was one example of creating an environment where everybody matters, everybody belongs, and everybody plays a key role (long snappers included), there were countless other initiatives that followed—several of which I'll share throughout this pillar and the next.

> *"Everyone wants to contribute. Trust them. Leaders are everywhere. Find them. Some people are on a mission. Celebrate them. Others wish things were different. Listen to them. Everybody matters. Show them."*
>
> **BOB CHAPMAN**
>
> CEO, Barry-Wehmiller, and author of *Everybody Matters*

No coincidence, following this shift in mindset the 49ers became recognized as one of the best places to work in the Bay Area. This was the first time in the organization's history it had received such recognition, and it's been repeated every year since.

The next time you look around your office, remember that every seat has a story. Will you get to know it?

THE GIFT OF LISTENING

To close the last chapter, you applied the playbook by answering the question, "What do great leaders DO?"

In my role as a leadership consultant and coach, I've had the fortune of asking this question to leaders across the world—and have uncovered a few golden takeaways.

First—whether on domestic ground or foreign soil, in public organizations or private, for profit or non-profit, among baby boomers or millennials, the responses to "What do great leaders DO?" are remarkably similar.

Second—there is a usual suspect that surfaces as a top-five response over 90 percent of the time: *Listen*.

Great leaders listen. Certainly not an earth-shattering answer. Then why so powerful? And why nearly unanimous?

When I've asked leaders these probing questions, there has been an unsettling response. One that leads to a candid admission that listening *can be* an amazing gift, but it's the rarity of that gift that leads to this yearning desire for more of it.

Better said, we all love being listened to—but it happens so infrequently that we have an even greater appreciation for it when somebody hangs on our every word. The power of listening is unquestioned. It's the discipline to empathetically and consistently do it that leads to the real power of what is possible when people feel heard.

SPEAK TRUTH TO POWER

During our cultural shift at the 49ers, one of the core practices implemented were listening sessions. Think of them as employee focus groups. They were held quarterly, on an opt-in basis, and became the foundation of the cultural transformation that followed.

After dozens of group listening sessions, there were several themes that emerged. One of the anchor themes was *trust*. There were some gaps in this area, but not for the reasons you would expect. The more typical gaps in organizational trust are results of poor relationships with a boss, lack of transparent communication, and behaviors that don't match what's preached. In this case, it was none of those.

As the stories within these listening sessions revealed, they actually started in a very happy place. A place that I dearly miss and think of often: the 49ers cafeteria.

This palatial cafeteria was designed to serve the players and the entire football operation. At some point in the years before I joined the organization, the gravy spilled over to the business side. We as employees now had dedicated hours where the players were elsewhere—typically practicing, in meetings, or with media—and we could dig into the king's feast. Swipe your badge, enjoy and congregate with your fellow colleagues—or, if in a rush, grab your to-go box, then on with your day.

It was these now infamous to-go boxes that led to an uproar in our listening sessions: "They took away our to-go boxes!" was voiced by countless team members, referring to the decision of management.

We've all heard the story of a few bad apples ruining it for all of us; this was a classic example of that. Of our two hundred-fifty employees, a handful decided to consistently eat lunch in the cafeteria, then pack a to-go box for that evening's dinner—clearly not the intent of the boxes.

What would any organization do in this case? Remove the boxes, of course!

Well, this didn't sit nicely with the rest of us. *The many* were being penalized for the actions of *the few*. There was no communication. No heads-up. One day, the boxes were just gone, like the act of a magician.

As the story was told inside our listening sessions, people used the platform to speak truth to power. This comment came from a session I participated in:

> *We work our asses off for the organization. There are days I have back-to-back-to-back meetings, at most five minutes in between—all in service of the team. I used to be able to go in and grab lunch to go. Now, I don't have the option or the time. I can't even count the days when I don't even eat.*

Stories like this were echoed by many.

When this feedback was brought to the team president, he was shocked. At the next all-hands, he announced, "To-go boxes are coming back!" He may have never received a louder standing ovation.

More important than any lunchbox, people felt that they had a voice, and there was action taken based on their feedback—leaving them to feel that they mattered. All it took was a little bit of listening.

In Chapter 9, we will take a time-out to integrate a listening session inside your team.

THE PLATINUM RULE

We've all heard of the golden rule: "Treat others as you want to be treated." What if that doesn't work? What if people don't respond to the same things you do?

These were some of my earliest learnings when transitioning from player to coach—before transforming from manager to leader. I had no perfect playbook to learn from. The advice received was generic. Rarely did it apply perfectly to my team and the individual players within it—whether a star or long snapper.

In my earliest stages of management, I had to learn through experience and by making mistakes—but thankfully had the awareness to know when things weren't right. I looked around the room, saw the talent, then looked at the scoreboard (our sales results), and something wasn't adding up.

It wasn't until I implemented the *platinum rule* that things took off.

The platinum rule is to "Treat others how *they* want to be treated."

This illumination would have never happened had I not taken advantage of the wise words from Eddie, who was on my inside sales team at the Clippers. Even though Eddie reported to me, there's no question I learned more from him, including this lesson I'm about to share.

Thank you, Eddie, for the wake-up call I needed.

BREAKING BREAD

I was stumped six months into my first leadership role. I went out for lunch with Eddie and shared how perplexed I was that a team that looked so good on paper was producing middle-of-the-road results.

Eddie asked, "What are we doing right now?"

Seeing the confusion on my face, he said, "We're breaking bread." Then he asked, "When's the last time you did this with anybody else on the team?"

I may never have a simpler yet more profound takeaway in my career. Eddie shined a light on the most obvious ingredient our team was missing, one I was blind and oblivious to: *relationships*.

Relationships are at the heartbeat of leadership—and I only had one relationship (with Eddie) on a team of a dozen. Shame on me for starting in that position. But now I was awake to the possibilities.

Eddie's words immediately reframed my entire approach—an approach that would go on to serve me for the duration of my leadership career in New Orleans, Sacramento, New York, and San Francisco. While there were still bumps in the road (some of which you've already read), this aha moment gave the relational foundation I needed. My approach was no longer results-driven; it was people-driven.

"You can make more friends in two months by becoming interested in other people than you can in two years by trying to get other people interested in you."

DALE CARNEGIE

author of *How to Win Friends and Influence People*

I built (and earned) an authentic relationship with each member of my team, which soon became a tribe. I learned what their personal and professional motivations were by leading with the platinum rule, and treating them how they wanted to be treated. Through the question "What is most important to you?" it revealed sides of them I had never seen. I gained insight into what got them out of bed; what they valued in life; what pissed them off; ultimately, how they wanted to be led so that they could show up at their best. That became the genesis of each relationship from that point forward, and it's been a key to my success to this day.

Now it's your turn. Let's unpack the power of your team, by unleashing the full potential of each member inside of it. You'll be amazed at what is possible when people feel that you care enough to customize a personal growth and development plan just for them. But the plan cannot come until you know who they are—and they feel like they matter.

APPLYING THE PLAYBOOK

CHAPTER 7: TEAM MEMBER VALUES AND TRIGGERS

In Chapter 3 of Applying the Playbook, we learned how to discover our own personal values. For more on a full team or organizational purpose and values discovery, see the Purpose Discovery FAQ at **WWW.POWEROFPLAYINGOFFENSE.COM**.

This section of Applying the Playbook will have two parts, each geared toward the individual as a member within a team. The first is a values exercise, the second a triggers exercise (learned at the Chapman & Co. Leadership Institute). This will help you understand the values and triggers of each team member to gain a deeper connection and relationship while having more empathy toward who they are.

Let's play offense and unpack each activity, starting with values.

VALUES TEAM ACTIVITY (APPROXIMATELY THIRTY MINUTES)

For starters, we will need a large base of values to select from. We can use this list from Chapter 3.

ACHIEVEMENT	EXCELLENCE	LEARNING
AMBITION	FAIRNESS	MASTERY
AUTHENTICITY	FAITH	OPTIMISM
AUTONOMY	FUN	PASSION
CARE	GROWTH	PERFORMANCE
CHALLENGE	HAPPINESS	PERSEVERANCE
COMMUNITY	HOPE	POTENTIAL
COMPASSION	IMAGINATION	PURPOSE
CONNECTION	INFLUENCE	RECOGNITION
COURAGE	INSPIRATION	SERVICE
DISCOVERY	JOY	SIGNIFICANCE
DRIVE	KINDNESS	TEAMWORK
EMPOWER	LEADERSHIP	TRUST

STEP ONE

Set up a ninety-minute team meeting called "Values and Triggers."

STEP TWO

Print out a copy of the values list so each person has the form in hand. You can download it at WWW.POWEROFPLAYINGOFFENSE.COM.

STEP THREE

Kick off the meeting by saying that this is an opportunity to get to know one another in a deeper way. It will span across our values (which highlight what's most important to each person in the room) and our triggers (which highlight our biggest pet peeve at work). Both are equally valuable and impactful in better understanding your fellow team members.

STEP FOUR

Have people find a partner (pairs are ideal; one odd group of three is fine if needed).

STEP FIVE

Have each person select three values (from the list) that most resonate with them.

STEP SIX

Have each person select one value (from the list) that they see in their partner.

STEP SEVEN

Have them discuss (for five to ten minutes) with their partner why they selected their own personal values and then reveal the values they chose for their partner and explain why.

STEP EIGHT

Bring the group back together and have a group conversation about their biggest takeaways. Two questions to guide the facilitation are:

1. When discussing values with your partner, were there any surprises or aha moments?
2. How easy or difficult was it for you to pick values for somebody else?

You'll notice that it always comes back to depth of relationship. When you know somebody well, it's easy. When you don't, it's difficult. This is a great opportunity to emphasize the importance of team members knowing one another beyond what's on the surface.

This is the value of values. Only when you know what's truly important to somebody will you have an opportunity to maximize the impact of the platinum rule: Treat others how they want to be treated.

That's the positive side . . . now let's talk about triggers (a.k.a. what pisses people off).

> **NOTE:** *I intentionally say "what pisses people off" to evoke a strong emotion. This has to be your biggest pet peeve at work. The one that gets your blood boiling. Had I said "your biggest frustration," you may not have gone there. Regardless, use the language with your group you're most comfortable with.*

TRIGGERS EXERCISE (APPROXIMATELY SIXTY MINUTES)

SUPPLIES NEEDED, SETUP, AND IDEAL MEETING SPACE

- One index card per person. As a facilitator, bring five sheets of paper, a pen, and tape.

- There will be five total pieces of paper. Write the following on each sheet. On the first paper, write, "At Peace." On the second paper, write, "Aware." And so on.

    1. At Peace
    2. Aware
    3. Anxious
    4. Annoyed
    5. Angry

- You'll see by the instructions below that a large wall will be needed for the activity, so ideally this is a large meeting space versus a small conference room. Base it on the size of your team.

STEP ONE

Have some fun with this intro! Literally say to the group, "Now that we got all the warm and fuzzies out of the way (values), let's talk about what pisses us off!" You'll get a good chuckle out of the group. It's time to dive in with instructions.

STEP TWO

Hand out an index card to each person. Ask them to write one thing that pisses them off (about work or people at work). In other words, what's their biggest pet peeve? When the response is people-related, emphasize that this is not about an individual person. It's a broad pet peeve related to many people, not what Brian or Mary specifically did. Share a few examples:

- When people are late to meetings
- When somebody is looking at their phone while you're talking to them

STEP THREE

While they're writing their cards, tape the five sheets of paper on a wall (spread them as evenly and widely as possible—in this order). The wider the gap between each of the five, the better.

AT PEACE	AWARE	ANXIOUS	ANNOYED	ANGRY

STEP FOUR

Now that you've taped the five sheets of paper to the wall, collect all of the index cards. Tell the group you need a minute to sort through them.

STEP FIVE

From the index cards, pick the five that you feel will lead to the strongest variance from person to person. As an example, being "late to a meeting" may be a huge deal to some but not to others. That's a good one to pick for this exercise. A different example like "people that are unethical and lie to get what they want" will likely lead to a similar feeling (annoyed or angry) among all people—therefore, do not select this one. The impact of the exercise will be maximized when there is a diversity of opinion and reaction (meaning some will be at peace while others will be angry—about the same trigger).

STEP SIX

Now that you have five index cards pulled out from the stack (meaning five triggers) that are about to be shared, explain the instructions to the group. A sample script is below:

I will call out one trigger at a time. After I call out the first trigger, I want each of you to process your immediate reaction based on the five that are on the wall. In other words, what is your instant feeling when I say the trigger? You'll see on the wall there are five options.

1. Are you at peace?
2. Are you aware?
3. Are you anxious?
4. Are you annoyed?
5. Are you angry?

Before we unpack the first trigger, let's start off with a softball. On a typical weekday (meaning it's a workday), how do you feel when you first wake up?

Walk to the spot on the wall that you most closely associate with in this example.

STEP SEVEN

You'll see the group disperse. After each person is standing in front of their reaction (at peace on one extreme, angry on the other), ask for a person standing on the far left side to share why, then question somebody on the far right; lastly, question somebody in the middle. So in an ideal world, you are asking Susan why she's at peace; Tom, why he's angry; and Mike, why he's either aware, anxious, or annoyed.

STEP EIGHT

Do this for each of the five triggers, time permitting. Within each trigger you will question both the left and right extreme positions, judgment call on the middle (based on timing and whether third perspective will add value). Here's what the flow looks like.

1. Read off first trigger.
2. Group disperses.

3. You question somebody on the far left side: "Susan, why 'at peace?'"
4. Then question somebody on the far right side: "Tom, why 'angry?'"
5. Move onto the second trigger. Lather, rinse, repeat.

STEP NINE (LEAVE FIVE TO TEN MINUTES FOR THIS DEBRIEF)

When all triggers are complete, ask the group what the biggest takeaway from this exercise has been.

What all groups eventually come up with is that all people are different. Different things are important. Different things give us meaning. Different things matter. Different things piss us off. We need to have empathy for one another's unique view and lens on the world. How well do we truly know one another? This exercise is a great launching point for these connections and realizations.

Only when you have this level of empathy will people feel that they are safe, that they belong, and that they matter. You've now paved the path for each person to unleash their superpowers.

UNLEASH YOUR SUPERPOWERS

In business, we often build teams through the lens of career achievement and performance to date, largely from a statistical point of view. In sports, while statistics are highly relevant, the best coaches look at the team as an ecosystem of players—a locker room, if you will—knowing that intangibles, chemistry, and complementary fit with one another will play equally critical roles in the team's ultimate success.

DREAM TEAM

When balancing performance with intangibles while constructing a locker room, there may be no greater example than the Dream Team. In the 1992 Summer Olympics, the USA men's basketball team set out to make history. These were the first Olympic Games where the United States Committee welcomed NBA players—which was timely, given the crushing bronze medal four years prior in the games of 1988, the first time the United States had not made the Olympics championship game in the sport it had invented.

Many would argue that this was the most special collection of individual talent ever assembled on a court. Each player was the star of his team, many were MVPs in the league, all but one destined for the Hall of Fame, and one player, Michael Jordan, was arguably the best the game has ever seen.

While the results of the 1992 Olympic Men's Basketball Tournament were an undefeated 8–0 record, chalked with blowout victories and the gold medal, perhaps the most significant victory was how the Dream Team gelled and integrated together. For all of the stardom and personalities, they created a flawless display of teamwork—so seamless that Coach Chuck Daly *never* had to call a timeout. Back in the NBA, these individual players were accustomed to fierce head-to-head competition. In this case, there was no conflict—only greatness.

If this team of legendary superstars can come together in such a self-sacrificing manner—to transform into long snappers for the greater good—what prevents us, as leaders, from doing the same?

Start by asking yourself, "*Are you on a team of leaders, or are you on a leadership team*?"

There is a distinct difference. A *leadership team* is comprised of individual business unit heads coming together, often with siloed agendas. A *team of leaders* is about team-first, representing the organization's best interests holistically to form a pact of unity around the boardroom.

There are several lessons we, as a team of leaders, can learn from the Dream Team experience if we want to build a similar locker room of greatness.

Fundamentally, the Dream Team started with a common vision, common incentives, and shared sacrifice. Are those characteristics that you would use to describe your team of leaders?

On a more dynamic level, the Dream Team played to their strengths while maxing out their natural gifts and talents so that they could display their superpowers (and medals) to the world. Some would call it the perfect balance of individual greatness coupled with team success.

In a similar vision, this chapter will unpack how we can expose these superpowers of our own.

BUILDING RELATIONSHIPS THAT WIN AND LAST

We've all heard the expressions *managing up* and *managing down*. Essentially, create a winning relationship with your boss (up) and your team (down). While I expected these relationships to be key to my success, I never realized that there was a direction missing until I was knee-deep in the leadership game. I eventually found that *managing left and right* (with fellow leaders) can be equally as critical and can position us greatly for growth and long-term achievement.

Relationships with fellow leaders can establish your brand and influence a higher level of water-cooler talk (at the leadership ranks)—which, in turn, has the following effects:

SUPPORT FOR YOUR IDEAS: This comes down to one simple factor—do other leaders like you? Sounds brash, but it's true. Just like people do business with people they like, people support ideas of people they like.

MITIGATE THE BAD NEWS: While there are no guarantees, when fellow leaders have your back, you're less likely to be the victim of internal politics, CYA emails, and siloed communication that hangs you out to dry.

PROJECT EXECUTION AND SUCCESS: When involved with cross-departmental initiatives, you'll need others' cooperation in the hopes that it will lead to genuine and proactive collaboration.

BRAND WITH EXECUTIVES: You never know who has the ears of the C-suite. The last thing you want is to have a fellow leader speak badly about you to their (or your) boss. Words of advice: Play nice in the sandbox.

INTERNAL GROWTH POTENTIAL: It's very difficult to grow internally without the blessing from those above. If your performance represents half of why you should get the next job, your brand and relationships with people are the other half—make them count.

LEADING IN ALL DIRECTIONS

My transition from the Clippers to Hornets was eye-opening in many ways. Personally, it was a move away from home for the first time, coupled with an adjustment into a new city—and not just any city—it was "The Big Easy." From the Pacific to the Bayou, Hollywood Boulevard to Bourbon Street, I knew I was in for one heck of a ride.

Professionally, I was welcomed in with open arms by an amazing team of leaders, making the personal transition even easier. We collaborated on all micro and macro elements of the business. Professional development and collective learning became the norm. We talked business philosophy and leadership over weekly team lunches—even going through a strength assessment that would customize our responsibilities in order to maximize our collective results. These were only some of the welcome memories that I experienced while being ingratiated into the Hornets' *team of leaders*.

Then came an unexpected disruption—the team owner's cancer diagnosis and subsequent NBA takeover while seeking a new, local owner.

Part of becoming more attractive and viable to a potential owner required a drastic overhaul of our revenue model—which was what led to the "I'm In" campaign detailed in Chapter 3. This trailblazing campaign was created in partnership with Hornets executives and the league's in-house consulting group, Team Marketing & Business Operations (TMBO), which was built to share best practices throughout the league. In this case, based on the dire conditions, Commissioner David Stern sent a handful of his top business executives to New Orleans full-time. Boots on the ground—inside our front office.

Just as you would expect with any major change, this was met with a mixed range of acceptance. My lens was one of optimism and eagerness to learn from some of the best and brightest in the league. I was a sponge in every meeting and took full advantage of this unique opportunity. One of the anchors of the "I'm In" campaign was to host one hundred events in one hundred days. These events were scattered throughout the region, which meant a lot of drive time. I always volunteered for these opportunities to drive, knowing it likely meant out-of-town league executives would join.

If time is the currency of leadership, I couldn't place a price tag on these drives—and the relationships they led to. Among the handful of NBA executives that I partnered with during this special chapter, a few relationships have stood the test of time; we're still good friends to this day. These relationships led directly to my next two opportunities, in Sacramento with the Kings, and then with Legends, a global sports agency that was based in New York at the time—leading to my opportunity at the NFL League Office.

> *"I believe that you can get everything in life you want if you will just help enough other people get what they want."*
>
> **ZIG ZIGLAR**
>
> author, salesman, motivational speaker

All this to say, relationships are at the core of leadership and at the core of life. To all the leaders that met me at the 50 along my journey, thank you. I wouldn't be where I am without you.

TIME-OUT: Identify one person in each direction (three total) that you're overdue to spend time and catch up with: Up is your boss (or senior exec); left/right is a leader at your level (ideally outside your department); down is somebody on your team (ideally a long snapper). Set up three coffees or lunches over the next sixty days. At the conclusion of these three meets, develop a cadence and keep them going, never blind toward any of the three directions of relationships.

A STRENGTHS-BASED APPROACH

Report cards are in. Take a peek.

A

A-

B

D

What is your *immediate* reaction?

Fix the D! Right?

Perhaps. But what if there was a different way of looking at it? Sure, let's address the D and pick it up. How much of an impact will that *really* make? Can the D ever become a strength? Or will we just beat our heads into submission to realize this isn't our jam?

I would never suggest completely ignoring the D, as a deep weakness can expose us. What I am suggesting is your natural strengths are *positively* exposed by the upper limits of your report card. That is where your maximized potential settles—until you take action against it.

What if you could *double down*, or, better yet, go ALL IN on the A?

By fully investing yourself into the A, you will exercise the potential of becoming the best, A+ version of yourself. Bigger picture: *Are you playing the game to be good enough or to be the best at it?*

You cannot be the best at it until you are your best self. The foundation of your best self is knowing what strengths got you to the A grade in the first place.

Let's see what the stats say on what happens when we play to our strengths.

ROI OF STRENGTHS-BASED DEVELOPMENT

In the research on strengths, this study performed by Gallup is the largest and most comprehensive to date.

Gallup studied workgroups using strengths-based interventions to examine the effects those interventions had on workgroup performance. This study included 49,495 business units with 1.2 million employees across 22 organizations in seven industries and 45 countries. Gallup researchers examined six outcomes: sales, profit, customer engagement, turnover, employee engagement, and safety. On average, workgroups that received a strengths intervention improved on all of these measures by a significant amount compared with control groups that received less intensive interventions or none at all. Ninety percent of the workgroups studied had performance increases at or above the following ranges:

10% TO 19%
INCREASED SALES

14% TO 29%
INCREASED PROFIT

26% TO 72%
LOWER TURNOVER
(high-turnover organizations)

6% TO 16%
LOWER TURNOVER
(low-turnover organizations)

3% TO 7%
HIGHER CUSTOMER ENGAGEMENT

9% TO 15%
INCREASE IN ENGAGED EMPLOYEES

22% TO 59%
FEWER SAFETY INCIDENTS

What's more, almost seven in ten employees (67 percent) who strongly agreed that their managers focused on their strengths or positive characteristics were engaged. When employees strongly disagreed with this statement, the percentage of workers who were engaged in their work plummeted to 2 percent.[21]

It's now easy to see the bottom-line impact of simply emphasizing strengths. All it takes is a mindset shift from *fix* the D to ALL IN on the A.

Playing to your strengths puts you in a position to thrive. It makes business sense *and* people sense.

> *"At Facebook, we try to be a strengths-based organization, which means we try to make jobs fit around people rather than make people fit around jobs. We focus on what people's natural strengths are and spend our management time trying to find ways for them to use those strengths every day."*
>
> **SHERYL SANDBERG**
>
> COO, Facebook

WHEN STRENGTH MEETS STRENGTH

Coming into a top Executive MBA program, I had no idea what to expect. I'm the sports business guy, head on a swivel. Over the years I had grown accustomed to being surrounded by heavyweights. But this was different. I was no longer lined by peers, bordered by the comforts of my industry. These were uncharted waters.

I stepped into orientation and realized that I was in a room of badasses. Each person was at the top of their respective field, climbing ranks, on their path to continuing their already massive success and achievements. Interestingly, I came to find out that others thought I was the badass because of my sports background. The feeling was mutual—and then some. While soaking it all in, I imagined how cool it would be to lock arms and learn from a chief surgeon, fighter pilot, and tech CEO—among countless others. I felt blessed to even be in the room.

It was a room of strengths, where we were all looking to enhance our abilities and become even stronger. As relationships formed, my comfort rose as I learned that underneath all of these inspiring resumes were regular people—just like me. There was no bravado, no ego, no flexing, no humble brags—just down-to-earth people showing up as lifelong learners, looking to level up our lives personally and professionally. This was my EMBA Los Angeles cohort from the University of Michigan and will forever be my wolfpack—my tribe.

My tribe taught me a lot about leadership. They taught me that there were different ways to lead. No judgment on right or wrong, no better or worse—in actuality, the hidden gems lay in the diversity of approaches. Michigan introduced us to a model of leadership that had four quadrants, each colored and categorized with a style of strength.

- **YELLOW** = the connectors and collaborators, a.k.a. "the people people" *(yep, that's me—guilty as charged)*
- **GREEN** = the visionaries and innovators, a.k.a. "the idea people"
- **RED** = the organizers and planners, a.k.a. "the process people"
- **BLUE** = the competitors and hard chargers, a.k.a. "the results people"

Throughout our twenty-one-month journey, as a locker room of leaders, we consulted and worked on countless projects, papers, case studies, and assignments. In looking back at which experiences turned out best, it was often those that had diverse representation across all four quadrants. While not an exact science, the model opened my eyes to a new type of diversity. Not the external diversity we most commonly hear about, but rather the internal diversity of our mindsets, personality traits, and cognitive approaches to teamwork and solving problems. Carlos could weigh in on numbers in a way that Erin couldn't. And Lynn systematized complex logistics like I could never do. We worked together to make the whole project better. By playing to our strengths, our most bold, confident, and authentic selves were able to show up in special ways, all in service to our fellow team members. Our individuality shone. Our contributions were memorable. Our impact was unquestioned.

My fondest recollection of these experiences was the egoless humility to express that we didn't have all the answers. In a locker room of badasses, the less we tried to take the lead, the more we became leaders.

> *"Keep learning; don't be arrogant by assuming you know it all, that you have a monopoly on the truth; always assume that you can learn something from someone else."*
>
> **JACK WELCH**
> former CEO, General Electric (GE)

STRENGTHS, TALENTS, AND PASSIONS

Recognize strengths as the table stakes for showing up as your best self. The other elements at play are your talents and passions—all of which we'll unpack in this chapter. Here's a brief description of each:

STRENGTHS: Consider strengths your functional, operating, and day-to-day powers of utility. Hands down, you're really damn good at these things. Through consistent application, practice, and experience over time, the strength among strengths emerge—your super-talent.

TALENTS: Consider talents the things in the world where you have unique gifts and the potential to be one of the greatest in the world. You begin to obsess over these things, which makes you work at them even harder. Over time, expertise and mastery have the potential to take form.

PASSIONS: Consider passions the love for what you do. Without passion, the maximization of your talents will likely not be possible because you will not obsess over your craft to the level of commitment that is required. This is the component that energizes you and makes you *feel alive*.

Many people will share your strengths. Few will share the combination of your strengths and talents. Almost nobody in the world will have your unique combination of strengths, talents, and passions. This is what makes it *your best self.*

Here's how you can visually think of it:

STRENGTHS + TALENTS + PASSIONS = YOUR BEST SELF

The beauty of this formula is that your superpowers are baked into each of these elements. Superpowers exist in your strengths, they exist in your talents, and they are super-charged when you're playing with passion. Organizations that know how to leverage this formula provide themselves with an incredible advantage. As Groupon founder Andrew Mason said, "Hire great people and give them freedom to be awesome."

The natural questions then become *what are my superpowers* and *where can I find them?*

Way ahead of you. That's exactly what we'll tackle at the end of this chapter in Applying the Playbook when you take your "Superpower Assessment."

Now that we've got your mind swirling around these amazing possibilities, here's the backstory on how I discovered (and recognized) my superpowers—including the messy parts. Your discovery may follow a similar path.

RECOGNIZING MY SUPERPOWER

From a young age, my family always told me I'd eventually be a sports agent or a lawyer. It was all rooted in my relentless pursuit of winning an argument—especially when there was a fire in my belly. No better way to fire me up than a sports debate. My family argued Lakers; I said Clippers just for the heck of it. They claimed Dodgers; I declared Angels. You get the drift.

It was clear from my earliest years that I loved sports and I could talk—or, as my family would say, "He just wouldn't shut up." We're *beginning* to see the connections to sales!

Years later, it became a reality that I could marry my interests of sports and business when the sales opportunity (coincidentally, with the Clippers) came about. Not only did I sell, but humbly speaking, I was also pretty darn good at it.

At this point, it became clear that I could identify one of my core superpowers. Birthed with a gift of gab, I could *communicate* effectively—that was my strength. Bigger picture and related to my strength, I started to recognize that I could influence and persuade, which is where the connection to sales comes in.

Now, before your mind wanders into how some perceive sales (e.g., the used-car guy), I will tell you I was keenly aware of that brand perception every step of the way. So much so that I over delivered on my commitments and promises to my team (and my character) because I never wanted to be perceived as the guy on the car lot, always reminding people how today was their lucky day!

Interestingly, my strength in sales began to illuminate what I truly loved about it. I didn't love the phone calls or the process. What I did love was the people that I did it with and could serve. Another's anticipated rejection within one hundred calls was my one hundred opportunities to connect and engage with people. The pursuit of relationships made me fall in love with people even more than I already had. The fact that sales was a strength and led to great results meant I could meet even more people on the back end—my clients.

It also meant that I was asked to mentor and groom younger sales executives because I was typically on top of the sales board. This mentorship began my infatuation with coaching. That love of coaching and grooming others became my obsession. An obsession that I poured myself into, soon realizing that not only did I have a passion for it, I was gifted at it. *Coaching* became my super *talent,* and that exposed me to the greater potential of doing it full-time. This progression welcomed me into leadership—and I've never looked back.

> *"You don't succeed because you have no weaknesses; you succeed because you find your unique strengths and focus on developing habits around them."*
>
> **TIM FERRISS**
>
> entrepreneur, podcaster, and author of *Tools of Titans*

ANOTHER SUPERPOWER EMERGES

As I navigated my career from sales to leadership, these same core competencies were equally critical. Instead of selling products and services, I began to sell a vision and ideas. When focused on my team, I sold a culture of inspiration and motivation. I sold the end benefits of career growth, purpose, impact, and fulfillment.

Then, as I rose up the leadership ranks, it led to more opportunities to double down on the roots of what made me great at sales—authentic communication and the ability to inspire others.

Formally, this grew into another supertalent—*speaking.* Known to be one of the top fears in the world, speaking became *my thing*. Initially, it was private, inside team and departmental meetings. Then, it became public at client events, organization-wide functions, and industry conferences. Just when I thought I was hitting my stride, I almost puked my guts out. (I warned you things got messy!)

While I was midspeech at a client event in the Sacramento Kings locker room, in walked the Maloof brothers, who owned the team at the time. You may recall them as the flashy and media-centric owners of the Palms Casino in Vegas, living the dream life. Well, let's just say that at their peak of fame, I got starstruck—then came the butterflies, and I almost lost my lunch.

After dodging this near-embarrassment, it became a great learning lesson. Up to that point, I had relied on my natural speaking talent; practice was secondary. Not fully internalizing the content led to the potential of nerves based on the inevitable curveballs (like the Maloofs walking in) that would continue to come. I now knew that if I was ever going to speak on larger platforms, I would have to over-prepare. This became my secret weapon, which turned into an obsession with the craft of speaking.

Roughly eight years later, I shifted a part-time gift of speaking inside the sports industry into becoming a global keynote speaker and launching my own business around it. I now rehearse a minimum of twenty times per speech, and record every moment—as painful as it may be. Try watching yourself on video for multiple hours per day, analyzing every word and facial expression! Ugh. But that's what's required if it's a supertalent and you strive for mastery.

While it's easy to connect the dots and play Monday morning quarterback, between my family highlighting my speaking abilities as a child, their asking me to speak at my grandma's funeral as one of the youngest family members at the time, and countless friends and business acquaintances complimenting my speaking, I never considered the larger meaning or impact of thought leadership. I just continued to get my reps in, keep my head down, and eventually it *called* me to go ALL IN and share my superpowers with the world.

PLAYING WITH PASSION

So far, we've covered the elements of what makes us special, unique, and great at what we do. Now it's time to unpack what you *love* to do.

Consider passion the fuel for your superpowers. You can be great at something; it doesn't mean you're going to love doing it *or* ever have the chance to find out.

Think of my story as an example. What if I didn't love the relational aspect of sales? What if that nearly humiliating moment in the Kings' locker room had derailed my confidence in speaking in public?

Being completely transparent, I still get the butterflies from time to time, but I consider it a natural part of the process. It's similar to the countless professional athletes who share how they experience jitters before every game—especially the biggest ones. The reason they push through is because they love what they do. They couldn't imagine not playing. There's a deeper purpose for *why* they do what they do. But it all comes back to passion. I think of how author, speaker, and self-described "eternal optimist" Simon Sinek describes it: "Working hard for something we don't care about is called stress. Working hard for something we love is called passion."

Passion is the fuel to drive the work you do behind the scenes so that you can potentially be one of the best in the world at it. It's all a cycle. Without passion, there's no permanent sacrifice. Without sacrifice, there's no greatness. Without greatness, there's no expression of talents. Without talents, there's no connection to your strengths.

Remember: Strengths + Talents + Passions = Your Best Self

You've heard about my journey; now, let's talk about yours.

LISTEN FOR THE CLUES

As you navigate the upcoming questions of reflection, you will have the opportunity to gain clarity about who you are on your best day when you fully max out your superpowers.

In retrospect, I've had the blessing of perspective and purpose. Ever since finding my 'Why' and challenging myself to bring it to life, I have found some answers on my own—but not all. The missing links came from the support of my inner circle. We're about to activate both for you.

Between your assessment of self, coupled with asking others about your strengths, talents, and passions, you will be able to recreate more of your best self in the future. You'll then be able to share your superpowers with the world—and have your team follow suit.

Before we unearth their superpowers, you must first find yours.

With that, let's apply the playbook.

APPLYING THE PLAYBOOK

CHAPTER 8: YOUR SUPERPOWER ASSESSMENT

IDEAL SETTING

Choose a private and calm space where you can fully focus and reflect, away from your daily working environment, free of technology.

STEP ONE

Fill out your self-assessment. If stuck, take notes of your loose thoughts. One note inspires the next. This is less about a fully curated answer today, and more about the process of internal reflection and discovery of themes as you revisit your first pass.

STEP TWO

Invite your inner circle into the process. Select one (or more) question from each section and reformat it so you can ask the question to others. As a few examples:

- What do you believe I'm exceptionally good at?
- If you saw me as a teacher of any skill in life, what would I teach?
- Of the things you've seen me most passionate about, what do you think I can invest more time and energy into?

STEP THREE

Look for the themes in your responses and the responses of others. These are the cues of your superpowers from which to focus on. Aim to select at least one superpower to create an action plan around. Until you reach this point, revisit these notes every 30 days until you land on one.

It's time to unleash your superpowers!

YOUR SUPERPOWER ASSESSMENT

STRENGTHS

- What are you naturally and exceptionally good at?
- What do people typically ask you for help in?
- What do you like *most* about yourself?
- What do you get complimented on most?

TALENTS

- If you had to teach something, what would you love to teach?
- What are some unusual skills you have?
- What did the most influential mentor(s) in your life see in you that you did not recognize in yourself?
- What comes especially easy to you?

PASSIONS

- What makes you *feel alive*?
- What are the things you obsess about, daydream about, wish you had more time to put energy into?
- As you were growing up, what did you most love doing?
- What activities make you lose track of time?

9

PEOPLE360: A BLUEPRINT TO BUILD A PEOPLE-FIRST ORGANIZATION

Who's coaching the coaches?

This question is one of the many that inspired this book. While I believe experience can be a great teacher (as many of my anecdotes to this point have illustrated), I also believe that there should be a "go-to" playbook for how to lead and develop talent.

In comes *The Power of Playing Offense*, where the endgame is to level up our leadership and be the best version of ourselves so that we can maximize impact in our workplace, community, home, and beyond.

MY LEADERSHIP DEVELOPMENT JOURNEY AND OFFER TO YOU

Until my most recent years, I was largely self-trained in leadership. Here's how my journey has evolved:

BUSINESS UNDERGRAD: Fundamentally theoretical, sans leadership courses.

INDIVIDUAL CONTRIBUTOR ROLES: I heard "Worry about it once you get there."

BREAKING INTO FORMAL LEADERSHIP RANKS: The message became "You'll figure it out" or "Learn from those around you—whether what to do, or what *not* to do."

MID-SPORTS CAREER LEADERSHIP RANKS: Leadership development finally came! Between two to five formal training days per year.

LATE-SPORTS CAREER LEADERSHIP RANKS: Same as mid-career.

EXECUTIVE MBA: Twenty-one-month crash course with leadership development interspersed.

LEADERSHIP INSTITUTE: Two years of daily immersion where I learned more about leadership than during all of the above combined.

BUSINESS OWNERSHIP: Everything I coach, I implement and validate on myself/my business first. It's the best course on leadership (and self-leadership) I've ever had.

LIFELONG COMMITMENT: I study leadership several hours per day. It's non-negotiable.

This chapter was written so that you don't have to wait as long as I did. I have minimal control over most university curriculums and can only influence leadership development programs within organizations I directly touch; that equation doesn't scale well enough to achieve a vision of impacting one million people, lives, and leaders by the year 2030.

This book is a key to maximize that impact. The learnings continue at **WWW.POWEROFPLAYINGOFFENSE.COM.**

Consider me a virtual coach for now—and of course, I'm always happy to have the conversation to meet at the 50 in person, however I can support you and your organization.

For now, let's roll up our sleeves and get to work.

"The business of business is people."

HERB KELLEHER

Co-Founder, former CEO, Southwest Airlines

PEOPLE360: A TRANSFORMATIONAL CYCLE

This blueprint is a compilation of *best practices* from organizations I have worked in, teams I have led, and client organizations that have served as great partners and case studies of mine. These *best practices* will include a mix of activities, exercises, methods, models, mindset shifts, frameworks, processes, and programs.

The blueprint is organized in a 360-degree cyclical fashion, where one element feeds into the next, from recruiting through retention (then back to recruiting). If the goal is to attract stars and keep stars, you'll entice new stars when you take care of your current ones. It's a cycle that keeps on giving.

People360 Blueprint. © 2020. *The Power of Playing Offense*, Paul Epstein.

Why are these five elements so important? Because each has unique impact—and most of it is left unfulfilled, never materializing due to gaps in our current people processes and systems. This blueprint is your way of overcoming these challenges in your team and organization.

For each element of the five-part cyclical blueprint, here's what to expect after a brief introduction:

- State of the Union—comprised of research, ROI, and more.
- Three actionable ways to install this phase of the People360 blueprint—as you see in the model below.

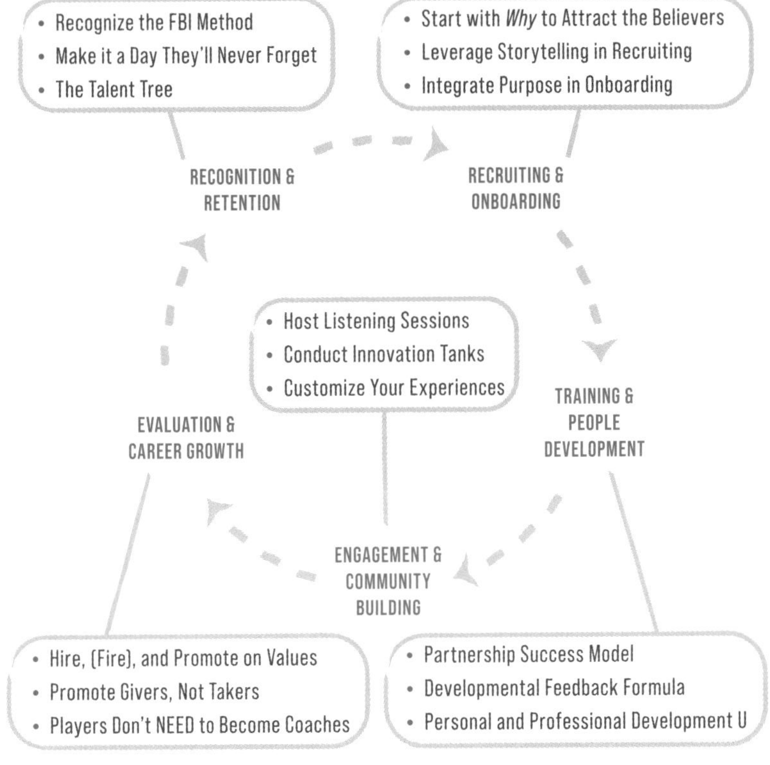

People360 Blueprint. © 2020. *The Power of Playing Offense*, Paul Epstein.

If you'd like to keep this People360 Blueprint handy, download or print it from WWW.POWEROFPLAYINGOFFENSE.COM.

RECRUITMENT & ONBOARDING

Talent wins games. The right talent wins championships.

This is as much about attracting the best talent in the marketplace as it is about selecting the right fit to enrich your locker room and ignite every person's superpowers—from star quarterbacks to long snappers.

The first side of the coin is recruiting.

Candidly, are the candidates you desire most interested in you?

Recruiting can be brutally competitive and word in the war for talent travels fast. With resources like Glassdoor, social media, and word of mouth via networks, candidates will know what you're all about in a few clicks of the mouse. The suggested practices below will help create the needed positive water cooler buzz about your organization beyond its four walls—so the *right talent* can find your tribe.

Once they're in, the fun begins. Everybody enjoys the *honeymoon period*—but honeymoons inevitably end. How can you welcome in the talent that you competed so hard to recruit, and ensure that they feel embraced, inspired, and energized, so that when they get past the honeymoon period, they are ready to authentically contribute with all their effort?

Treat them right from day one.

STATE OF THE UNION: RECRUITING & ONBOARDING

Top candidates **STAY AVAILABLE FOR JUST** 10 days before getting hired.[22]

48%

of businesses say their top quality hires **COME FROM EMPLOYEE REFERRALS.**[24]

Organizations that invest in employer branding are

3x

MORE LIKELY TO MAKE A QUALITY HIRE.[23]

33%

of employees **KNEW WHETHER THEY WOULD STAY WITH THEIR COMPANY LONG-TERM AFTER THEIR FIRST WEEK.**[25]

33%

of new hires **QUIT THEIR JOB AFTER SIX MONTHS.**[26]

69%

of employees are more likely to **STAY WITH A COMPANY FOR THREE YEARS IF THEY EXPERIENCED GREAT ONBOARDING,**

yet only

12%

of employees strongly agree that their organization **DOES A GREAT JOB OF ONBOARDING.**[27]

START WITH WHY TO ATTRACT THE BELIEVERS

The choice is yours. If you want the same candidates you're already getting, keep posting a paragraph about your company, then a dozen or so bullets about the position and job requirements.

Alternatively, you could start with *why*. Why does your company exist? Why do you serve? What is your collective purpose? What cause do you stand for? What are the beliefs you share?

Do that, and you will hire the *believers*.

Your purpose and vision cast an inspirational message to the like-minded and like-hearted believers in the marketplace. They embody who you will collectively be as an organization once they join. It's easy to hire for the blue skies; hire the people that will stick with you through the storm. As believers, they joined you for the duration of the journey, not just the destination.

> *"If you hire people just because they can do a job, they'll work for your money. But if you hire people who believe what you believe, they'll work for you with blood and sweat and tears."*
>
> **SIMON SINEK**
> author of *Start with Why*

LEVERAGE STORYTELLING IN RECRUITING

Once you hire the believers, you'll start to see the superpowers shared in the last chapter come to life. Strengths, talents, and passions will emerge in abundance. Also remember that *every seat has a story*. Capture the stories of your people on their best days, about how they are able to express their superpowers, how they feel a part of something bigger than themselves, what the organization means to them, and how the organization has provided for them.

Capture it all in print and video if possible. Work with your marketing and communications teams to bring it to life, then evolve it and let it be a staple for how you communicate to the outside world. Your people are your greatest gifts and recruiting tools. They will feel more invested in the locker room when they're helping to fill it with fellow members of their tribe. As for candidates, people buy people. Make sure to always keep your most inspiring and authentic stories out there for the world to see.

We will dive deeper on the power of storytelling in Chapter 10.

INTEGRATE PURPOSE IN ONBOARDING

Just as we did in the 49ers Academy, at the culmination of your formal onboarding (which likely consists of functional and technical training, FAQs, and welcoming activities), end the process off-site. Carve out a half day and lead your new hires through an exercise or two from Applying the Playbook in our first pillar, Live with Championship Purpose. A four-hour investment of time expresses the purpose and care needed at this foundational stage. If you'd like to learn more about facilitating a Purpose discovery as a part of your onboarding process, please see the Purpose Discovery FAQ at **WWW.POWEROFPLAYINGOFFENSE.COM**.

TRAINING & PEOPLE DEVELOPMENT

Your locker room is inspired. They feel purpose, believe in the vision, serve as proud ambassadors, and are ALL IN on the mission. Now, how do they level up?

One of the key drivers of retention is the feeling that you're getting better each and every day—personally and professionally. When you know the organization is wholly invested in you, it creates a bond and social contract that you can't put a price tag on.

Most organizations have training programs. They invest in the advancement of skill, function, and execution of the daily tasks in the hopes of mastery within their best talent. I'm going to leave that side of the training equation to the experts in your field—you. What we're going to talk about is people and leadership development. You know—the other side of business. The side that probably attracted you to this book.

Do what other organizations won't if you want to develop the people they can't.

STATE OF THE UNION: TRAINING & PEOPLE DEVELOPMENT

68%

of employees say **TRAINING AND DEVELOPMENT IS THE COMPANY'S MOST IMPORTANT POLICY.**[28]

40%

of employees with poor training **WILL LEAVE THE COMPANY WITHIN THE FIRST YEAR.**[29]

In the US and UK, an estimated **$37 billion** is **SPENT ANNUALLY TO KEEP UNPRODUCTIVE EMPLOYEES WHO DON'T UNDERSTAND THEIR JOB.**[30]

24%

HIGHER PROFIT MARGINS can be the result of companies who invest in training.[31]

74%

of employees **DON'T BELIEVE THEY ARE REACHING THEIR FULL POTENTIAL.**[32]

PARTNERSHIP SUCCESS MODEL

Commit to each and every one of your employees that they will leave better than when they arrived. This is your version of my Clippers Constitution from Chapter 5. Cocreate what the core controllables are with your team (e.g., work ethic, positive attitude, being coachable). That's their end of the bargain. In exchange, you will commit to their personal and professional growth—holistically. This starts by creating a custom training and development plan for each individual. If they give you the controllables, you commit to delivering the training. Now there's skin in the game on both sides, and nobody (on your team) will be able to say that they weren't leveling up if they did the foundational things that were expected—which should be table stakes for the job regardless. This is your partnership success model.

DEVELOPMENTAL FEEDBACK FORMULA

S-B-I-N (in this order):

S—situation

B—behavior

I—impact

N—next

This is the formula for delivering constructive feedback so that your people can develop, and they are inspired toward better action. As much as I've been guilty of sugarcoating and compliment sandwiches, I realize that people need to hear what they need to hear (not what they want to hear)—me included. For more on the topic of what researcher Kim Scott coined "radical candor," refer to her phenomenal book by that name.

From Kim's model, radical candor happens at the intersection of caring personally and challenging directly. This intersection is where feedback is best received, and thus increases the potential of positive change as the outcome.

The key question you first need to answer is whether you have a foundational relationship where your team member knows it's coming from a good place. If not, start there before you pull out the battering ram.

If you have the relationship equity established, proceed with this feedback formula:

S—What is the situation? Be specific on occasion and frequency.

B—What is the behavior? Notice I didn't say judgment. A behavior is "you're late to work." A judgment is "you're lazy" (your perception of them because they're constantly late to work). To avoid unnecessary arguments and personal attacks, keep it to the black and white behaviors—not judgments.

I—What is the impact of your behavior? (Financial, relational, team, trust, time, morale, etc.)

N—What actions can we co-create so that we don't end up addressing this same behavior in the future?

Here's what this could look like:

"Johnny, every Monday morning (situation) you're coming in late to work (behavior). Our team is starting to lose trust (impact) in whether we can rely on you for some of these early week deliverables. I personally want to see you have the best possible brand inside our team and the company. This is small for now, but small things add up, and I wouldn't want your growth to be hurt in the long run because of these minor and controllable things. What can we do to avoid you being late to work in the future?"

As a coach, this is your "go-to" formula when delivering developmental feedback. Stick to it. Your team will undoubtedly develop—and trust will inevitably be built.

TIME-OUT: Before your next round of conducting one-on-ones, carve some time out on your calendar to craft these messages in advance so that you are prepared to deliver this developmental feedback formula as needed.

PERSONAL AND PROFESSIONAL DEVELOPMENT U

From my days at the 49ers, we started "49ers U." This was a multimonth, university-style speaker series that featured guest presenters (typically executives and department heads) to share insights unique to their space. This spanned contract negotiations and managing the salary cap and player analytics, along with a plethora of business topics.

While you may not have the sports industry at your fingertips, you have the same opportunity.

I propose that every organization create a *Personal and Professional Development U.* Create a monthly thought leadership series of internal and external experts to train and speak on themes such as leadership, team building, culture, emotional intelligence, mindset, purpose, resilience, managing conflict, success, and personal growth—the list is exponential.

Separate from core job topics, how can you develop the people side of your business? This will help groom and build the leaders of today and tomorrow. Think of it as *Leadership U.* Whether you call it that or not, you're creating leaders inside the office (no title required) and beyond.

Cherry on top, by promoting a learning program, it will organically create internal teaching opportunities—and as we've often heard, the best way to learn is to teach. The content of the U can be taught in each and every department and team, further expanding and sustaining the learning capacity of your organization beyond the U.

ENGAGEMENT & COMMUNITY BUILDING

You've taken your talent, people, and leadership to the next level—that's HUGE.

Now, how do we keep them engaged in between these high-mark points? Ultimately, the day-to-day experience will own their mind space. It will be the factor of work that will influence how they feel on the drive in *and* the drive home, what they say at the dinner table and at happy hour.

Better yet, if you build a strong enough community, they may choose to spend some of this social time with each other, where there isn't a barrier between personal and professional. It makes people sense and makes business sense as the research by Gallup shows that having a best friend at work increases the overall engagement, retention, trust, innovation, and performance of the organization.

An engaged community is one that wants to do the work—they don't need to be told to do the work. It isn't the carrots and sticks that drive them, it's the authentic belief in what they do, why they do it, whom they do it for, and whom they do it with.

The endgame: Gone are the days of silos. In are the days of connection and communication, where you'll have a thriving community of happy, productive, and engaged employees.

STATE OF THE UNION: ENGAGEMENT & COMMUNITY BUILDING

$550 billion IN LOST PRODUCTIVITY EVERY YEAR DUE TO DISENGAGED EMPLOYEES. But let's call these employees what they really are: people who have quit without actually quitting.[33]

54% of employees say A STRONG SENSE OF COMMUNITY (great coworkers, celebrating milestones, a common mission) KEPT THEM AT A COMPANY LONGER.[35]

53% of Americans are CURRENTLY UNHAPPY AT WORK – costing American businesses over $300 billion per year.[34]

56% of the POSITIVE CHANGES IN COMMUNICATION PATTERNS WITHIN THE WORKPLACE can be accredited to social interaction outside of the workplace.[36]

Companies and organizations that COMMUNICATE EFFECTIVELY ARE **4.5x** MORE LIKELY TO RETAINTHE BEST EMPLOYEES.[37]

HOST LISTENING SESSIONS

Similar to the 49ers lunch box story in Chapter 7, listen to those closest to the work. By asking what's going well and what could be better, you will unearth change in three forms:

Do More—Do Better—Do Different

In response to what is going well, now you're aware of it! Do *more* of those things.

In response to what could be better, you now know what needs course correction—whether it can be slightly *better* or should be completely *different.*

Your people will feel heard, they will have a platform to speak truth to power, and you will have the opportunity to act so that people feel like their voices matter and can make a difference in their daily environment. You never know where the lunch box example may be hiding in your team or organization—until you ask.

TIME-OUT: Identify one thing you will do more, one thing you will do better, and one thing you will do different. Jot each down. Now, let's loop the team in and create some positive change together.

Identify a date roughly ninety days out where you can carve out a half day (or full day) off-site for your team. In between now and then, see the appendix for a guide on how to best facilitate your first listening session (including tips and framing so it doesn't turn into a vent session). You'll be amazed at how much you'll learn about what really matters to your team. After you learn what you can collectively do more/better/different, raise a glass and celebrate the off-site. When back in the office, it's time to put it in action.

The timing of ninety days is strategic. By then I anticipate you will have finished the book and can now customize an entire half or full day *Playing Offense* experience for your team. The listening sessions will take roughly two hours, the rest of the agenda is a blank canvas. For off-site agenda ideas, I'd recommend a selection of your favorite Applying the Playbook and/or Time Out exercises; there are dozens to choose from, and all are highlighted in the appendix. Select a few that will resonate with your team and get planning!

CONDUCT INNOVATION TANKS

We typically think of innovation as a grand idea—something groundbreaking that is *Shark Tank*–worthy. To achieve these innovative and progressive outcomes, it is less about the size of the idea, and more about the process to get there. This is not a story about the emperor in an ivory tower; rather, it is about the village coming together so that everybody's fingerprints are on the blueprint.

Innovation tanks are opt-in working sessions with a blank canvas to brainstorm about the future of the business. It can focus on a system, a process, a product, a strategy. Ideally, you have a master facilitator who can manage the flow, interactivity, organization, and advancement of the conversation. There should be a mix of people by department, tenure, and ideology. At your next all-hands, present the top idea from each innovation tank to recognize who inspired it and create a *pull strategy* for participation in the next tank.

Whether a listening session or an innovation tank, these are only two (of many) examples on how you can engage and value your team, give their voices a platform, recognize courageous and bold ideas, and create an inclusive culture of belonging, contribution, and impact.

CUSTOMIZE YOUR EXPERIENCES

Believe it or not, not everybody wants a ping pong table in the office!

After working in Silicon Valley for years, I can endorse this theory to be true. While certain benefits or experiences can create a "we want it, too" movement, they typically will fade as soon as the next fad hits.

We've all heard the saying "give the people what they want." While fair in spirit, the challenge is we all want different things. Your yoga retreat is somebody else's jelly of the month club.

There's only one solution to the problem: the power of customization. Create a diverse menu of options, even poll your employees for what should be on the menu—THEN people will truly get what they want.

Your team members will choose the experience and incentives that matter most to them. Some will elect flexibility to work from home once a week. Others will elect health and wellness benefits. Others may actually want the ping-pong table!

There is no right; there is no wrong. Empower your team to make these small elections, and watch their engagement take off.

Lastly, keep the community in mind when crafting your benefits. Fun and social gatherings should be a must. Your next one might even be where you announce these new perks.

PS—While I'm a massive fan of customizing experiences and incentives, even more important is the daily work environment and opportunity for growth. That's the greatest motivator of them all—even beyond financial rewards, as research from McKinsey & Company has shown: "Praise, attention from leaders, and opportunities to lead projects are more effective motivators than performance-based cash rewards."[38]

EVALUATION & CAREER GROWTH

Now comes the moment of truth. We've provided inspiration, purpose, opportunities for contribution and impact, personal and professional development, and a seat at the table.

As coaches, we get paid to make tough decisions and have tough conversations. People's careers are in our hands. There's an extraordinary responsibility in that.

So, how are we grooming and molding our leaders of tomorrow? What is expected of them? Do they know what winning and success look like on a daily basis? How are we keeping score along the way? What are the factors for how we evaluate *and* what we evaluate?

If we're going to dangle the carrot of formal career growth, there should be no surprises when sitting on the other side of the table. These practices to follow will help create a transparent and consistent platform to create, build, and grow a locker room you're proud of.

STATE OF THE UNION: EVALUATION & CAREER GROWTH

76%

of employees **PLACE CAREER GROWTH AS A TOP PRIORITY** and key determining factor in staying at company.[39]

Only **17%** of employees say their **MANAGERS ARE ACTIVELY INVOLVED IN THEIR CAREER DEVELOPMENT.**[40]

WHEN ASKED IF THEIR COMPANY MAKES IT EASY AND TRANSPARENT TO UNDERSTAND OPPORTUNITIES FOR ADVANCEMENT WITHIN THE ORGANIZATION,

26%

say "not at all" or "hardly ever" and another

27%

say "only from time to time."[41]

3/4

say they **WOULD STAY WITH THEIR CURRENT EMPLOYER IF THEY KNEW THEY HAD A CAREER PATH.**[42]

2/3

of **MANAGERS FAIL TO ACTIVELY ENGAGE IN THEIR OWN CAREER DEVELOPMENT.**[43]

HIRE, (FIRE), AND PROMOTE ON VALUES

Hiring is the easy part: Promote your organizational values externally, and watch the attraction begin.

Firing is where it can get messy. Often, it's because performance clouds our lens. Superstars typically survive. Middle-of-the-pack performers with strong values and intangibles are a coin flip. I'm not denying the natural temptation of this gray space; however, you *cannot* be a values-driven organization if it's *not* the governing lens for your actions, behaviors, and decisions.

Lastly, promotions. As you conduct evaluations that lead up to these career growth conversations, are you reviewing more than KPIs and metrics? Are values factored in?

If not, today is an opportunity to start. Until others in your organization see that values are, the driver of how you hire, fire, and promote, they're just words on the wall. Once values are activated within your organizational DNA, then consistently practiced and embedded over time, you will be able to proudly say that you are a values-based organization. Then, never look back.

> *"We believe that it's really important to come up with core values that you can commit to. And by commit, we mean that you're willing to hire and fire based on them. If you're willing to do that, then you're well on your way to building a company culture that is in line with the brand you want to build."*
>
> **TONY HSIEH**
>
> CEO, Zappos

PROMOTE GIVERS, NOT TAKERS

All around us, there are people who *take* at every opportunity. You know exactly who I'm talking about.

There are others that *give*, fully generous, no agenda, and don't "keep score."

This leads to a divergence in culture: one side built around scarcity—the other built around abundance.

If you want to continue to fight for perceived finite resources, including time, money, and information, skip to the next section. If you want to create an environment where you shift from "I don't have the time" to "I'll make the time," from budgeting considerations being holistic versus siloed, and where information is shared versus hoarded, then recognize this giving philosophy as a core message in your organization.

A simple way to embed this is in your performance evaluations, especially at the leadership level. If a leader's contributions are 100 percent inside their department, that's a sign of prioritizing "taking" over "giving." Takers don't get promoted. Those who get promoted are the givers—those who create value for the organization beyond the four walls of their team and their department.

Once implemented, this practice can transform the value created from within your organization overnight, from scarcity to abundance. Giving will lead to willing reciprocity. The virtuous cycle takes over from there.

PLAYERS DON'T NEED TO BECOME COACHES

The best players rarely become the best coaches. But in business, that's exactly what we do. We default to promoting the highest achieving "doer" to supervise or manage the *doers* of that space. We're not shocked by the role-player in sports who becomes a legendary coach (see, for example, Steve Kerr, Golden State Warriors championship coach, Chicago Bulls role player), but rarely give the same *look* to businesspeople who are non-stars. In sports, coaching is a different skill set from playing, and we acknowledge that fact. Yet in business, players become coaches overnight for being the top scorer (i.e., producer), regardless of a known ability to lead.

It all comes back full circle to Personal and Professional Development U, a.k.a. Leadership U. If it is implemented, you now have a platform to develop high-potential team members into future leaders—to train them on model leadership behaviors versus pure focus on functional and technical expertise.

After the university launch, embed a *leadership behavior evaluation* across your organization for every employee that aspires to be in the formal leadership ranks. This behavioral scorecard can be used for existing leaders as well. After all, they're the ones conducting the reviews!

You've now embedded leadership DNA into the fabric of your organization. Here are some eye-opening stats to highlight the importance of maintaining a focus on developing your leaders and yourself. There's very little traffic on that road.

STATE OF THE UNION: LEADERSHIP DEVELOPMENT

ONLY **62%** OF EMPLOYERS HAVE A LEADERSHIP DEVELOPMENT PROGRAM IN PLACE for their new managers.

38% do not.[44]

58% of MANAGERS SAID THEY DIDN'T RECEIVE ANY MANAGEMENT TRAINING.[45]

The **TOP 2 REASONS** PEOPLE GET PROMOTED ARE UTTERLY UNRELATED TO THEIR TALENT FOR MANAGING PEOPLE:

1) because they were successful in a previous role, and

2) because they have a lot of tenure or experience.[46]

RECOGNITION & RETENTION

Homestretch. People know where they stand and what's in it for them.

Now it's time to shine a light on the bright spots within your team and organization. Let everybody know they matter, especially the long snappers. It's your opportunity to make them feel special and provide moments and memories that will last a lifetime.

Speaking of lifetime, it's time to start thinking about how you want to be remembered. When all is said and done, will you leave everything and everybody you impact better than you found them? Will you pay it forward to inspire the next wave? You will never know when somebody has their own breakthrough, but you invest in their potential regardless. When you take care of people in this fashion, word travels fast.

Back to our introduction of the 360 cycle. What's your *keeper* strategy? If the goal is to attract stars and keep stars, you'll entice new stars when you take care of your current ones. It's a cycle that keeps on giving.

> *"Appreciate everything your associates do for the business. Nothing else can quite substitute for a few well-chosen, well-timed, sincere words of praise. They're absolutely free and worth a fortune."*
>
> **SAM WALTON**
>
> Founder of Walmart and Sam's Club

STATE OF THE UNION: RECOGNITION & RETENTION

The **#1 REASON** **PEOPLE LEAVE THEIR JOB** is that they don't feel appreciated.[47]

65% of Americans reported **RECEIVING ZERO RECOGNITION** for good work in the last year.[48]

51% of **MANAGERS SAY THEY DO A GOOD JOB OF RECOGNIZING A JOB WELL DONE**, yet only **17%** of employees from the same companies in the study say that their managers recognize them for a job well done.[49]

The **ORGANIZATIONAL COSTS OF EMPLOYEE TURNOVER** are estimated to range between **100%** and **300%** of the replaced employee's salary.[50]

Managers who give frequent recognition and genuine encouragement see a **40%** **INCREASE IN PRODUCTIVITY.**[51]

More than **80%** of employees say they're **MOTIVATED TO WORK HARDER WHEN THEIR BOSS SHOWS APPRECIATION** for their work.[52]

RECOGNIZE THE FBI METHOD

It's time to catch somebody doing something right. Similar to developmental feedback, there's a formula for affirmative (positive) feedback, a.k.a. recognition: F-B-I. While I hope you never get interrogated by them, do use the formula.

F—feeling B—behavior I—impact

Unlike the developmental feedback formula, these elements can be used in any order; I-B-F works just as well. The key here is to not forget the F (*feeling)*. That is the secret sauce.

Most recognition messages are crafted solely around the behavior. Fewer recognize the impact of the behavior. Few say what it actually means to them, their feeling. As an example:

> *"Susie, thank you for staying late last night to craft our presentation (behavior). Because of you, we were so well prepared for the client meeting today that they signed on the spot (impact). We're so thankful to have you on the team, and you continue to inspire us (feeling) to do our part because we trust that you will always overdeliver on yours."*

A few tips as you're crafting your next recognition message: It's easy for many of us to recognize achievement. Some us acknowledge the process, but it's important to do so regardless of the results (as this example with Susie highlights). If she did everything in her power to achieve the desired result and we didn't land the client, we should still recognize her efforts. Most importantly, recognize the behaviors you want to see if you want to see them more often—and recognize the values you want to see if you want them to stick.

Bonus: kick each team meeting off by catching somebody doing something right. Simply ask, "Who caught somebody doing something right?" and watch the recognition flood in. We did this at the Clippers, and it worked wonders. Your turn.

MAKE IT A DAY THEY'LL NEVER FORGET

Short, simple, and sweet. For the most significant recognitions of the year, (confidentially) invite their immediate family. Make it a surprise—this part is key! When the presenter is concluding their remarks, ask their family to join them as a grand reveal. The more difficult the logistics of getting their family there, the more impactful it will be.

Make sure to have some tissues nearby!

THE TALENT TREE

If you want to retain the best, you'll have to take care of your best. Extrinsic motivators like money and titles will only get you so far. It works in the immediate, and then there's another benchmark set out to achieve.

What has the potential to last is your genuine commitment to growing people. When you have their best interests at heart, you look after them personally and professionally. You inspire their best. You believe in them wholeheartedly. You elevate their potential beyond levels they knew they had in them.

The end result is authentic service, commitment, and dedication in return. This will often lead to increased production and performance, which naturally increase the probabilities of formal growth opportunities. If internal, you're always a happy camper. If external, there can be mixed feelings. You can shun it, or you can applaud it—just like my boss at the Kings did.

A true leader should be measured by more than the score on the board. They should be measured by whom they have grown along the way. Think of it as a *talent tree.*

Who has worked for you, in your span of care, that has now grown to greener pastures? In this upcoming exercise in Applying the Playbook, you'll put pen to paper on this question.

This selfless approach to doing what's best for your people—even if it stings your team and organization in the short run—is the sign of what makes a great leader. Just like you would never want to be held back, let those around you fly as well—and never clip their wings. This will become your ultimate legacy as a leader.

Now let's go draw that tree!

APPLYING THE PLAYBOOK

CHAPTER 9: YOUR TALENT TREE

"Someone is sitting in the shade today because someone planted a tree a long time ago."

WARREN BUFFETT
investor, philanthropist, CEO, Berkshire Hathaway

What do you want your leadership legacy to be? What's the story you will be able to tell when you hang your cleats at the end of a long, hard-fought career? How will you be remembered?

No doubt we all want to achieve business results—otherwise, career growth would be scarce. That said, I'd like to expand our view on what success and impact look like for a leader. Is it only about the trophies and hitting metrics? Or will it be the people that we've impacted along the way? The people that are now positional leaders in their own right, paving their own path, grateful that we played a part in their growth and development along their journey.

If you envision your legacy and leadership brand being both results and people you've grown, this exercise is for you. I trust you'll handle the results. Let's tackle the other side by playing offense and filling out your talent tree.

NOTE: *This exercise assumes you are in a positional leadership role. If not, all good—can't wait for you to get there. Absorb the spirit of the exercise and use it as a motivator for your leadership brand and legacy when you are formally leading a team in the near future.*

STEP ONE

Identify all the people that you have promoted over the course of your career. It can be internal or external. If it's a short list, no worries—this is a career-long exercise going forward.

Make a list with their name and where they were promoted to (organization/position). This information will be used in the next step.

STEP TWO

Draw a tree that resembles the one on the following page with the below information (just like in a real tree, all parts are connected and rely on one another for growth and support):

- Your name in the top of the tree
- Names of your current team members in the trunk
- Names of your past promotions in the roots (one person per root)—include their name, organization, and position
- Strategically draw a few roots with no information next to them. Consider these motivational placeholders as this information will be updated in real time going forward. The only question is "Who's next?"

YOUR TALENT TREE

PAUL EPSTEIN

CURRENT
TEAM
NAMES

NAME
ORGANIZATION
TITLE

NAME
ORGANIZATION
TITLE

NAME
ORGANIZATION
TITLE

WHO'S NEXT?

WHO'S NEXT?

The list below is what initially inspired me to start a talent tree of my own.

While not in the exact same format, this career growth chart is what we used at Legends and the 49ers to showcase all of our people growth within the sports industry. This, as much as the billion-dollar revenue target (which was achieved), became a sign of the project's success. What makes business sense, makes people sense. The same can apply anywhere.

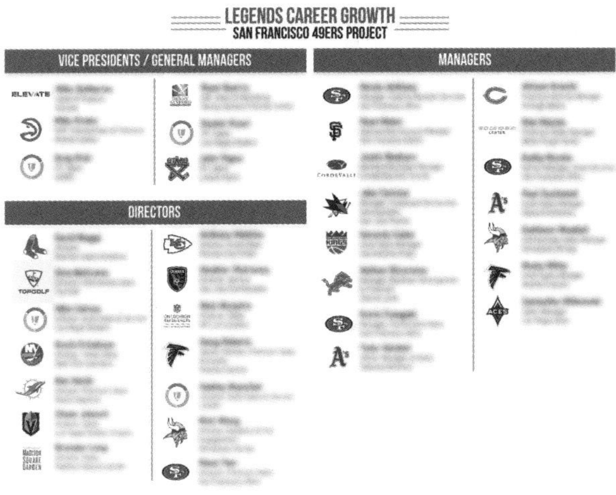

You don't need to see their names to see that we were proud of our impact at the 49ers as our people elevated through the sports industry.

It's time to use your tree for future inspiration, impact, and gratitude.

- The **INSPIRATION** is creating your leadership brand and building a legacy you're proud of.
- The **IMPACT** is the way you will touch the lives of everybody on your tree. Every day, you have the ability to impact the lives of each name in the trunk of your talent tree (your current team). You have already made a major impact in the lives of each person in the roots of your talent tree.

- The **GRATITUDE** is a way for you to stay connected to every person within your tree (especially the ones you don't see every day), to simply say, "thank you" and "I wouldn't be where I am without you." Share this exercise with them and encourage them to draw a talent tree of their own.

Keep your tree visible as a daily reminder that this is what matters. Your legacy and how you will be remembered are a direct reflection of the lives you've touched and the careers you've grown. People may forget a trophy, but they'll never forget who took care of them along the way.

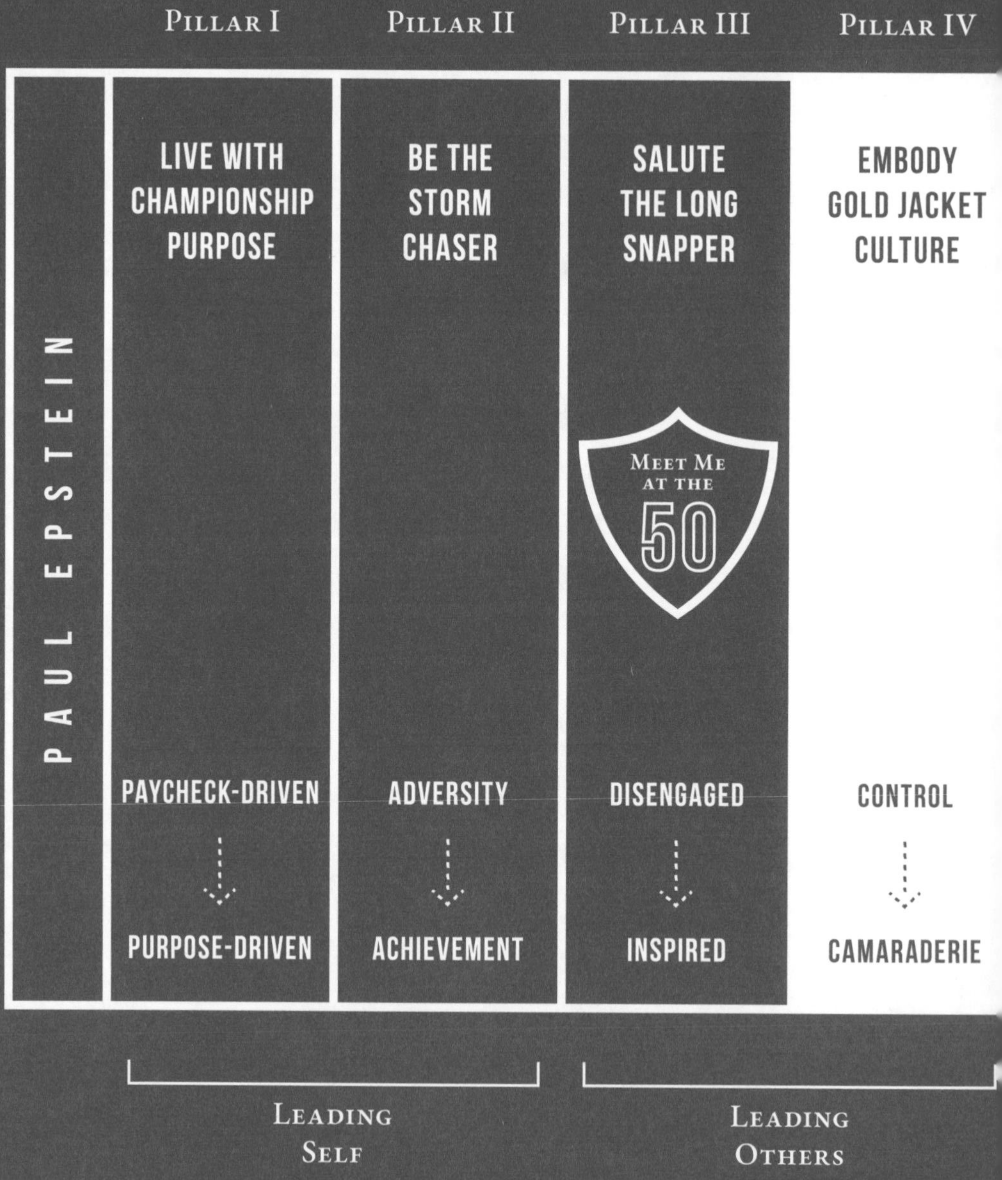

	Pillar I	Pillar II	Pillar III	Pillar IV
PAUL EPSTEIN	LIVE WITH CHAMPIONSHIP PURPOSE	BE THE STORM CHASER	SALUTE THE LONG SNAPPER	EMBODY GOLD JACKET CULTURE
			Meet Me at the 50	
	PAYCHECK-DRIVEN → PURPOSE-DRIVEN	ADVERSITY → ACHIEVEMENT	DISENGAGED → INSPIRED	CONTROL → CAMARADERIE

Leading Self (Pillars I–II)

Leading Others (Pillars III–IV)

Pillar V

PLAYING OFFENSE

LEAVE IT BETTER THAN YOU FOUND IT

SUCCESS

SIGNIFICANCE

Leading the Future

EMBODY GOLD JACKET CULTURE

NFL players and leaders who leave an indelible mark on the game and its surrounding culture are granted the sport's highest honor—inclusion in the NFL Hall of Fame. When this happens, they're gifted an iconic gold jacket that represents the honor bestowed on them by their peers. It's a form of unmistakable recognition for having reached the mountaintop.

Now, imagine you're leading a Gold Jacket Culture, one where every member of your team believes in their ability to do Hall of Fame–worthy work, unleashing their full potential by exercising their strengths, talents, and passions every day. Together, we will explore the path to showing your team that they have the support system to make it happen, resulting in an environment of high trust and intrinsic motivation. You will meet your team at the 50 because you are a leader who is willing to do the real work as a partner rather than direct orders from the top floor.

In the first pillar, you transformed your team from paycheck-driven to purpose-driven. In the second pillar, you embedded a mindset for how to transform adversity into achievement. In the third pillar, you transformed the disengaged into be inspired. This pillar brings it all together.

We started by mastering the *inside game*. Then, we focused on maximizing an individual's potential. Now, we form a team (but not just any team—a Hall of Fame–worthy team) by embodying Gold Jacket Culture. This pillar is where we will conclude winning the *outside game* by transforming the organizational norm of command and control to one of camaraderie and connection.

CHAPTER 10 *will establish how culture can become your ultimate competitive advantage.*

CHAPTER 11 *will deliver a framework for how to design an environment of intrinsic motivation and build a high-performance team—including a case study of the 49ers Academy, where it was implemented.*

CHAPTER 12 *will demonstrate how to transform your culture from mindset, to structure, to action planning.*

With that, let's dive in.

10

CULTURE IS THE COMPETITIVE ADVANTAGE

In January 2017 the 49ers welcomed General Manager John Lynch, a Super Bowl champion as a player and a former NFL broadcaster. After the introductory press conferences and other media obligations, something unanticipated happened—something that would infuse our sales culture with motivation (and cool stories) for months to come.

As our head of public relations for the club was walking John around the front office, I saw them enter our sales area. Just as John turned the corner, the room was about to erupt, but not from our new GM being there; rather, one of our newest Sales Academy members, Greg, was about to close his first-ever sale with the organization. John could sense that a special moment was about to take place.

I walked over to him and whispered the highlights. Moments later, the sale was officially closed.

Instinctively, John walked over to Greg to give him a fist bump, then asked if he could hop on the call. Like a deer in headlights, Greg handed over his earpiece.

Our general manager of only a few days asked, "Hello, who am I speaking to?"

After hearing his name, John continued, "I understand you just became a 49ers season ticket holder. Welcome to the family! I'm fired up to be here, I hope you are, too. Special times are ahead for all of us."

With that, the call ended. John instantly became the leader we had hoped for and set the tone for something much larger simply by the way he *showed up.*

Two of the newest members of the 49ers: Greg from the Sales Academy and GM John Lynch.

BRICK BY BRICK: FROM 2-14 TO NFC CHAMPIONS

In January 2020 the world saw the 49ers become NFC champions en route to Super Bowl LIV. While the world saw the success on the field, I saw the origin of the success off the field, inspired by what was built in the locker room. This Super Bowl berth was a credit to the team's ultimate competitive advantage: *culture.*

You could hear it in every interview: There was a special brotherhood on this team. When General Manager John Lynch and Head Coach Kyle Shanahan were hired in early 2017, they inherited a 2–14 team and an organization that was yearning for universal leadership. Until that point, we—like most sports organizations—operated as church and state: Business did their thing; football administration did their own. When John and Kyle arrived, that all changed. The wall was gone. Barriers were dismantled. We were now ONE team—one organization, one family, with a single mantra.

Brick by brick.

John shared these words at an all-hands gathering. "We will build this organization brick by brick. It applies to our culture. It applies to our locker room. It applies to everything we do."

What John had done on the sales call earlier that week was an example of what it would take to live up to the new rallying cry—how we would have to *show up* for one another. It was evidence that our actions behind the scenes would dictate how our culture would ultimately take form for the world to see. There was no job too small, even for our general manager. We all had to do our part. *Brick by brick*, we built.

On the business side, bricks were already being laid. One of the keys to our success was a shift in mindset when we had opened up Levi's Stadium a few years prior. Our then chief operating officer and now president, Al Guido, said, "We will become an organization of *yes, if* versus *no, because*."

No, because is a typical response in business where we rely on past norms to effect nonaction because "that's just the way we do things around here." In our new environment, now managing a multi-billion-dollar enterprise versus the old days at Candlestick Park (with one-tenth the budget and one-third the staff), that mindset just wouldn't cut it. The message from Al was clear: Transform from an organization of operators to an organization of builders, growers, developers, and visionaries to inspire the path forward through a *yes, if* mentality. With this outlook, hurdles and obstacles were removed—and possibilities and opportunities were in front of us.

No coincidence, this business transformation was amplified after the work we had done the prior year around our organizational 'Why.' We had our North Star to guide us and a *yes, if* spirit to attack each day. Coupled with football administration carrying their load in parallel, I felt blessed to have a front-row seat and experience it first-hand.

Reading this on the outside, it may sound like a fairy tale, as if all of these dominos fell perfectly into place at the ideal time. On the contrary, it was a slow, methodical, often difficult and laborious process—but we had a few things working in our favor: Clarity, alignment, vision, and purpose—all fueled by ONE team, one organization, and one family. With a single mantra to live, lead, and operate by:

Brick by brick.

That's how Gold Jacket Culture is built—one person at a time.

> *"Individual commitment to a group effort—that is what makes a team work, a company work, a society work, a civilization work."*
>
> **VINCE LOMBARDI**
>
> former Green Bay Packers head coach, five-time NFL champion

CULTURE IS HOW YOU SHOW UP

As a consultant in the space of organizational culture, I often get asked to define culture. Frankly, one of the challenges we face when we address culture is that we overthink and overcomplicate it.

Microelements such as values, beliefs, norms, perceptions, desires, expectations, assumptions, and attitudes all boil under the surface, and we try to associate them with culture. That's a lot to juggle, and it muddies the waters, leaving us confused about what culture is and the work we can do to better it.

I'm not suggesting these elements don't influence culture, but I am suggesting that we can simplify them by bringing everything to the surface level for us to easily see.

Simply put, culture is *how you show up*. How you show up is comprised of your actions, behaviors, and decisions. As a result:

CULTURE = ACTIONS + BEHAVIORS + DECISIONS OF ANY GROUP

These groups can be your direct team, your department, your organization, even a group you associate with outside of work—each has its own local culture. More on this in Chapter 12.

What makes culture more empowering is that all core elements (actions, behaviors, and decisions) are fully in your control.

That's the internal context. Now let's add some external context.

Think of any competitive advantage that exists in your team or organization. Then, ask yourself:

- Can it be outsourced? *If so, it's not your competitive edge.*
- Can it be disrupted from an external source at any time? *As an example, can a competitor copy or mimic your advantage? If so, it's not your ultimate edge.*
- Is it reliant on an uncontrollable customer preference that may shift away from your advantage over time? *If so, it's not your sustainable edge.*

Using these external lenses, competitive advantages such as product, technology, features and benefits, labor systems, or process are difficult to distinguish and endure as the edge you need over time. They're too easy to disrupt or lose control of.

What's not easy to disrupt are the unique elements of your internal assets: the people in your locker room. Their distinctive mix of strengths, talents, and passions *cannot* be replicated. Your people and *how they show up* define your culture.

- You can't outsource culture.
- Culture cannot be disrupted unless you do it to yourself.
- Culture doesn't rely on external stakeholders.

Culture is an *inside game* and is birthed from the depths of the organization. The strongest indicators are typically behind closed doors, as this example from my time at the 49ers will illuminate.

THE WEDDING THAT ALMOST DIDN'T HAPPEN

While working at the Hornets, I took a Memorial Day trip in 2011 to Las Vegas. It was in Sin City, at a pool party and nightclub (I have to stop there, or she'd kill me), that I met my beautiful wife, rock, and best friend, Mayra. No doubt, she's the best thing that has ever happened to me and inspires me each and every day. I can even trace the initial inspiration back to a single moment. When I met her, I pulled the "I'll call you" line after getting her number (to make sure she didn't give me a fake). It not only rang, it was a SportsCenter ringtone—now I knew I'd met *the one*!

Following our experience in Vegas, we withstood three years of long distance, as she had just started law school. It was when I eventually joined the 49ers that we moved in together and finally enjoyed each other's company every day.

Engagement already locked in, it was time to get married. Our wedding vision was always to make it accessible for our families (largely in Southern California and Mexico), while also making it a getaway where everybody could let loose and enjoy, so we vetted out Napa Valley right in our backyard. As we checked out venues in wine country, we quickly hit some roadblocks that became deal breakers. Turns out there's a 10:00 p.m. noise ordinance at most vineyards. Curfews weren't our thing, especially for two celebratory families of proud Mexican heritage; 10 p.m. is when the party starts! So, we pivoted and now consider it a "champagne problem."

At this time, I was overseeing the special events department at Levi's Stadium, which prompted Mayra to ask, "Don't you do weddings at the stadium?" I'll spare you the rest of the details, but let's just say I took a few jabs over the coming months to sarcastically ask, "How would you like to get married at *your* workplace?" In due course, I was outvoted 1–1; we were getting married at Levi's Stadium!

The date was set: March 12, 2016. A month after it hosted Super Bowl 50, we'd be married on the same field. The stadium calendar was clear—the stars were aligned perfectly. Until they weren't.

There were monster truck races scheduled for weeks after our wedding, and the load-in calendar unexpectedly flexed, with no wiggle room. Our COO and my boss, Ethan, got word.

Ethan called me into his office. I could see it in his face. Something was off. He said, "Dude, you're never gonna believe this. Remind me of the wedding date?"

Oh boy.

We talked details. I was sweating bullets. Mind racing. *Do I tell Mayra? Do I not?*

Ethan closed the meeting, saying, "Give me some time. I got this."

That upcoming week felt like a year. In my head, I was thinking, *Of all the things to cancel a wedding, monster trucks! Really?*

I eventually got the call, and Ethan said, "You're good to go, bro."

In this case, it was a figurative *lifesaver*. He felt like a superhero with a golden cape instead of a gold jacket. Ethan *showed up* for me in a way that I'll never forget. He epitomized culture. It wasn't about talk. It was about actions, behaviors, and decisions.

Ask me why I love the 49ers so much—it has nothing to do with the wins, business card perks, or Super Bowls. It's because of how I was treated behind closed doors. Culture is a closed-door game.

Icing on the cake: The wedding was magical. Two hundred loved ones gathered on the field. Seeing our families' faces when they first stepped on the grass was a moment I'll never forget. Footballs thrown around during cocktail hour. We even had a late-night taco bar and mariachi band—a first in Levi's Stadium history. Most importantly, she said, "I do!"

A wedding day to remember—Mayra and I on the field of Levi's Stadium.

Since no pets were allowed, we got our two labradoodles there in spirit.
Arthur and Oliver on the videoboard!

BRINGING YOUR CULTURE TO LIFE

We all have a workplace. Some settings may be grander than others, but ultimately, no matter how beautiful a physical space might be, it never has heart or soul until it's animated by its employees. People are at the heart of our culture's brand and identity. Our people become the culture champions and evangelists needed to inspire our internal locker room so that we can eventually win over the marketplace.

So, where do we start? Is culture a top-down initiative? Or is it a groundswell from the front lines?

The reality is it's a combination, but it does lean toward one of the two dynamics. While the top-down message and vision are important, culture is by no means a "push" program. There is no wand to inspire employees to love the company and one another. People need to make those decisions willingly and on their own terms.

So, if it's less about the top-down approach, how do we inspire the front lines to animate a gold jacket culture and bring it to life?

As a refresher from Chapter 1, the answer lies in the Latin definition of inspire: *to breathe life into.*

Breathe life into your employees, and they will breathe life into your culture.

"You can dream, create, design, and build the most wonderful place in the world . . . but it requires people to make the dream a reality."

WALT DISNEY

co-founder, Walt Disney Company

WOW MOMENTS

The Ritz Carlton has evangelized their most prized resource—people. Or as they refer to them, "ladies and gentlemen." These forty thousand ladies and gentlemen not only embrace the culture that has been passed down, but they also contribute to growing the culture every day. As president and COO Herve Humler says, "Our people own the future of their company." To realize this, Herve has created a culture that is not measured by industry awards and recognition (though their trophy case is quite full) or traditional revenue metrics (again, doing quite well); rather, he believes in the ongoing investment in nurturing strong internal culture—aligning organizational words and employee action, putting its ambitions and beliefs on display for the entire world to see, mobilizing believers, and empowering those believers to add to the brand's story.

So, how do they accomplish this and take these aspirational thoughts and ideals into actual brand behavior? They call them WOW moments. Look no further than the Ritz-Carlton Dubai for a prime illustration.

There was a young guest who arrived in a wheelchair. Even though he had never walked a day in his life, he spoke in the lobby about swimming in the ocean. The problem? Between the hotel and the beach is a two hundred-meter stretch of sand—one that you couldn't push a wheelchair through. The hotel engineer heard about the wish, and three hours later, had built a wooden walkway to bring the wheelchair down to the ocean. For the first time in his life, that fourteen-year-old boy went swimming.

What's most impressive about this heartfelt act is that nobody told the hotel engineer to do this. He was empowered to act independently, as a proud ambassador of the Ritz.

Perhaps this was an isolated case? Surely, this level of service and culture is difficult to organically scale from one property to another. In typical cultures, true. But at the Ritz, another WOW moment surfaced soon after at the Kyoto, Japan, property.

A traveling journalist was at the tempura counter in the on-site restaurant being guided through a sake-tasting experience when she struck up a conversation with the beverage manager, who learned of the guest's particular taste in an extremely rare and unique sake. This led to a Mission Impossible–like sake search. Countless local sake stores and suppliers were contacted, to no avail.

The guest was now due to check out and shared great compliments with the staff about her overall stay, holding no discontent about the failed search. While many hotels would have thought, *Valiant effort, but we missed our window,* this beverage manager continued the search. She reached out to a brewery over fifty miles away. She got the news they might have it. Driving across town to verify, she found the sought-after bottle. The hotel then shipped it to the US guest's home with a handwritten card and photo of the eventual destination where the bottle was found, weeks after the checkout date.

Once again, the Ritz empowered and invested in their people, providing the resources and autonomy to bring their culture to life, establishing their own competitive advantage on and off property.

If culture is the total sum of the actions, behaviors, and decisions of an organization, I'd say the Ritz is showing up remarkably—thanks to their ladies and gentlemen.

TIME-OUT: Create a WOW moment for somebody internal to your team. It can be big or small—but make it meaningful, based on something personal or important you know about them. When you deliver that WOW moment, if possible, do so in front of the rest of the team. It will light up the room.

Once this is done, develop a cadence and make sure to deliver these moments in an equitable fashion across your entire team.

FROM COMMAND AND CONTROL TO CAMARADERIE AND CONNECTION

What's most amazing about these examples from the Ritz is the authenticity of service and dedication to the brand, and the people they touch. You can give this playbook from the Ritz to your employees and tell them to replicate it—but it won't work. Your culture has to be unique to you.

This is *not* a command and control game, as business often becomes. It is a camaraderie and connection play, if you want to win the game *and* sustain your cultural excellence over time.

The value of camaraderie and connection is they unify the efforts of the collective cultural mission, which enables the impact to be maximized internally and externally. Think of these same two examples from the Ritz. If the engineer wants to build the ramp but is surrounded by "push-back," that fourteen-year old boy doesn't have his first swim. If the ambitious beverage manager is told to "stay in her lane," the sake is never found and enjoyed to create a customer for life.

Your culture can only be as strong as the weakest link. It is the ultimate team game. In the best of cultures, some would call it a tribal game.

TRIBAL BONDS

What if your product, brand, or service isn't as inspiring or glamorous as the Ritz? Can culture still be your competitive advantage?

Ask Garry Ridge, CEO of WD-40. He would argue it's even more critical and the potential is even greater—because it's so unexpected.

WD-40 is a crown jewel in the space of organizational culture, where they call their employees tribe members. From an individual to an organizational level, they aspire to model the behaviors of a tribe, with shared values, knowledge, and belonging, and everyone is recognized for their contributions that benefit the greater tribe. The end result: WD-40 is a self-sustaining place where people want to stay and grow.

> *"A tribe is a group of people connected to one another, connected to a leader, and connected to an idea. For millions of years, human beings have been part of one tribe or another. A group needs only two things to be a tribe: a shared interest and a way to communicate."*
>
> **SETH GODIN**
>
> author of *Tribes*

The reason they feel this way is based on the tribal foundation of their purpose. As Garry states, "We know that purpose mobilizes people in a way that pursuing profits alone never will. The reason for this is simple. A company with a clear sense of purpose ignites the passion of its employees and inspires the trust of its customers."

That is culture in a nutshell. How can you win the inside game to ultimately win the outside game?

WD-40 has cracked this code by establishing these tribal bonds. They have cultivated a highly engaged workforce who live their company's values every day—values serving as the actionable elements of their purpose.

As we all seek to model a culture of camaraderie and connection, here's what it looks like from a collective employee perspective at WD-40—they call it their maniac pledge, and you can find it on WD-40's company website,[53] under "Our Tribe."

> *I am responsible for taking action, asking questions, getting answers, and making decisions. I won't wait for someone to tell me. If I need to know, I'm responsible for asking. I have no right to be offended that I didn't get this sooner. If I'm doing something others should know about, I'm responsible for telling them.*

Do you have a pledge for your team? If so, awesome. If not, here's an idea on how to bring this to life.

TIME-OUT: If culture is the total sum of the *actions*, *behaviors*, and *decisions* of your tribe, create a pledge around these core elements. Set a meeting in the next two weeks. Call the meeting "Our Tribal Pledge."

Begin your gathering by asking, "What is the pledge that we will commit to each and every day?"

Some questions to guide the conversation:

- What *actions* will we take for each other?

- What *behaviors* will we commit to for each other?
- How will we make *decisions* for each other?

Similar to WD-40, consolidate it into one paragraph or less. Keep the pledge visible to your team every day, and have these words serve as the spirit for how you will *show up* for each other—as all great tribes do.

Is the impact of tribes working for WD-40?

Just take a quick glance at their employee engagement scores, where a resounding 94 percent[54] of team members self-report they're fully engaged at work, when our nationwide engagement scores have hovered around 30 percent for decades. It's now our turn to unpack this current state of engagement and how it can be a driver of our internal culture.

THE ROI OF CULTURE

"Culture eats strategy for breakfast." Infamous words by legendary management consultant and author Peter Drucker. While I'm heavily on Peter's side of this argument, we'll let the numbers do the talking.

But first, allow me to explain the connection between the stats and empirical research I'll present. Leaders are the tone setters of culture, and culture sets the tone for the entire employee experience. The level of employee experience will drive their ultimate performance. Every employee makes a decision on how much they pour themselves into their work. A highly engaged employee serves with passion, purpose, and intent. A disengaged employee has the potential to become toxic, participates in negative office politics, rarely contributes their best ideas, does not feel safe, and will seldom (if ever) take the initiative to break down silos and connect with others.

Where does the employee get most of their social cues about culture? Their leader. You set the tone for your employees' experience and their ultimate performance. You dictate whether your team pours in discretionary effort or does just enough to get by. You determine the health of your team, and when you add this effect of each leader on their respective teams, you get a culture. A culture is healthy, or it's not. There's no in between. Here's an illustration of this dynamic and the numerous feeders into organizational health.

This is how health shows up in both scenarios, followed by key statistics and research on the enormous influence engagement has on our bottom line and our people.

HEALTHY ORGANIZATION = Employees are happy, productive, and engaged. They're working harder and, as a result, are performing at a higher level. Your culture and leadership inspire the workplace to be their best. Impact is maximized. Fulfillment is felt at the end of each day.

UNHEALTHY ORGANIZATION = Employees are stressed, burned out, and disengaged. They're doing just enough to not get fired. They clock in and out, nothing more. Your culture and leadership have drained their positive spirit and belief in the company. Morale is low. Trust is broken. They'll likely be gone within six months—they're already looking.

THE REALITY AND IMPACT OF EMPLOYEE ENGAGEMENT

As you can see from the following engagement trends, employee disengagement has been rampant in our workplace cultures for decades.

US EMPLOYEE ENGAGEMENT TREND[55]

(ANNUAL AVERAGES)

● % ENGAGED ○ % ACTIVELY DISENGAGED

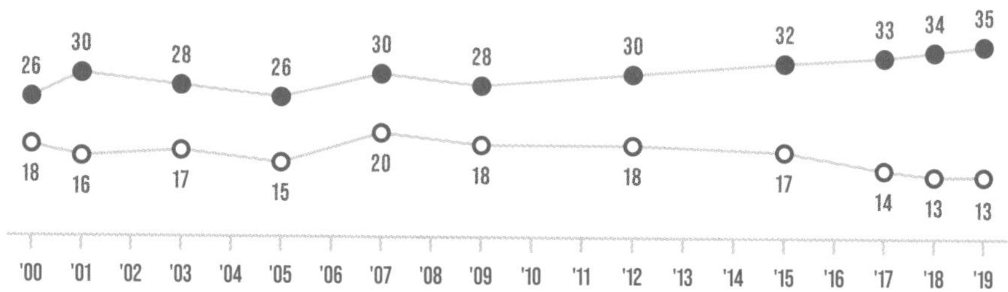

While engagement has improved in recent years, there's a long way to go. As of 2019, 13 percent of employees were actively disengaged and 52 percent were disengaged; only 35 percent were engaged (as shown above). We always hear the terms, "rowing," or "pulling a rope in the same direction," when talking about a team of people who are working in unison for a common goal. On the contrary, this is what disengagement looks like:

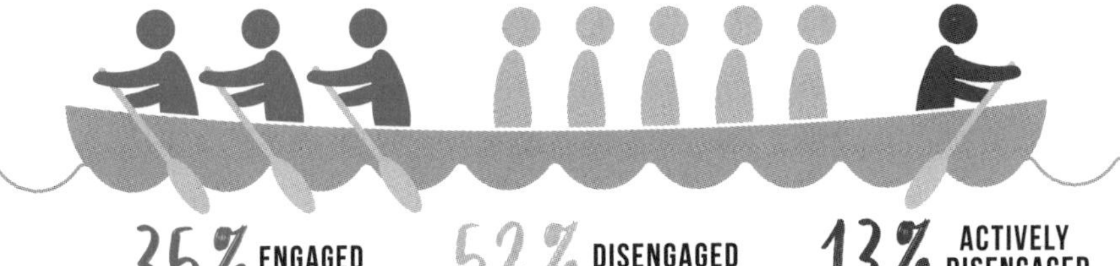

35% ENGAGED 52% DISENGAGED 13% ACTIVELY DISENGAGED

It will certainly be tough to win the long game if we're all rowing and pulling in different directions. But if we are aligned and engaged, here's the impact:

Those teams who score in the top **20%** in engagement realize a **41%** **REDUCTION IN ABSENTEEISM,** **AND 59%** **LESS TURNOVER.**[56]

Research revealed engaged companies have **5x** **HIGHER SHAREHOLDER RETURNS** over five years.[57]

Organizations with **ENGAGED EMPLOYEES OUTPERFORM** those with low employee engagement by **202%.**[58]

THE IMPACT OF LEADERSHIP ON ENGAGEMENT

Now that we have an overall view of the impact engagement (and disengagement) has in our working world, the key question is how much of this disengagement is impacting our managers. The research is consistently alarming. Only 35 percent of the overall population is engaged at work, and the same percentage holds true for leaders—35 percent. So, what happens to the employees who report to the other 65 percent?

The ripple effects are evident as managers account for at least 70 percent of the variance in employee engagement and 80 percent of employees who are dissatisfied with their direct manager are disengaged on the job.[59] This disengagement is leading to "hidden turnover," meaning leaders have no reason why they're losing people at the rate they are. As Leigh Branham, author of *The 7 Hidden Reasons Employees Leave*, revealed,

89% of bosses believe employees quit because they want more money.

The reality is, only

12% of **EMPLOYEES REPORT LEAVING FOR MORE MONEY.**[60]

Still not convinced?

1 in 2
employees
HAVE LEFT THEIR JOB TO GET AWAY FROM THEIR MANAGER.[61]

Employees who are supervised by highly engaged managers are
59%
MORE LIKELY TO BE ENGAGED than those supervised by actively disengaged managers.[62]

When followers trust their leaders, 1 in 2 are engaged.
WHEN FOLLOWERS DON'T FIND LEADERS TRUSTWORTHY, ONLY
1 in 12
ARE ENGAGED AT WORK.[63]

58%
of people report they would **TRUST A STRANGER MORE THAN THEY WOULD TRUST THEIR DIRECT LEADER.**[64]

69% who strongly agreed that their leaders made them "feel enthusiastic about the future" were engaged.
ONLY 1% **OF THOSE WHO DISAGREED WITH THE STATEMENT WERE ENGAGED.**[65]

"NON ENGAGED" MANAGERS COST US COMPANIES between
$77 billion TO $96 billion
annually through their impact on those they manage. When you factor in the impact of "actively disengaged," those numbers jump to
$319 TO $398 billion annually.[66]

THE ROI AND IMPACT OF CULTURE

Let's bring it all together. Disengagement is impacting nearly every organization, and leaders have a long way to go to become part of the solution instead of the problem—as leaders set the tone for culture, culture sets the tone for people, and people drive our business. So, if leaders like us set the tone of culture, what bottom-line effect can we create? We aren't just trying to find the warm and fuzzy side of business; we're looking for results.

Thankfully, Gallup has helped gather these insights on the connections between culture, engagement, and financial performance. Here's what the research shows:[67]

VS

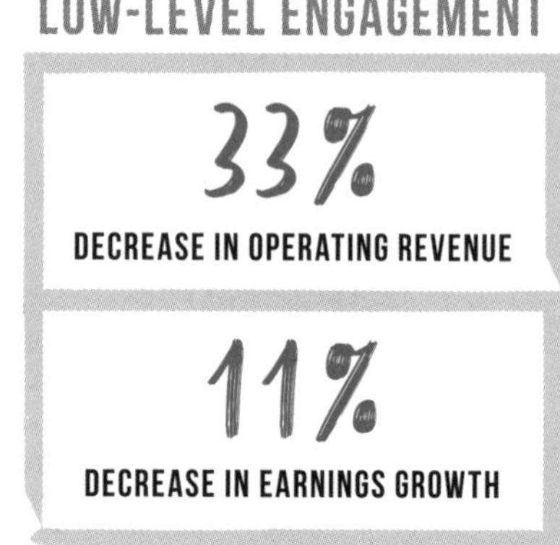

Organizations that purposefully craft and develop their culture experience a

14%

TURNOVER RATE, whereas organizations that ignore their culture experience a

48%

TURNOVER RATE.[68]

41%

cited workplace culture as the aspect of their talent strategy that would make **THE GREATEST IMPACT ON ATTRACTING AND RETAINING THE PEOPLE NEEDED TO REMAIN COMPETITIVE.**[69]

Having a culture that attracts high-talent can lead to

33%

HIGHER REVENUE. Part of this comes from hiring talented managers, which leads to

27%

HIGHER REVENUE PER EMPLOYEE.[70]

87%

of people report **LACK OF MOTIVATION OR UNHAPPINESS AT WORK.**[71] Companies with happy employees outperform competition by

20%

and are

12%

more productive,[72] **AN IMPACT OF OVER**

$300 billion.[73]

WHO'S DOING IT RIGHT?

Start with the Fortune list of Great Places to Work, a list highlights the strongest organizational cultures and takes into account a blend of these core factors: leadership effectiveness, values, trust, innovation, and financial growth, all rolled up into a score that expresses these companies' abilities to maximize human potential. Not only are companies on the list doing it right, they also generate three times more return compared to the overall stock market.[74]

The following companies have been recognized as a Great Place to Work every year since the inception of the list. This is a *massive* accomplishment. Raise a glass for the culture champions who are leading the way!

- Nordstrom
- Four Seasons
- Wegmans
- Cisco
- Goldman Sachs
- Marriott
- Publix
- REI
- TD Industries
- SAS
- Whole Foods
- Gore

THE NEED TO ALIGN PERSONAL WHYS WITH TEAM CULTURE

What distinguishes best in class cultures, like the ones we just highlighted, is they know *why* they exist. Tribes bond around a greater purpose—and cultures are fueled by purpose. Each member of your team should feel like they are a part of something bigger than themselves. They should know (and deeply believe in) *why* your team serves.

As illustrated in Pillar One, each member of your team should also know *why* they serve—and how that aligns with your greater team purpose. Until this fusing of individual and collective purpose takes form, you are operating two independent North Stars. Possible to win the sprint as a sprint may take place solely in blue skies. Impossible to win the marathon, as over the course of a marathon, you'll inevitably run through storms that will test your will, your fortitude, and your belief in *why* you're running in the first place.

You're more likely to win the race when you care deeply about the race, but that level of care is only possible when it's rooted in purpose—at all levels.

"Purpose keeps you on the treadmill, especially on the days you want to get off."

PAUL EPSTEIN

YOUR BEST DAY

The best process to unearth your collective team purpose is to know who you are on your best day. Similar to the individual "Superpower Assessment" in Chapter 8, this is the team and organizational version. It also serves as an anchor for finding your team 'Why.'

I led this experience for over one hundred business executives at SoFi Stadium (home of the Los Angeles Rams and Los Angeles's Chargers) to find our 'Why.'

More than one hundred business executives from Legends and SoFi Stadium found their 'Why.'

The experience was centered around best days working for the organization, contributions of service toward the greater team, and the impact created from those contributions. What brought these elements to life was the color in the stories shared over the course of the day.

Storytelling can be an amazingly powerful platform of communication, inspiration, and purpose.

Who is your team on its best day? Who is your organization on its best day?

Let's find out by Applying the Playbook.

APPLYING THE PLAYBOOK

CHAPTER 10: BEST DAY STORYTELLING

Knowing who you are on your best days allows you to have more of them. Said in the opposite way, if you don't know who you are on your best day, there is no road map for you to repeat. The same applies for a team.

When a team can answer the question "Who are we on our best day?" with clarity, this is the play pattern they need to repeat—over and over. In sports this is the play that the coach keeps calling, and the other team can't figure out a way to stop them, even when they know it's coming.

Correlating it to business, this results in an empowering feeling for each member of the team.

That leads to higher performance, increased engagement, and an elevated connection to one another because each person is now after the same thing—contributing to the team's best day.

Let's play offense and bring this to life for your team.

IDEAL SETTING

Off-site, whether a retreat or kickoff to a team-building day (i.e., a Friday experience out of the office)

TIME

Ninety minutes

SUPPLIES NEEDED

Flip chart and marker as a facilitator; small notepad and pen for every person

MEETING KICKOFF

Open up briefly to share your thoughts on why it is important to understand who you are on your collective best day. Feel free to use some of my thoughts in the intro to this exercise, as well as a teaser that what you discuss today will serve as the foundation for a future conversation in which the team will gather to form a team "Why Statement."

MEETING FACILITATION

STEP ONE: Have people pair off; one odd group of three is fine.

STEP TWO: In advance of the meeting, write the below four questions on a single flip chart page.

1. When have you felt most proud to work for this organization/team? Note: If this is with your fellow leadership team, use "organization." If it is with your positional reporting team, use "team."
2. What does the organization/team look like at its best?
3. What's inspired you the most while working here?
4. What keeps you coming back?

STEP THREE: Have each person privately reflect on these questions (which should be visible to the group).

STEP FOUR: Have each person take notes for a few minutes on their responses, including the stories most closely associated with their responses.

STEP FIVE: Have each pair (or single set of three) share their responses with their partner(s)—five minutes per person.

STEP SIX: Facilitate a group debriefing and organize your notes in the following fashion. On the flip chart, draw a vertical line down the middle to create two columns (left and right). On the top of the left column, write the word "Contribution" and underline it. On the right column, write "Impact" and underline it.

Ask the group: "Who has a story that captures the essence of what our organization/team is on its best day?"

STEP SEVEN: After each story, ask the entire group:

- "What was the major contribution toward others in that story?" Jot high-level notes in the left column on the flip chart.
- "From that contribution, what was the impact?" Jot high-level notes in the right column of the flip chart.

STEP EIGHT: After most (if not all) have shared and the flip chart page is filled with notes on contribution and impact, ask the group what themes have emerged or jump off the page. Try to highlight the words of contribution and impact that resonate most. These highlighted words are the anchors for the team's eventual "Why Statement."

Thank the team for their time, and set an expectation for when this group will gather back together to form their collective 'Why.' For now, it's time to enjoy the rest of the off-site gathering!

BONUS ACTIVITY

Now that you've captured a natural high with this group, it's time to make it last. Take a few minutes on the side with each person and record their biggest personal takeaway (from the session you just experienced) in an organic video on your phone. This can be great material for future culture exercises, team building, recruiting, or recognition ceremonies.

PS: If you'd like to see this all the way through and form your team "Why Statement," email CONTACT@PURPOSELABS.US for the template and action steps going forward.

11

BUILDING *HIGH-PERFORMANCE* TEAMS

In August 2014, the 49ers ushered in the next chapter of a franchise that already owned a storied past. After more than forty years in Candlestick Park, we upgraded our home to the state-of-the-art Levi's Stadium in Santa Clara.

Leading up to the stadium's grand opening, team performance was at a peak level on the field, front office personnel had nearly tripled in size, and revenue performance across all major categories was fast approaching the league's top ranks. With such strong performance throughout the organization, all seats and suites (two of three primary revenue drivers) in Levi's Stadium were swiftly sold through.

Within the first two years of operation, shifts in market conditions, team performance, and consumer sentiment, along with the conclusion of the "honeymoon" period of the new facility led to a pivotal change on the revenue side of our business.

We faced a monumental task: create a strategy to sell and recoup all lost revenues from this downswing while developing an optimal and sustainable sales structure going forward. Out of this necessity and opportunity, our executive team and sales leadership team emerged with an all-encompassing game plan.

The sales side of the business underwent a substantial re-org, including hiring new personnel, realigning management, and launching a Sales Academy intended to serve as a long-term talent incubator for the organization's revenue departments.

A CASE STUDY TO BUILD AN ENVIRONMENT OF INTRINSIC MOTIVATION

I was the proud founder of the 49ers Sales Academy. While not anticipating this case study would be written years later, the learnings I am about to share have since been transported and coached into other organizations (both in and out of the sports industry). Several elements will look familiar from the People360 Blueprint you learned in Chapter 9, as the Academy was the incubator for many of these practices.

This is the playbook for how you build an environment of intrinsic motivation—which sets the table for sustained high performance.

Imagine a working world where you didn't have to *hold* your people accountable? In this world, they hold themselves accountable. Sounds great, right?

The best part of this hypothetical—but achievable—world is that you're the reason why. You have created and built this environment. Because you were accountable to your team, they are now accountable to the business.

Gone are the days when you solely relied on carrots and sticks as external motivators for your team. In are the days where you inspire an environment of intrinsic motivation. Your team is genuinely dedicated, fully responsible, and *leaning into* their work at all times.

Carrots and sticks just don't work anymore. This old-school methodology creates a needless dependency on carrots, with the potential of entitlement. Watch out for the backlash when the carrots disappear. Sticks can be equally, if not more, damaging. You're either viewed as controlling or as creating a culture of fear. Neither is a winning game plan.

What will win (and last) is an environment where people show up wanting to fix the problems, do what's expected (and then some), and aspire toward stretch goals. Not because they crave a carrot or fear a stick, but rather because they give a damn about what they do and whom they do it for.

These philosophies were the gaps I saw as I studied many cultures (in and out of industry) prior to the launch of our academy. It was this environment of intrinsic motivation that inspired me to systematize a portable and transferable set of cornerstones that can apply to any organization. You are about to learn them over the course of this chapter.

First, we will unpack these four cornerstones of intrinsic motivation within the academy, with one recommended practice per cornerstone.

Then, we will share external organizational examples of these same cornerstones.

Lastly, we will add the closing ingredients that fuel high-performance teams.

THE INGREDIENTS OF INTRINSIC MOTIVATION +
THE INGREDIENTS OF HIGH-PERFORMANCE TEAMS =
A RECIPE FOR GOLD JACKET CULTURE

Let's get started.

FOUR CORNERSTONES OF THE 49ERS SALES ACADEMY

Here are the four essentials, all transferrable to your team, toward building an environment of intrinsic motivation:

PURPOSE

CHOICE

PROGRESS

IMPACT

1. PURPOSE

START BY ANSWERING THE QUESTION: Does your team feel a deeper meaning toward what they do?

AN ACTION ITEM TO CONSIDER: Incorporate Storytelling and Visioning in Recruiting

From the job posting to the screening calls, the narrative of the 49ers' business transformation from Candlestick to Levi's Stadium was front and center. It was described as a Mount Everest that had already been climbed, the honeymoon of the new stadium gone. As we flipped the page, we were now on a *new* mission—to reignite the glory days and build your (the candidate's) brand within the storied franchise. This vision inspired the *right* team members to join, given where the organization was. To use a sports analogy, we were not rebuilding, we were reloading. That attracted certain people, and repelled others—both wins in our book.

BONUS: To really take it up a notch, conduct a personal 'Why' discovery for each member of your team. As part of the academy's onboarding, I took the inaugural group to my home (pizza, beers, jumping Labradoodles all included) and conducted their own 'Why' discoveries. I want you to experience the same magic with your team.

2. CHOICE

START BY ANSWERING THE QUESTION: Does your team have a say in how their work gets done and the environment they work in?

AN ACTION ITEM TO CONSIDER: Use Interviews as Qualitative Research Opportunities

From the initial interview forward, their fingerprints were on the blueprint. If they ended up hired, they saw their inputs realized (as a surprise on their first day). If they weren't hired, it was still valuable market data to learn what matters most to people in our recruiting landscape. This was a chance to put the platinum rule into practice. Questions revolved around their ideal leader, ideal development program, ideal culture, ideal working environment, ideal schedule, ideal tools, and benefits most desired. This qualitative feedback was taken into consideration and molded our eventual training programs (see more under "Progress," below), health and wellness benefits such as the flexibility to attend personal fitness sessions at the neighboring 49ers facility, and adapting my own coaching style to maximize their strengths. I even committed to the infamous ping-pong table (something I thought I'd never do).

"Winning means you're willing to go longer, work harder, and give more than anyone else." This table was a tone-setter for the 49ers Sales Academy, and Jerry, Steve, Ronnie, and Joe got to watch some epic ping pong matches.

3. PROGRESS

START BY ANSWERING THE QUESTION: Does your team feel they are better when they leave the office versus when they walked in?

AN ACTION ITEM TO CONSIDER: Create a Robust and Diverse Training Program.

Beyond functional and technical expertise, we included a combination of "skill and will" exercises, personal development sessions, leadership and executive presence, personal brand coaching, industry best practice study sessions and think tanks, and an internal and external speaker series leveraging cross-departmental executives, football administration, as well as local Silicon Valley business leaders. This was bigger than the professional. This was designed for the *whole* person.

> *"Employees who believe that management is concerned about them as a whole person—not just an employee—are more productive, more satisfied, more fulfilled. Satisfied employees mean satisfied customers, which leads to profitability."*
>
> **ANN MULCAHY**
> former CEO, Xerox

4. IMPACT

START BY ANSWERING THE QUESTIONS: What difference did your team (and each member) make? How did you leave your team better than you found it?

AN ACTION ITEM TO CONSIDER: Create Your Version of a Gold Jacket

This was the birthplace of what led to the phrase "Gold Jacket Culture." The difference between the last player on the roster and the person in the Hall of Fame (where they receive a gold jacket) is the Hall of Famer accomplished something *special*. Something legendary. Something iconic. That mentality is how we recruited into the academy. On recruiting calls, I still remember saying, "If all you want to be is the next great sales executive, this isn't the job for you." That shocked candidates, and some, thankfully, walked away. My pitch continued, "But if you want to do something *special* in your career, if you want to develop to become a better leader, a better person, and are obsessed with doing something *special* in your life, then we'd love to continue the conversation. One day, you could have a gold jacket of your own."

Nick and Nick from the 49ers Sales Academy earn their coveted Gold Jackets at our promotion ceremony in the 49ers Media Auditorium.

For the right candidates who decided to meet us at the 50, this vision was music to their ears. A program to create massive impact in their lives, as a person and a pro. A program where they could become the best version of themselves. A program that wouldn't stress the *how* as long as they lived up to their 'Why.' A program where the score would take care of itself, because that's what their coach believed and how he led.

As I reflect back, I am proud that we created an inspiring culture that was authentic to the foundational cornerstones we set out to implement.

- We inspired the academy around a common *purpose*.
- There was personal *choice* in every aspect of the sales playbook and working environment.
- *Progress* was tracked through personal growth and professional achievement.
- *Impact* was made in the lives of every person that fully invested themselves into the program.

Here's how it looked on the books and in the locker room:

- On the business side, we surpassed revenue expectations by 20 percent.
- On the people side, former members of the academy have already reached director levels in the industry, while others' purposes connected them to the path they were always supposed to be on.

By those measures, I'd say gold jackets were earned—and then some.

Now, let's see how these four cornerstones have shown up outside the academy.

POWER OF PURPOSE

Purpose is the foundation of an intrinsically motivated team and environment. People must know *why* they do what they do. There must be a deeper meaning—a spark that gets them out of bed.

How are you, as a leader, embedding purpose into your day-to-day culture?

Are your people connected to the 'Why' of your team and organization?

Do you know their personal 'Why?'

If not, that would be a great place to start. Otherwise, we're stuck in this vicious cycle of carrots, sticks, and holding people accountable. Your choice.

THE LEGENDS WAY

In October 2008, Dallas Cowboys owner Jerry Jones and the late New York Yankees owner George Steinbrenner announced a joint venture, Legends Hospitality Management. I was welcomed into the mega-agency now known simply as Legends in 2012.

From the moment I joined, I knew I was a part of something bigger than I had ever been accustomed to. Come to find out, the feeling from my counterparts was mutual. Whether representing the inaugural teams at AT&T Stadium with the Cowboys, or the new Yankee Stadium, or the gauntlet of clients that have emerged since, it had the feel of something extraordinary. Since the earliest days, consulting and operating partnerships have emerged at One World Observatory at One World Trade Center, Levi's Stadium, Mercedes-Benz Stadium, Banc of

California Stadium, SoFi Stadium, Allegiant Stadium, Notre Dame, the Rose Bowl, the University of Oklahoma, the University of Southern California, and numerous other professional and college properties.

I show this list not to be boastful but rather to show the magnitude of the scale of these monumental partnerships, each with their own ability to change the landscape of the industry's revenue and operating models.

This grand vision set the tone for all partnerships, especially those with the highest stakes—typically new billion-dollar-plus venues or major premium renovations. If Legends delivered on the mutually agreed revenue targets, the well-known domino effect was that the key players representing Legends on these projects would be taken care of—primarily from a career standpoint. As a result, recruiting the all-star team of business executives was not the hard part. Similar to my experience in the NFL League Office, the challenge was in delivering these astronomical results. But those were the table stakes to enter these projects. In the words of our executives, "This is your chance to be Legendary."

I personally experienced this process at Levi's Stadium and have countless friends and business acquaintances who were a part of each of the projects mentioned above. While each had its own unique backdrop, there was one thing all projects held in common: *purpose*.

We held to a purpose bigger than ourselves. No question, there were extrinsic motivators that pulled us in to join, but it was the intrinsic motivators that got us through the toughest days.

Regardless of the flash of the book cover (i.e., the industry, company, or venue), it's the feeling when I flip the pages (i.e., the day-to-day experience) that I remember most. In this case, the projects were significant—but they paled in comparison to the people to my left and right that I went to battle alongside. That was a purpose worth fighting for. I may forget the goal, but I'll never forget the relationships I built along the way.

When we focus on people over place, purpose becomes much more accessible to us all.

POWER OF CHOICE

When you have a say in what you do and how you do it, you elevate your level of engagement.

As a coach in this scenario, you have two options:

"Here's the playbook; go execute."

OR

"Let's create the playbook together."

Which do you believe will get the best response from your players?

This is the power of choice. When people are personally engaged to have a say in their work, their environment, and how they get things done, it exponentially increases their level of buy-in, dedication, and commitment. The endgame: authentic ownership and accountability.

Here's an example of how inclusion can help design your culture of choice.

FINGERPRINTS ON THE BLUEPRINT

It's a typical day at the office, full-grind mode. One of your managers walks in during the thick of it. Just when you thought it was going to be another fire to put out, she asks if you have a minute. She opens the conversation by going on about how much of a Justin Timberlake fan she is. She'd like to follow him on his year-long nationwide tour!

Major problem—she's a full-time associate marketing manager on your team.

As a prominent benefit, your company is proud that employees are able to tweak their workdays to suit their lifestyles. But this request isn't about one morning. She wants to be out of the office for a *full yea*r!

How do you even respond to that? We know what traditional business would do. A year out of the office just doesn't happen.

Here's the response this JT-enthused manager heard in real life: "Cool. Have so much fun. Send some pictures. I'm sure you'll get your work done."

This is not a fairy tale.

This happened at HubSpot, a high-growth developer and marketer of inbound marketing and sales software, generating north of $500 million annually. Recently ranked as the third best tech company to work for—behind only Google and

Facebook—according to Glassdoor's annual Employee Choice Awards, while being second in the tech space amongst other culture and employee-driven surveys.

Managerial and personnel decisions like we just described are no easier for leaders at HubSpot than they are for you or me. But what HubSpot has figured out is that culture is the lens through which they will make their decisions, especially the toughest ones.

From their view—whether you like it or not—you're going to have a culture. Why not make it one you love?

What's remarkable about this philosophy is how HubSpot has harnessed the balance between internal employee culture and external customer culture. They set the tone from the inside out, even equating culture to their core product: "*Culture is to recruiting as product is to marketing,*" states the HubSpot Culture Code.

Customers are more easily attracted with a great product.

Amazing people are more easily attracted with a great culture.

To realize this great culture, HubSpot touts that its employees have HEART: They are humble, empathetic, adaptable, remarkable, and transparent.

An example of living their value of transparent: HubSpot's entire culture playbook, the Culture Code, is online, which presented an opportunity to be transparent internally as well. The Culture Code is known to be a perpetual "work in progress," as it's updated by its employees periodically—twenty-five times and counting. The endgame: to build a culture that every employee feels connected to.

- How are you connecting with your employees in this fashion?
- How are their fingerprints on the blueprints you're asking them to go execute?
- Do they have a say in the future of their work?

It doesn't have to be a year away to see JT concerts. It can be the simplest acts of embodying a Gold Jacket Culture and empowering *choice* each and every day.

POWER OF PROGRESS

As human beings, we are momentum machines. We love seeing progress. We love knowing where we stand so we can keep score and continue to level up. This progression gives us fuel—the carrots and extrinsic motivators become less of the reward, and the internal drive to compete within ourselves and make progress takes over.

Are you, as a leader, measuring progress for your team along the way? In a major project, are you recognizing and celebrating the milestones along the journey? Do your people know what winning and success look like each day, week, and month?

If each day represents progress along the path and an opportunity to build momentum, there is a higher likelihood that people will want to join you for the duration of the journey.

THEY GAVE US WINGS

While I was consulting at Legends, my first project was to serve as head of sales for the MLS club the New York Red Bulls. This partnership opened my eyes to a side of the business world I had never seen. Red Bulls was edgy, hip, adventurous, bold, risk-taking. From a marketing perspective, it worked—for the energy drink. The soccer club was a different story.

There was such little awareness in the market. When we introduced ourselves on a sales call, they literally thought we were trying to sell them cans of Red Bull. Brutal start to a conversation! Aside from the youth soccer community and soccer fans in Northern New Jersey (largely from international backgrounds), there was nominal interest in attending our games.

In comes the expert agency for challenging environments like this—Legends.

On paper, the partnership made total sense. In reality, it was a partnership of two worlds. Red Bulls was a culture of hoodies, beanies, and casual o'clock. Legends was suited and booted; if you weren't five minutes early, you were late. Inspired by our Dallas Cowboys ties, we subscribed at Legends to the philosophy of Deion Sanders: "If you look good, you feel good. If you feel good, you play good. If you play good, they pay good."

Buttoned up, we entered the scene. We recruited an all-star sales crew to bolster the sales team already in place. Once hired, we rolled out an intensive sales bootcamp training—on the same level as if it were a billion-dollar-plus new NFL stadium project. Post–bootcamp, the playbooks were implemented. Campaigns rolled out. Execution was fully underway.

Although the early results were promising, there was an unspoken tension in the organization. It felt like two disparate worlds trying to lock arms, but we were speaking different languages. The criticism was less about what we did (as there was clear progress); it was more about our brand in doing it. For the first time, I faced a cultural challenge through a different lens. I was now the outsider. I was "the consultant," as in-house managers tend to call us. I know because I've been on the team side.

While I was wearing a different hat, it felt eerily similar to the experiences that had groomed me up to this point. I knew exactly what to do.

Over the following months, I made it my personal mission to build relationships with the key leaders of the Red Bulls, primarily the newly hired president and tenured CFO who ran the business operation.

While this may seem like a general strategy of building relationships, I took a very customized approach. The CFO spoke Spanish, so I brushed up on mine, which hadn't been used in years. I stumbled through conversations, but I showed the effort. It opened up a connection that likely was not otherwise possible, as we got to reminisce about childhood experiences in Mexico. Ultimately, these key relational bridges were built.

I understood how to find a happy medium. From the suit jacket becoming a Red Bull pullover to an integration of our cultural best practices with the strengths of the Red Bull culture, this proved to be an amazing chapter—a case study for me to understand how culture can work when two worlds merge. It boiled down to the same ingredient that worked at the Clippers and every place since: relationships.

With the relationship equity now built, it was time to shine. The sales campaigns powered by our blended culture initiatives took off. The needed boost on the books materialized, resulting in all-time record revenues and attendance for the club. More people in the stands meant more Red Bull cans sold—so everybody was happy!

To that point, I had always measured progress as a metric and indicator on the books. I now learned that progress can also be measured off the books. Just as there can be progress in results, I now measure progress in relationships. If an external consultant can do it, anybody internal can do it.

The currency needed in this case was *time:* Time to build a relationship. Time to listen. Time to earn trust.

Time can be the greatest currency of leadership—and thanks to the Red Bulls, who met us at the 50 and gave us the wings we needed to succeed, as partners.

TIME-OUT: If time is the currency of leadership, identify one person you need to spend more time with and get a coffee on the books over the next two weeks. Unlike as in the Time-Out in Chapter 8, feel free to expand beyond the three-directional lens of boss, peer leader, and member of your team. This can even be a personal relationship–as leadership is a trait of business and life overall.

POWER OF IMPACT

We each must decide what impact means to us. What is the *difference* we want to make?

For some, there are personal and professional drivers. For others, social and societal causes. When it comes to impact, there is no right or wrong—it is solely a matter of whether we have identified the impact and difference we seek to make.

In my case, *impact* was the value that inspired my leap of faith from sports to the Chapman & Co. Leadership Institute. I asked myself, *Can I create* more impact *within the walls of the 49ers, or beyond?*

Through this lens, the decision became easy. I no longer wanted my impact to be limited by four walls. I was now on a quest to create impact wherever there was a willing party to meet me at the 50.

CONNECTING INTRINSIC MOTIVATION TO HIGH-PERFORMANCE TEAMS

The following framework is a combination of the four cornerstones you just read *plus* a few elements I learned from the Chapman & Co. Leadership Institute that will help to operationalize them.

To recap, the four cornerstones of an intrinsically motivated environment are:

1. **PURPOSE**
2. **CHOICE**
3. **PROGRESS**
4. **IMPACT**

To optimize this environment for high performance, there are two missing marks:

- ✓ **SYSTEMS**
- ✓ **CAPABILITY**

In sum, these are the six elements of intrinsically motivated and high-performance teams:

1. **PURPOSE**
2. **CHOICE**
3. **PROGRESS**
4. **IMPACT**
5. **SYSTEMS**
6. **CAPABILITY**

Let's explore this further by applying the playbook.

APPLYING THE PLAYBOOK

CHAPTER 11: HIGH PERFORMANCE TEAM SCORECARD

This is your high performance scorecard. You can download it at **WWW.POWEROFPLAYINGOFFENSE.COM**.

HIGH PERFORMANCE TEAM SCORECARD

SPHERE OF LEADERSHIP	PURPOSE	CHOICE	PROGRESS	IMPACT	SYSTEMS	CAPABILITY
YOU	1 2 3 4 5	1 2 3 4 5	1 2 3 4 5	1 2 3 4 5	1 2 3 4 5	1 2 3 4 5
YOUR TEAM	1 2 3 4 5	1 2 3 4 5	1 2 3 4 5	1 2 3 4 5	1 2 3 4 5	1 2 3 4 5

Across the left side is the sphere of leadership, starting with leading yourself, then moving to leading others (your team). Across the top are the six drivers of high performance teams. Populating each field is a 1–5 scale from which you will score yourself and then your team relative to each column.

Prior to gathering your team, fill out the scorecard (Q1: You, Q2: Your Team) on your own by answering the following questions:

PURPOSE: The level of meaning at work (feeling of being a part of something bigger)

Q1: On a scale of 1 to 5, how much purpose do you feel in your work?

Q2: On a scale of 1 to 5, how much purpose does your team feel in their work?

CHOICE: The level of say you have at work (feeling that your fingerprints are on the blueprint)

Q1: On a scale of 1 to 5, how much choice do you feel in your work?

Q2: On a scale of 1 to 5, how much choice does your team feel in their work?

PROGRESS: The level of positive momentum at work (feeling of measurable advancement and evolution)

Q1: On a scale of 1 to 5, how much progress do you feel in your work?

Q2: On a scale of 1 to 5, how much progress does your team feel in their work?

IMPACT: The level of making a difference at work (feeling of service and contribution)

Q1: On a scale of 1 to 5, how much impact do you feel in your work?

Q2: On a scale of 1 to 5, how much impact does your team feel in their work?

SYSTEMS: The level of procedural efficiency and effectiveness at work (feeling of ease and alignment)

Q1: On a scale of 1 to 5, how would you rate the systems in your work?

Q2: On a scale of 1 to 5, how would your team rate the systems in their work?

CAPABILITY: The level of resources and training at work (feeling of capacity and competence)

Q1: On a scale of 1 to 5, how would you rate the capability in your work?

Q2: On a scale of 1 to 5, how would your team rate the capability in their work?

Now that you've filled out your scorecard, it's time to bring the team together and see how their responses measure up.

STEP ONE

Set a ninety-minute meeting called "Core Drivers of High Performance Teams." If you don't get through all six drivers today, book another meeting for one week from today to continue the conversation. Keeping momentum is key.

STEP TWO

Explain that you've already filled out your scorecard personally and for the team, but the team ratings primarily matter based on the alignment with what they think—which is why you're all gathered today. As an example, if you as a leader thinks the team is at a "5," and the highest team rating is a "3," something has to change. It starts with an honest conversation about the gap. Ensure your team has a safe space—as candid feedback is necessary to elevate the team to its highest levels of potential and performance. All responses will be visible but remain anonymous.

STEP THREE

Introduce the six core drivers with a brief description of each (provided in this exercise).

STEP FOUR

Hand out the scorecards and give them three to five minutes to fill them out. Once every one is complete, ask them to pass their rating sheets back to you at once (so they remain nameless and anonymous).

STEP FIVE

Once you've gathered all sheets, take a minute to scan their results so you spot the high marks and low marks (establishing a range).

STEP SIX

Now, unpack each of the six high-performance drivers, starting with "Purpose." Share each team member's number next to "You" under "Purpose." Then share your number from the same space. Move on to the second row: "Your Team" under "Purpose." This process will be repeated for each area.

STEP SEVEN

Facilitate a conversation for each of the six drivers, especially for "Your Team" results. If both your rating and the team rating is high, the discussion may only be a few minutes long.

IMPORTANT NOTE: *When there is a gap (one way or the other), the conversation can last ten to fifteen minutes. You booked the meeting for ninety minutes; the key is not to rush. Better to stay in a conversation about a gap for twenty minutes than rush and squeeze all six drivers into the ninety-minute window. To reiterate, if you don't complete all six conversations in ninety minutes, book another meeting for one week from that day.*

STEP EIGHT

Once all conversations are complete, revisit this scorecard with the team once per quarter. Evaluate changes and progress. Most importantly, provide them a voice and a seat at the table to have a say in the daily culture of their team. As a leader, in this platform of "actively listening," you have the opportunity to build bridges with your team that otherwise wouldn't be possible. Listening and taking action based on what your team shares can be as powerful as the six drivers of high-performance teams combined.

12

TRANSFORMING YOUR CULTURE

This book was written during the 2020 pandemic. From a financial perspective, between jobs lost, businesses shut down, furloughs, industries collapsing, and unemployment hitting record levels, an economic recession seemed inevitable. I'm sure you've felt the massive effects of it at whatever time in the future you're reading this.

But wait—you thought you were diving into a chapter on culture transformation. This is the intro?

One hundred percent—and here's why. Moving a culture from an A– to an A+ (while great) is *not* transformation. For transformation to materialize, we're coming from the cellar, baby!

That said, if you're currently an A– culture, come along for the ride anyway. Getting to A+ will still be pretty sweet.

It's too easy to talk about the rainbows at the end of culture transformation. The only way to learn is to study the depths of culture and what happens during the storms, pretransformation.

You're about to see an example of how culture can begin in the darkest of days, when many on our team and organization feel helpless, uncertainty surrounds us, and tomorrow's paycheck is not guaranteed. This backdrop is when some companies *play offense* to intentionally build culture and double down on their values, while others continue to *play defense* and let the market dictate the terms.

This is a story about an organization that transformed its culture based on how it showed up during the Great Recession of 2008–2009, which has given many organizations a playbook on how to handle our latest recession in 2020.

I know this story to be true because I've personally met the people impacted and transformed by it.

A RECESSION TURNED CULTURE TRANSFORMER

When the financial crisis hit in September 2008, it impacted us all. Barry Wehmiller, a $3 billion private manufacturing company grown through over one hundred acquisitions to date, was no different. Initially, leadership took stock of their business units and had a sense they would be ok.

However, five months later, the company faced a 40 percent drop in new equipment orders. CEO Bob Chapman was expected to react how Barry Wehmiller (and most companies) historically did—by laying off team members in the affected areas to "right-size" in response to the decreased orders.

While that would have been the easy lever to pull, Bob thought of an experience from the early 2000s, when he and his colleagues formed their Guiding Principles of Leadership, which offered a view of what success looked like. The headline?

"We measure success by the way we touch the lives of people."

With this overarching mission, when called to consider the appropriate reaction to this dramatic drop in revenue in light of how it touches lives, their guiding principles offered the guidance to think, feel, and respond as their mission called them to.

Bob Chapman's heightened awareness of stewardship of those in his span of care gave him a clear sense of purpose and clarity through which to view the situation. In Bob's words: "We're a family at Barry Wehmiller, so we need to act like one. What would a responsible family do in this crisis? A loving family would share the burden."

The financial directive was in. The company had to shed 10 percent of its costs. The easiest line item to cut: personnel. This was the domino every frontline worker expected; what they heard was quite different.

A furlough program was introduced (at a time when this was not common) where every person in the organization had to take four weeks of unpaid time off. For some, this was a massive financial burden—and their team members knew it. Still, much better to not lose your job completely.

The reaction to furloughs turned out to be extraordinary.

As the organization didn't place parameters around how the time needed to be taken off, countless team members offered to take double furloughs—stepping up to "take the time" for their coworkers who could not afford the loss of pay. A shared sacrifice in the end didn't seem like much of a sacrifice because it meant saving a team member's job.

This familial act of sacrifice and generosity ultimately helped get the organization financially through the crisis and storm of the recession.

"In this ever-changing society, the most powerful and enduring brands are built from the heart. They are real and sustainable. Their foundations are stronger because they are built with the strength of the human spirit."

HOWARD SCHULTZ

former CEO, Starbucks

In reflection at the Global Economic Forum years later, Bob shared that the best reward of all was what the company received from its team members as a result of the response to the economic downturn: "Because we walked the talk, they rewarded us with something truly priceless: their trust."

How you lead in crisis is how you will be remembered. Thanks to leaders like Bob, we can measure success by the way we touch the lives of people, especially in the toughest times. In my two years of service for Bob Chapman (as a part of the Chapman & Co. Leadership Institute), I can vouch that stories like this only scratch the surface of the impact he's made for the twelve thousand-plus people in his span of care.

TIME-OUT: In your next team meeting, share the visionary statement, "We measure success by the way we touch the lives of people" with your team. Ask each team member to come up with one way they touch the lives of people. I think you'll find they can't stop at one. This is an amazing way to reframe what success is all about.

ALL CULTURE IS LOCAL

Part of the beauty of working for Bob's Leadership Institute was the size and scope of organizations we got to partner with. There was one client in particular, a major airline, that had over one hundred thousand employees—and we were responsible for training their six thousand–plus leaders. Those in my network familiar with the work I was involved with frequently asked, "So, what's their culture like?"

I'll admit, prior to engagements like this, I was led to believe culture was a top-down game. The C-suite gets behind a mission/vision/values initiative, we roll through some workshops, communicate, integrate, measure impact, and BANG—the culture is transformed. Not the case at all.

In reality, *all culture is local*.

Tell me who the leader is. Tell me what department. Tell me what location. Tell me what floor of the building. THAT'S the culture! On floor three, people are high-fiving. One floor above, radio silence, watch out—the boss is coming around the corner. For the same company in the same building, there are micro-climates and micro-cultures.

Each leader and local culture has its own weather system. There is challenge in this reality, but there is also opportunity.

The *challenge* is that transforming a large-scale culture takes time, because the hard work happens at a local level, then organically has to surpass the tipping point to be embraced by the whole company—more on this later in the chapter.

The *opportunity* is the responsibility that you as a leader have regardless of what is happening upstairs or downstairs. Your local culture is counting on you. How you *show up* determines the forecast for that day.

Think of your favorite class in school; how much of an impact did the teacher have? How about your favorite youth sports experience as you were growing up; how much of an impact did the coach have? In either setting, replace that individual with a different teacher or coach. It's a drastically different experience. Each group has its own culture. This is the impact you, as a leader, have.

AMAZON: A CULTURE OF TWO STORIES

How is it possible that the culture of a company that is consistently in the top ranks of LinkedIn's Top Companies to Work For list can also be described as . . .

Bruising. Relentless. Painful. Frequent combat. Burn and churn.

A 2015 *New York Times* article reported stories about employees crying at their desks, suffering from incredible stress, struggling to keep up with the intense pace of the company—or being fired for failing to meet the standards and metrics set by management.

Some have called this organization a workplace bully, while others have come to the organization's defense—most notably, their existing employees.

How can both sides be right?

The answer: *All culture is local.* Especially at the global giant Amazon—a company and leadership team that I have been blessed to work with. One of my EMBA cohort members, Oumar, worked for Amazon and brought me in for a leadership development workshop in 2019.

As I entered the building, I felt sharper just breathing in the air. I could sense the fast tempo. The design and office layout spoke to the innovation and logistical brilliance of the company. The people had a special energy to them—moving swiftly, with purpose.

As I engaged with respective leaders across different verticals of the organization, it was as "switched-on" a group as I had come across. There was a curiosity that was well above the norm—leading to a thirst for more knowledge and spirited conversation, then onto the next agenda item. Time was always of the essence.

Over coffee breaks I gathered that expectations were sky high. People were stretched and challenged, but most communicated it in a positive light. The most common saying was, "We know what we signed up for." Now, on the flip side, I understood that this wasn't necessarily reflective of the entire organization—solely the sample size that was in attendance.

Full disclosure, this leadership workshop was optional to attend (customary company policy). So, you could say that these were the most engaged leaders, those who chose to level up their skills and aptitude to engage and inspire trust in their team—which was the focus of the workshop.

"Paul helped Amazon understand the core values at the center of leadership, such as Compassion, Character, and Trust."

—OUMAR DIAGNE

former Amazon senior manager,
senior director of Global Operations Finance, Honeywell

This room was filled with leaders who took the time to invest in themselves so they could pour the value back into their local culture.

For as much as I'd heard about Amazon's culture in the media, news, or industry chatter, I found it to be quite the opposite. Not bruising, relentless, painful, frequent combat, burn and churn.

I am not denying the potential validity of those claims—for the sake of this case, let's assume they're true. Even more reason to recognize and appreciate that *all culture is local*. Each of these leaders took the responsibility to show up so they could create the best version of their micro-climate. What other leaders outside of this room were doing, I'll never know.

The news media will continue to describe Amazon the way they do—and that's their perspective. I can only speak from my lens and say that their culture seemed pretty awesome.

TIME-OUT: If somebody parachuted into your local culture, how would they see it? How would they describe it? Better yet, ask your team.

With your team, have a real conversation about what your local culture is as of today. Then, set a vision for what you ideally want your culture to be. Whether you're already nailing it or there's some work to do, write down what your visionary local culture looks and feels like. Synthesize it into a paragraph or less. Keep this culture statement visible for each team member to ensure accountability and establish commitment to transforming your local culture—brick by brick.

PARTNERS, TOURISTS, AND PRISONERS

Let's have some fun here.

In any large group of people, there are figurative partners, tourists, and prisoners. Let me explain by using my workshops as an example—where the CEO will hire me, and all leaders go through a program.

PARTNERS: They're sitting front row. Leaning forward. Their vibe is positive. While they don't have to agree with everything, their positive engagement and participation keep the day going.

TOURISTS: They show up open-minded. Fork in the road, some will go left, others right. Things go well, happy they came. Things go badly, blame the tour guide (a.k.a. me).

PRISONERS: Back row. Arms folded, 5:30 p.m. can't get here soon enough. They were *voluntold* to be here.

Partners, tourists, and prisoners are all around us. They may all be represented in your team. Certainly in your organization.

Allow me to share a perspective on how I lead and invest in these three groups, which may guide how to lead them in your world.

A RECIPE FOR CULTURE TRANSFORMATION

When I entered the space of coaching and consulting culture transformations, I had it backward.

I initially came in believing that it was about converting the non-believers—the prisoners. In my mind, if we could flip them, the bad seeds were now on the right side, you tipped the scales, and the transformation took care of itself.

Boy, was I wrong. Not only does that not work, it's exhausting and depleting, leaving you no energy to focus on those who are eager and inspired toward positive change—the partners.

Focusing on prisoners doesn't work because you can't force somebody to believe in or join a movement. Either they care about your culture or they don't. That's it. It's the classic cliché of leading a horse to water; you can't make them drink it.

Frankly, I would take it up a notch in this context as to why this philosophy in particular won't work. When it comes to culture change, transformation, and infusion of best practices, you don't want to muddy those waters with people who *don't* want to be a part of that process. Authenticity, genuine engagement, and the spirit of opt-in are all key to creating the positive shift you're seeking. Simply put, ignore the prisoners—so long as they're not hurting those to their left and right. A silent prisoner is ok. A toxic one is not and should be addressed.

I realized I had it backward, and I changed my approach.

I now focus on the partners. They are the bright spots. They are the ones who will authentically lean in. They will commit to change—because they chose it. They will inspire others to join, without having to be asked to do so. And that's the golden ticket toward building majority.

Partners will attract the tourists—simply by how they *show up*.

As a reminder from Chapter 10:

Culture is *how you show up*. How you show up is comprised of your actions, behaviors, and decisions. As a result:

CULTURE = ACTIONS + BEHAVIORS + DECISIONS OF ANY GROUP

If you want to transform your culture, focus on the partners. They will showcase the highlights of your culture. This will magnetically attract the like-minded tourists to join—and that becomes *your recipe for culture transformation*.

Oftentimes, we fail at these transformations for three reasons:

- We lose hope when the culture of the greater organization does not match our desired local culture.
- We don't organize our entire community into these three buckets: partners, tourists, and prisoners—leaving no clarity on roles (or lack thereof) within the transformation.
- We think it can happen overnight—then get discouraged and give up at the first setback.

Let's tackle these one-by-one.

- We now know that all culture is local. Start with what you can control (consider yourself the partner); it will inspire other local culture leaders (partners and like-minded tourists) to do the same.
- You also know to not waste your time or energy by focusing on changing the prisoners.

- Lastly, while signs of change can happen in weeks and months, true transformation may take a year (or more, for larger organizations). At least you know it's a marathon, and you can prepare your mindset and team to weather the storms accordingly.

With these lessons in hand, you're ready to take the next step. Focus on the bright spots so they can scale.

SCALE THE BRIGHT SPOTS

Shine a light on the bright spots in your culture so that others know what the model looks like. This process of awareness and recognition can take many forms.

Public-facing recognition of the people who are modeling the way is something you can begin immediately—at your next all-hands meeting, in your company newsletter, or at the upcoming awards banquet. Recognize the behaviors and values you want to see more often.

The private side is less publicized, but can be equally, if not more, impactful. Just as we acknowledged that leadership is who you are behind closed doors, the same can be said for culture. Culture is a closed-door game. Conversations of affirmation for partners to champion the behaviors that set the tone for the rest of your team and organization can go a long way. This will inspire them to continue paving the path because you can rest assured, they are outnumbered by the prisoners and tourists. This will lead to moments of discouragement, where they ask themselves what's the point and flirt with the temptation to give up as a partner in the culture transformation journey.

Once your culture champions and ambassadors (a.k.a. partners) feel valued, appreciated, and that you, as their leader, are inspired by them being a part of the movement, you may not be outnumbered for long.

TIME-OUT: Call a fellow cultural partner into your office now just to say thank you, that you believe in them and what they stand for. Take a moment to empathize that you appreciate them treating culture like it's a full-time job—because it is. That peace of mind to continue to make culture a focal point will go a long way.

START ON THE INSIDE TO TRANSFORM THE OUTSIDE

Why play this long game of culture? After all, it's just a soft topic with a set of soft skills that have no connection to the bottom line, right?

While the research in Chapter 10 states otherwise, allow me to illustrate it with an example of an organization that prioritized its people and culture early and the transformation that followed. What makes it more impressive is the industry they come from—grocery—was highly disrupted and volatile (pre-pandemic) due to higher costs, failing productivity, and race-to-the-bottom pricing. Industry experts reported that 50 percent of the grocer's economic profit vanished between 2012 and 2017, resulting in over $1 trillion in lost earnings.[75]

Even through these financially dismal times, there was a player in the grocer space generating over $9 billion annually, executing an ongoing expansion plan, and on *Fortune's* annual 100 Best Companies to Work For list EVERY year since it first appeared in 1998—once finishing #1.[76,77]

Welcome to Wegmans. Where hundreds of staffers are sent on trips around the world to become experts in their products, including to Argentina for beef, France for cheese, and Italy for cookies. You can rest assured that all cashiers have a minimum of forty hours of training before their *first* interaction with a customer (not the norm in a churn-and-burn labor model), employees enjoy flexible scheduling, broad career-track opportunities, no mandatory retirement age, and they have *never* laid off workers.

Gravy on top, every cent of their profits is reinvested in the company or shared with employees—including an employee scholarship fund that has now risen to over $80 million in educational assistance to support more than 25,000 team members.

While all of this is happening on the inside, Wegmans has developed a cultlike following of their customers on the outside—fiercely loyal, always ready to tell you they feel like Wegmans is "their store."

Alec Baldwin once said on the Letterman show that his mother refused to leave upstate New York for Los Angeles because there was no Wegmans in LA!

The Food Network has recognized Wegmans as its Best Grocery Store, Consumer Reports voted Wegmans the top grocery store every year running since 2006, and when Market Force surveyed over ten thousand grocery shoppers nationwide, Wegmans was rated "America's favorite grocery store."[78] Customers have lined up overnight in the thousands for a new store opening, while others regularly write love letters to the store headquarters to ask for one to open in their area.

Ask the Wegman family (the business has stayed family-owned from day one) what their secret sauce is. No question, it's their people. Their senior vice president of HR, Kevin Stickles, shares that "our employees are our number one asset, period!" The first question they ask when facing any business decision: "Is this the best thing for the employee?"[79]

That's a totally different model from the industry standard. But in reality, the model is simple: A happy, knowledgeable, and superbly trained employee creates a better experience for customers. Extraordinary service builds tremendous loyalty—and that loyalty leads to high volume and tremendous profits.

Wegmans is a classic example of how to embody a Gold Jacket Culture on the inside so we can all enjoy it on the outside. Even in a highly disrupted industry, they found a way for culture to be THE competitive advantage needed.

What makes it most remarkable is their ability to scale this across one hundred–plus locations—meaning one hundred–plus local cultures. How did they reinforce it all, and maintain it during an ongoing expansion?

It was always Wegmans's consistent philosophy that all decisions *had to* be filtered through the *employee-first* lens. This non-negotiable was the anchor to their transformation.

FROM SCARCITY TO ABUNDANCE

Tell me if this sounds familiar: You hire an all-star. Slated to be your next high-potential up-and-comer. They sign on the dotted line, you welcome them in, pour yourself into the onboarding process—then watch them go.

The first time they're off script, you tell them that's not the way things are done around here. You're essentially telling them to stay in their lane. Figuratively, you're handcuffing their natural abilities—you know, the ones you hired them for. Over time, they are reminded of this feeling, becoming paralyzed to take action, take risk, or present their best ideas for fear of backlash. They protect what little they have. They are fully in survival mode, putting in no discretionary effort, doing just the bare minimum to get by. This is a culture of scarcity.

Wave a wand. Let's go back to that magical hire date. Only now, they find meaning in their daily work, and show up ready to contribute. They gain some early wins, and look to continue the momentum. Their superpowers—you know, the ones you hired them for—are on full display. They are thriving and seek collaboration at every opportunity. This is a culture of abundance.

After experiencing both cultures firsthand, I choose abundance.

The choice is yours.

THE POTENTIAL OF RECIPROCITY

When you have a culture of abundance, people *play loose* and *feel alive*. Their strengths, talents, and passions are embraced and enhanced by those around them. They feel valued and recognized, fortunate to be part of your team and organization, grateful for the opportunity.

Do you believe a person with this profile will show up with a giving mindset? Do you feel this person will share their best ideas, resources, and knowledge to support a fellow member of their tribe?

Of course they will.

The challenge is—are we asking? And in turn, reciprocating.

By studying the power of reciprocity, I learned what is possible when we are open and vulnerable to share an experience with others, where they can help us (personally and professionally), and let their value of generosity take over. The end result: After you help (by giving to) somebody, they are authentically invested to help you. This is what's possible when you participate in the Circle of Reciprocity.

> *"We make a living by what we get. We make a life by what we give."*
>
> **WINSTON CHURCHILL**
>
> former Prime Minister, United Kingdom

Let's apply the playbook.

APPLYING THE PLAYBOOK

CHAPTER 12: THE CIRCLE OF RECIPROCITY

This exercise can be shared with any tribe of people. While I will share how to conduct the exercise with your professional team, know that you can just as easily share this experience with a group of family members, friends, or any other form of community or cohort.

The premise is that each person identifies one personal item and one professional item that they'd like to share with the group, with the hopes that somebody can offer help, support, guidance, advice, resources, or information.

Personal examples include tips on what to do for an upcoming trip you're planning to Italy, referrals for contractors to help with a major home renovation, or recommending a personal fitness coach.

Just think of a personal item for which you currently don't have the information or resources you need and about which you'd like to ask for the group's help. If there are twenty people in the group, that's twenty potential opportunities for support that you would never have had access to had you never asked. This exercise provides that opportunity to ask.

On the professional side, you may be in the market for a trainer in a space where you have few contacts, you may be looking for a book recommendation on a topic that is heavily impacting your industry, you may be in the midst of a research project and need some advice on best resources to explore, or you may be planning a large conference and scrambling to find a great speaker.

Whether the item is personal or professional, only you know what support you need. Now is your time to ask. As apprehensive as you may be initially, you will soon realize the power of reciprocity and how amazing it feels to be able to help somebody in your tribe.

Let's play offense and activate your circle of reciprocity.

SUPPLIES NEEDED

Lots of colored Post-its (two colors minimum)—ballpark ten Post-its per person. Have each person bring their own notepad and pen.

ROOM SETUP

Group sitting in circle, in a way where everybody can see one another

STEP ONE

Gather your team (time will vary based on size of team). Ninety minutes is typically enough.

STEP TWO

Explain the purpose of the exercise based on some of my introduction above, followed by the instructions detailed below:

- Each person will share one personal and one professional item that they'd like the group's help with.
- As each person is talking, if you can help them, write some notes (on provided Post-its), including whom you can help and how. It is important you do this in real time as it will be tough to remember the details once everybody has shared. Rest assured, you won't be able to provide support for every person in every situation; only write when you can add value and help.

STEP THREE

Begin the sharing; you lead off. Start with your personal ask, followed by your professional ask. Then proceed clockwise until the group is done sharing.

STEP FOUR

Once all sharing is complete, create a circle of Post-its on the wall that mirrors the seating order of the room. Have a single color of Post-it for all of these names.

STEP FIVE

You'll now go back around the circle in the same order in which you shared (start with the person that shared after you, so you can go last). Let's assume Andy is next to you. Ask Andy in ten to fifteen seconds to remind the group of his personal and professional ask, then ask for one person to share how they can help personally, another to share how they can help professionally. While this is happening, encourage anybody else that can help Andy to write down how they can help on their Post-it. No long explanations is needed. It can be as simple as somebody writing their name on the top of the Post-it, then a phrase on how they can help. For example, if Andy asked for Italy recommendations, Maria could write "Maria—have some Italy recs for ya!" on the Post-it. It will then be on Andy to follow up.

STEP SIX

In this example, after Andy shares and hears who can help, have each person that can help Andy go up to the wall where everybody's name is and put their Post-its up under Andy's name. In my previous example, Maria would take her Post-it and stick it under Andy's name on the wall.

Repeat this cycle for each person—starting with Andy, ending with you.

STEP SEVEN

When everybody has gone, have a look at the wall as a group. Take a moment to soak up the incredible amount of support and help that has just been shared among the team. This is what's possible when we ask for help and realize the power and strength of a team. Without this exercise, all of this impact is never created. The bonds and relationships aren't as connected as possible—and the reciprocity may never fully take form.

STEP EIGHT

Urge the group members to continue to ask for the support of one another, whether personal or professional. You don't need a circle of reciprocity every time; it's the spirit of the exercise that matters.

PAUL EPSTEIN

Pillar I	Pillar II	Pillar III	Pillar IV
LIVE WITH CHAMPIONSHIP PURPOSE	BE THE STORM CHASER	SALUTE THE LONG SNAPPER	EMBODY GOLD JACKET CULTURE
PAYCHECK-DRIVEN	ADVERSITY	DISENGAGED	CONTROL
↓	↓	↓	↓
PURPOSE-DRIVEN	ACHIEVEMENT	INSPIRED	CAMARADERIE

Meet Me at the 50

Leading Self (Pillars I–II)

Leading Others (Pillars III–IV)

Pillar V

LEAVE IT BETTER THAN YOU FOUND IT

PLAYING OFFENSE

SUCCESS

↓

SIGNIFICANCE

Leading the Future

Over the course of life, we will engage with thousands of people and places. The question is, did we leave them better than we found them? Or were they the exact same (or worse) when we walked away? That difference is the impact we make in the world—the mark we leave that will determine how we are remembered. In other words, our legacy.

In this pillar, we will climb the two mountains of life that embody success and significance. Do you find success by what you see in the mirror, or what you feel on the inside? Can you simultaneously experience both? And is that what you strive for? We'll delve in soon.

So far you've explored mastery of the inside game (in pillars one and two) and the outside game (in pillars three and four). This pillar combines the power of all four to inspire people in every encounter and contribute in meaningful ways. Consider it a culmination of all your efforts that generates massive impact because you are focused on making a difference—to leave people, places, communities, and perhaps the world better than you found it.

Ultimately, how do you want to be remembered? By the close of this pillar, you will have a framework and process to give you clarity around your answer.

CHAPTER 13 *will pave the path from a life of self to a life of legacy.*

CHAPTER 14 *will deliver personal development habits and rituals to level up your leadership potential.*

CHAPTER 15 *will pay it forward by honoring and connecting with those who left us better than they found us.*

With that, let's dive in.

13

A LIFE OF SELF TO A LIFE OF LEGACY

There comes a pivotal time in life when we face a massive fork in the road: Are we living for ourselves or for others?

On a personal level, many say this leap happens when becoming a parent.

On a professional level, this is the challenge of career growth.

We all start as individual contributors. Our job is to excel so we can climb to the next rung up the ladder. We are players in the game. Then, we are faced with the decision of whether to become coaches and lead a team ourselves.

For your entire career up to a point, it's been about you. And then you realize it's no longer about you. It may never again be about *just* you.

This welcomes us into a space where we think of leadership in a new light, namely, as a servant. Many of us are familiar with servant leadership, where the central goal of the leader is to serve. A servant leader doesn't believe you work for them; the leader works for you. A servant leader shares power, puts the needs of others first and helps people develop and perform as highly as possible.[80] A servant leader believes that your success is their success.

For that reason, servant leaders take an immense pride in the service of coaching. If you embrace coaching, questions begin to percolate about what type of goals you will have in this new selfless seat. What type of impact will you create? What legacy will you leave behind? Ultimately, how will you be remembered?

A CELEBRATION OF LIFE

I stand here before you today as we celebrate the life of a man who lived it to its fullest—a man who lived with purpose, inspiration, and passion. A man who will be with us in spirit forever as his impact and contributions are unquestioned.

He loved his family more than words can describe, and considered himself to be the luckiest person in the world for the love and support received from those closest to him. He chose to keep an intimate circle of friends but also chose to touch the lives of millions through the course of his daily work—which he was called to.

A lover of people. A lover of dogs. A lover of good times. He loved life. Most importantly, he felt alive.

When he walked in the room, you could sense a special energy. He breathed life into every person he touched and every place he passed through. He believed in people, even if they didn't always believe in themselves. In those moments he brought out their best potential. He believed that people all had gifts to share with the world, and it was up to him to help them find them.

He looked at each day as an opportunity for growth. This mindset took him far in life. You never heard him talk about the limits of life; he only spoke of the possibilities of life. Life never happened "to him;" he said it always happened "for him."

If there was one word to describe him, it would be authentic. Approaching each day with a genuine spirit is what gave him his fuel. When this value of authenticity was matched by others, he would stop at nothing to support these people, his authentic tribe. If you wanted to give him a gift, all he asked was to live true to your values and true to your purpose.

For all of the adversity experienced in life, he had a visible courage to stand tallest when fear and risk were highest. In the most uncertain of times, he showed up with strength for himself and to serve others. While others considered his service brave, he believed it was his duty to support people in their lowest of times, to uplift them personally and professionally.

He was on a daily quest for impact. Any opportunity to make a meaningful difference got him out of bed with an extra spark. He made decisions through this lens constantly, sacrificing material resources so that he could stay authentic to his value of impact. This trait was passed down from his family and will continue to be his calling card for others that he has undoubtedly impacted toward the future.

Partnership is how he built relationships. He always believed that it takes two parties with an equal investment of energy in one another to make a true partnership work and last. This led him to ask potential partners to meet him at the 50.

This is the life of Paul Epstein, and this is how we will always remember his time with us.

Every day I am working toward this legacy existing as reality.

"Think about your legacy because you are writing it every day."

GARY VAYNERCHUK

entrepreneur, speaker, influencer

SUCCESS IS FLEETING

My career has humbly taken me to places where I have hit the loftiest of goals I had set and won the biggest of trophies in my field. But then, I often found myself at the top of a mountain with a feeling deep in my gut, asking myself, "Is this it? All that for this feeling?"

Not fulfilled. Not satisfied. Already pointing myself to the next Mount Everest. The reality is you never reach the peak in business. You never score the final goal of the game. You hit one goal, and there will always be another. The goal posts keep moving.

Success works the same way. One promotion only leaves you wanting the next. One pay raise only leaves you wanting more. There's no end destination—and no magical moment where "you made it." I've felt this personally, and heard it from countless senior executives across industry—many left to question what it all even means when reflecting on their careers.

Success is forever fleeting. This is the endless cycle when you play the game for yourself.

However, the game shifts when you decide to play for others—as great leaders do.

Will you play the game for your own gains? Or will you bring your team with you? Better yet, will you inspire your team to play the game as you coach with passion from the sidelines? Isn't that what leadership is all about?

MY BIGGEST BREAK TURNED OPPORTUNITY

In my pursuit of breaking into sports (as detailed in the first pillar), I completed an eight-week revenue management course with Sports Management Worldwide. Their assurance was that top students would get plugged into their network of clubs, and they delivered—calling the Los Angeles Clippers to set up an interview. This was my shot.

I was suited up walking into Staples Center. As I entered the Clippers boardroom, I expected it to be the hiring manager and me. Instead, I saw several other equally eager faces. Come to find out, this was a group interview. My mindset immediately went into *Rocky* mode: Eye of the tiger. Only the strong survive. And every other competitive sports cliché you can think of.

Minutes later, in burst the hiring manager. He introduced himself, strolled up to the front of the room where there was a flip chart—and started to educate us on the position, the market, and the opportunity. Then we dove into overcoming sales objections.

We had been in the boardroom for almost ninety minutes. Still no interview questions. At this point, I was thinking about the time since I had to get back to work. Expecting it to be a traditional interview, I'd built in a window of several hours. I could now tell I might need to call my boss and get creative.

The hiring manager said, "Okay, folks, time for a break." I immediately raised my hand and asked, "What time do you think we'll be through the interview?" He emphatically responded, "Interview? This is your first day. Welcome to the Clippers."

Huh. First day? Are we getting Punk'd *(for those who remember the MTV reality show)?* That's what I thought on the inside.

On the outside—cool, calm, and collected. I didn't know if it was an honest mistake, but at this point, it didn't matter. We sat there the rest of the day "in training," filled out some paperwork, and I was officially an inside sales executive for the Los Angeles Clippers.

Within weeks of starting, the same hiring manager (my boss) announced he was leaving for an external promotion. Now it all started to make sense. My gut told me he already had the position when we initially met, and he may have been so deep in planning his cross-country move and next opportunity that our group interview was mistaken for a first day on the job. Sounds crazy, but that's my theory.

To this day, I have loosely kept in touch with my boss of only a few weeks. I've never brought up this story to him. I guess he'll find out when he reads the book!

> *"Luck is what happens when preparation meets opportunity."*
>
> **SENECA**
>
> Roman philosopher

There's no denying the luck dynamic at play, but I still had to take advantage of the opportunity.

As former Microsoft executive Qi Lu said, "Luck is like a bus. If you miss one, there will always be the next one. But if you aren't prepared, you won't be able to get on."

A fare is always required to get on the bus—and then stay on board. The fare can be preparation, skills, or sweat equity. It may be information, or surrounding ourselves with the right people.

In this case the ongoing fare was performance. Even with the luck of the opportunity, I still had to close deals and sustain my results. Without finishing first on the sales board four consecutive months, I likely wouldn't have earned the promotion into the full-time ranks. The rest of my sports career may have never taken off.

Case in point, I was the only one in that group interview (where we all received the same luck) to make it past the second month on the job.

I call this out not to disparage anybody else. I'm calling out the reality of how a track record of success is built—we have to perform. Regardless of whether luck is involved, we have to be able to seize the opportunities.

Will you have the fare required the next time the bus pulls up?

FROM SUCCESS TO SIGNIFICANCE

Is life about success or significance?

Success is how many of us are raised. Often, it's reflected by title, money, responsibilities, social status, where you go to school, or the brands you work for. Achievement is the name of the game. We serve ourselves to climb the first mountain of life. The mountain of success.

We need each and every experience in this first mountain to mold us, to grow, to fall, and to give us perspective. Often, we find that this perspective leads us to the second mountain—where we realize there is more to life than our individual gains or resumes.

We now have a yearning for purpose, for impact, and for contributing toward something beyond ourselves. When this is realized, we then have the feeling of fulfillment—and significance—to know that we mattered because we left our part of the world better than we found it.

While life tees up the first mountain to be about success, I would argue it's the second mountain of success *and* significance that we're all supposed to be on.

Success and significance are not binary. They can live in harmony. Even better, one can fuel the other—but it typically goes in one direction.

An obsession with success can often blind us to the significance of why we do it. However, when we are focused on significance, success tends to be a natural part of the evolution. The correlation is clear—significance amplifies success.

Significance doesn't just add to success—it increases it three times, four times, ten times, if not hundreds or thousands of times. This multiplying effect is what's possible when you combine the powers of success and significance. The impact of your success expires when you expire because you've only served yourself. When you serve others, they then pay it forward to others, and your impact becomes unlimited. On this second mountain of life, purpose, impact, fulfillment, and legacy are all maximized.

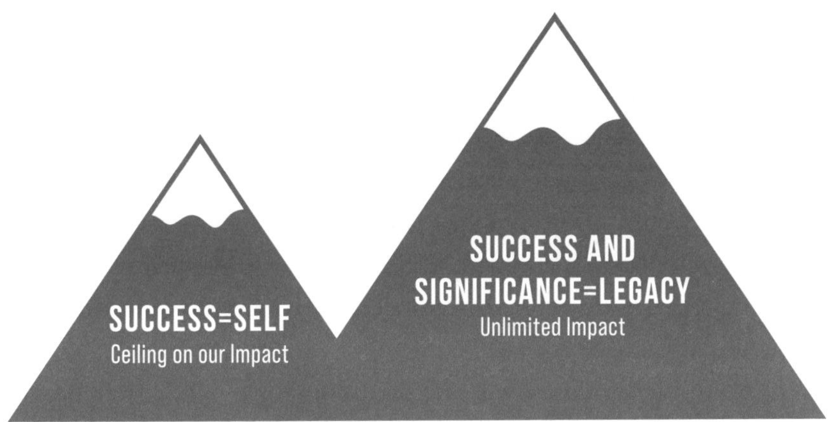

As this illustrates, the second mountain of life is where exponential growth and impact are possible. Only then can we fully transform from a life of self to a life of legacy.

"Success is when I add value to myself. Significance is when I add value to others."

JOHN MAXWELL

leadership author, speaker, pastor

Why not do both?

A TALE OF TWO MOUNTAINS

"The merchant of death is dead."

As the inventor of dynamite, you opened the newspaper to this headline in the obituaries in 1888. The worst part, your name is under the headline as you read your own death notice!

Your name: Alfred Nobel.

While many of us know Nobel to be the inventor of the Nobel Peace Prize, it was the nature of his earlier inventions that led to this false report of mistaken identity. In actuality, his brother had passed. But this journalist took it upon himself to send a message to Alfred. This French newspaper that published the obituary described him as a "merchant of death who had grown rich by developing new ways to mutilate and kill."

None of us may ever know what it's like to read our own death notice with such lethal words—but Alfred did.

It was all predicated on how he made his riches on the first mountain of life, inventing dynamite and sending explosives throughout the world, which ultimately branded him as a merchant of death.

But then it all changed. Alfred started to think about legacy and how he would be remembered. From that day forward, he dedicated the rest of his life to playing offense through a noble cause. One that led him to create the Nobel Peace Prize—investing every cent of his riches to his new life's work.

Many of us may have never known about Alfred's first mountain in life, but we will always remember the second. He dedicated and committed himself to a purpose bigger than himself. He created something worthy of being etched forever in the history books long after he was gone.

Alfred Nobel's story teaches us a principal lesson. He had all the success in the world and was rich beyond our wildest imaginations, yet hollow on the inside once he read the obituary and saw how he would ultimately be remembered. He understood that his memory would be lacking in significance.

As you reflect on your life to date, perhaps you're still on the first mountain of success, or perhaps you're already on the second mountain of success and significance. Regardless, these two mountains of life present opportunity. If you're still on the first, make tomorrow the first day you take intentional steps toward the second. If you're already on the second, stay disciplined and focused on not reverting to the former.

I encourage you to think of life as a book, with each day as a blank sheet, waiting for you to author it—starting with tomorrow.

What will you write?

> *"The great use of life is to spend it for something that will outlast it."*
>
> **WILLIAM JAMES**
>
> American philosopher and psychologist

HONORING YOUR PATH

As you author your story, it often requires a look in the mirror to see how you got here. Did you go at it alone, or did you have support along the way? Were you on an island, or did it take a village?

These questions often illuminate that we wouldn't be where we are without those who paved the path before us—those who left it better than they found it.

My path is no different. I am grateful, honored, and stronger for being molded by several industry trailblazers who took me under their wings and groomed me.

While I think it's cool that I've worked for people who had a hand in bringing the Olympics back to Los Angeles, negotiated nine-figure player contracts, or booking concerts with the likes of Jay-Z and Taylor Swift, that's not what I'll remember.

What I'm most proud of goes beyond the association with the above events and accomplishments. I'm most proud of being able to call these leaders my friends, mentors, and coaches. Many of them took a chance on me, they believed in me, and this book is written as a thank you to them, as my opportunity to pay it forward for the next wave of leaders.

CRAFTING YOUR SIGNIFICANCE

As important as knowing why you do it—know whom you want to serve. If you are a leader in a business environment, this largely is directed at your team. I've spent the majority of my career serving my team.

It was out of circumstance that I came across a different way of looking at this lens of service. While it started inside of the sports industry, speaking allowed me access I otherwise never would have had. I expected to speak at industry conferences, and that provided a level of inspiration and fulfillment—but then it was outside of the ballroom where I started to feel an even deeper level of impact. It went beyond business impact. This was life impact.

While still in sports, I was asked to speak at local schools and non-profits. This felt different, not just by the looks on the audience members' faces as I spoke but also by the level of appreciation as I walked off stage and by the level of impact that I heard in one-on-one conversations afterward. In underprivileged schools I heard how disadvantaged backgrounds turned into a loss of hope and belief. In urban non-profits, I heard about lacking resources to create an impact to fulfill their missions.

These conversations crushed me in the moment yet served as inspiration over time. I didn't know I would become a keynote speaker years later, but as soon as the world of speaking became a full-time reality, I remembered these off-stage conversations from years prior. It even took me back to my childhood.

I started to think about the earliest days with family in Mexico, and I vowed to never forget where I came from. I quickly learned that resources as simple as motivational speakers didn't frequent places like these schools and nonprofits—perhaps where they're needed most. From that day forward, I made an internal commitment that I would always *make the time* to balance my impact. While the corporate engagements create massive impact in our workforce, I also wanted to create impact beyond the walls of business.

This clarity about whom I want to create impact for has changed my life view. I now care about access and inclusion on a parallel path with impact—to amplify the significance in my world.

So now, let's focus on you—through the prism of your what, how, why, and who.

Like me, you already know what you do and have external indicators (success, promotions, growth) of how well you do it. I encourage you to emphasize the latter two buckets: your 'Why' and identity (from Pillar One) and your internal and external 'Who.' Take some time to process the below:

- Why do you do what you do?
- Does your 'Why' align with where you work?
- Who are you at your core?
- Whom do you want to serve?
- Whom are you inspired to create impact for?

These answers will unlock your path toward significance.

WHAT IMPACT LOOKS LIKE

Reflecting on past events I've had the pleasure to attend, I'd like to take a moment to detail the thought-provoking information I gained from a speaker last month:

A highly motivated individual can set their mind up to achieve wanted success. However, it takes a consistently self-reflective person to be able to step back and review their innermost core values that give them the answer 'Why.' These kinds of people wake up in the morning and ask themselves, "Why am I working toward this ultimate goal?" "Why am I passionate about my career?" and "What is the story behind the decisions I've been making?" If that person can uphold the values that make them so unique, their attitudes, behaviors, and choices will positively be affected thereafter. At the end of the day, everyone should be able to confidently say, "I love my life" as a complementary addition to the phrase "I feel alive."

I read this note after speaking at Dodgers Stadium for an engagement hosted by WISE (Women in Sports and Events). There isn't a price that can replace what it feels like to absorb heartfelt messages like this.

She is an example of why I do what I do, and we have stayed in touch ever since.

Speaking to Women in Sports and Events (WISE) at Dodger Stadium.

Similarly, when I'm speaking to a two-thousand-person audience in a massive ballroom and fifty wait around to connect individually after, those fifty people are the fuel that keep me going.

My goal of serving as a speaker allows me to create impact on a path toward inspiring millions of lives. My vision toward legacy is to always be somebody who gives back. I try to be accessible and a leader who puts no limit on my potential to make a difference that matters—on my terms. That is a life worth living. It's what I've been called to do.

Paul is a wonderful, service-driven human with genuine aspirations to help people grow within themselves. Paul's genuine life ROI is seeing others thrive, a truly rare trait in our world. People from all walks of life can learn a thing, or two, or ten from Paul Epstein. His message to find my 'Why' in life changed my path and outcome forever.

TIME-OUT: This is a time out for the future. Going forward, keep a folder (physical and/or digital) for all thank you cards/emails, testimonials, recognition messages, or notes of appreciation you receive. Create this folder and put your first item in it now.

As you compile over time, read these notes for positive affirmation of your service and value, and start to look for themes—specifically around contribution and impact.

- Do you see patterns in what you contribute?
- Do you see patterns in the impact you make?

These indicators are further evidence of your significance. All of these notes will come in handy as you're living and leading with purpose.

ALIGNING YOUR GOALS TO YOUR LEGACY

As you author your future:

- What goals will you prioritize?
- Are those goals aligned with the impact you want to create?
- Is that impact aligned with the legacy you want to be remembered for?

Knowing the answers to these questions will bring your internal purpose to life. Your purpose shows up through your values. Your values are the lens for your actions, behaviors, and decisions (which, as you recall, can be summarized as *how you show up*).

Now, it's time to align these even further by connecting your purpose and values to your macro goals and beyond.

Let's apply the playbook.

APPLYING THE PLAYBOOK

CHAPTER 13: AN IMPACT-DRIVEN LIFE

In Chapter 3 of Applying the Playbook, you formed your operating values as a lens for how you "show up" through your actions. Consider this outer layer of the "Identity Model" below, the daily representation of how you activate your purpose.

This playbook exercise will provide you with something tangible to activate. Once you are sourcing your values from your purpose—and your daily actions reflect that—it's now time to expand this to an external level by applying the "Impact Model" below. In this model your purpose and values are a source for your goals to create greater impact and build the legacy you'll leave behind. This congruence between models will fully align your identity with your impact.

Simply put, the "Identity Model" is your compass for today. The "Impact Model" is your compass for the future.

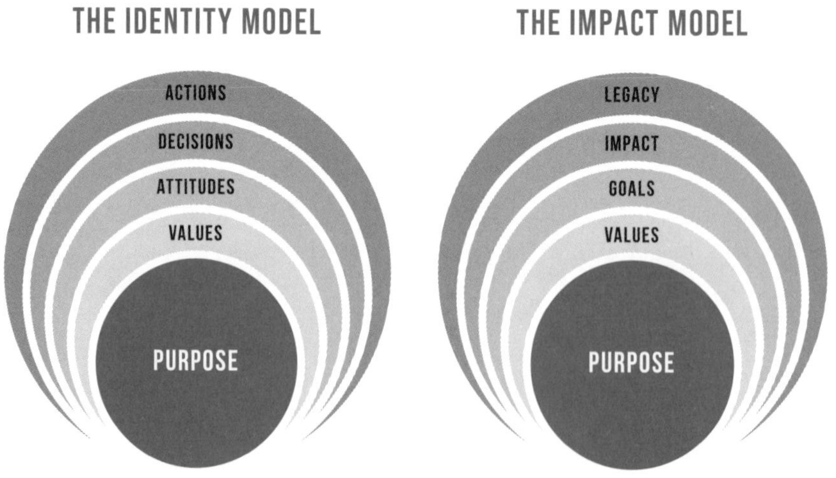

Give yourself at least an hour of quiet space for this exercise. The more tranquil the environment, the better. It requires deep thought, converting your thoughts to written notes, and reflection. At the end of the day, this can be one of the most powerful visioning exercises you do because it gives you a roadmap for your goals of today and forms congruence with your impact and legacy of tomorrow.

It's time to play offense and make this a reality.

STEP ONE

Your purpose and values are a starting point for this exercise. As a reminder, for all information on a purpose and values discovery, see the Purpose Discovery FAQ at WWW.POWEROFPLAYINGOFFENSE.COM.

Once you've identified your purpose and values, we move on to goals. The key is not only to identify goals but align and connect them to your core purpose and values. Begin by asking yourself:

- What are your top three goals in life?
- Is each goal aligned with your purpose and values? *If the goal is not tied to your core purpose and values, the result of this process may not be as impactful or meaningful. My recommendation is to go back to the drawing board until your (top three) goals are tied to your purpose and values.*

STEP TWO

Once your goals have been detailed, connect them to impact. Ask yourself:

- For each goal, what is the impact it will create?

STEP THREE

Now we'll shift to legacy. These are intended to be stand-alone questions (answered independently of your responses above). Ask yourself:

- At your retirement party, how do you want to be remembered? Describe in as much detail as possible.
- At the celebration of your life, how do you want to be remembered? Describe in as much detail as possible.

The answers to these questions will provide clarity on the legacy you want to leave behind. How you will have impacted people. How you will leave this world better than you found it.

STEP FOUR

Now we will *reverse engineer* the model to connect and align all layers.

For the legacy you want to build, connect it to your goals and impact. Begin by asking yourself:

- What is the single goal (of three identified) you are most inspired by?
- What is the impact created by achieving this goal? Already answered in step two.
- How will your legacy be strengthened by making this goal and impact a reality?

If you are inspired by the answers to these questions, you now have your action plan. It is tied to your core purpose, true to your values, authentic to your identity, and aligned with your goals to create an impact that is meaningful to you, so you can start to build your legacy *today*.

MY PERSONAL APPLICATION

I personally went through this exact process in the earliest days of the 2020 pandemic. Here are my open notes, in reverse order based on the outcome:

- My **LEGACY** is to inspire purpose and positively impact the lives of others, just like Dad did when he was alive.
- The **IMPACT** I want to create is to transform the working world as we know it today, where the journey of working one hundred thousand hours will give us fuel versus deplete us of our fuel. I imagine a working world where we are inspired to go into each day, contribute in ways that are meaningful to our purpose, create impact on something that is bigger than ourselves, all in order to be fulfilled on the back end of each day—excited to do it again the next. I *will* impact one million lives by 2030.
- The **GOAL** I will execute on over the coming months is writing my first book to make this vision come true.

This exercise made *The Power of Playing Offense* a reality.

PERSONAL DEVELOPMENT HABITS AND RITUALS

Let me tell you a story about 3:00 a.m. Paul.

When I got to the 49ers, I wanted to fit in and impress. In my earliest executive leadership meetings, I looked to my left, I looked to my right, and I saw a powerhouse team. Most had been hand-selected to lead the organization through a four-to-five-year run-up to the grand opening of Levi's Stadium—a journey which resulted in winning "Sports Facility of the Year" honors at the 2015 Sports Business Awards.

One of my earliest responsibilities was sending out daily sales reports on behalf of all revenue departments (tickets, suites, tours, events, corporate sponsorships). Typically, these reports were only sent to members of revenue departments, but I proposed that we send the reports out to formal leaders across all departments. Knowing that in order to pay off the debts of construction, revenue was the single most important factor leading up to ribbon cutting, I wanted us to be transparent about our performance at all times. Since people across the organization were constantly asking where we stood, my vision was to bring other teams along for the journey—for connection, camaraderie, empathy, morale, and a good, old-fashioned sales referral when called upon. In spirit, right thought. In execution, not my proudest practice.

Every morning, I woke up to my alarm, shot out of bed, and by 3:10:00, after my first cup of coffee, I started to organize the prior day's sales results. My goal: hit send by 3:59:59—no later.

Why 3:59:59?

Because I thought it was good for my brand to be known as the guy "grinding" at 3:00 a.m.

The crazy thing is, nobody ever asked for a report at this time, or expected it. It could have just as easily hit send at 9:00 a.m.

This 3:00 a.m. pattern was not sustainable. But not because of the hour. Because of the mindset.

I had to make a change. I had to stop playing defense.

"Be more concerned with your character than your reputation because your character is what you really are, while your reputation is merely what others think you are."

JOHN WOODEN

former UCLA men's college basketball coach,
winner of ten NCAA championships

IT WAS TIME TO PLAY OFFENSE

I stopped looking to my left. I stopped looking to my right. I stopped trying to impress. I stopped worrying about what other people thought (even if it was in my mind). I started to do things wholly on my terms. I permanently took the mask off—and threw it away.

The irony is, I still wake up between 3:00 a.m. and 4:00 a.m. Only now, it's 100 percent because I want to, and I believe in *why* I'm doing it. I wake up at that time because my mind and thoughts are clear and I can focus without interruption before others are awake.

This opening hour has now become my personal development window. Every day I see a reminder: "Own your morning." It's my time in the day where I can work on myself to level up every twenty-four hours.

We all have worked tremendously hard to get where we are. You're reading this book—in part, I would assume—because you want to take your leadership game to the next level. If that's the case, you're going to need enough energy in your tank, so that you can pour your energy and best self into others. Your team, your organization, your inner circle, and your family are counting on it.

Here's a good energy test to measure where you are:

If you're working extremely long hours (which I *don't* believe is a requirement for success), you likely get fatigued from the neck down. There's a point in the day you inevitably hit a wall.

In that moment, how are you feeling from the neck up?

Three a.m. Paul at the 49ers was fatigued in both directions. Now, even when I'm exhausted from the neck down, I've never *felt more alive* from the neck up. The reason is, I'm being true to myself. The energy is authentic. It's not to prove anything to anybody else or look a certain way—all signs that I'm playing offense.

HABITS TO OWN YOUR MORNING

"Be where your feet are."

This is advice I was given by an old boss, to be present at all times. He always said, "When you're at work, you work. When you're at home, you're home—physically and mentally." This didn't mean no exceptions, but these were the ground rules—

and 90 percent of the time, they matched reality. With the fast pace and heavy travel demands of my work, this advice has turned out to be priceless.

The challenge is, it's difficult to be fully present once the world is up, and every email, text, social media notification, or call is another interruption in a world filled with distractions. What I have experienced is the majority of this inbound noise is about other people's agendas. So, how do we flip that to manage our own agenda—if only for a small window of time?

It all starts by owning your morning. Once we let other people's agendas enter our day, to an extent we're on their watch. Here are a few tips I would suggest, after personally applying and practicing them over the past few years.

For the first sixty minutes of each day:

1. No cell phones or email (difficult at first—but this is the only way to eliminate outside noise).

2. Create a routine around personal development—journaling, mindfulness practices, and reading). From there, dive into your favorite thought leadership content if time allows.

If you want to play offense each day, own your morning. One of my go-to thought leaders, Ed Mylett, once shared that we must "take inventory of our current habits and rituals in order to begin taking steps to immediately control them." Once the above steps become habitual, you will have accomplished five things:

1. You are now starting every day on your terms. On your agenda.

2. You are growing (by developing yourself) every day. Imagine the progression possible once you stack this for a week, a month, and then a year. This is leveling up.

3. Your habits and rituals are what will keep you accountable and consistent to personal development, especially on the days you aren't motivated.

4. Ideas in, ideas out. This frequency and volume of thought leadership content will inspire ideas of your own. This has been a massive game changer for my creative work.

5. By the time you get into the office, you've already worked on yourself for the day. You now have the time to selflessly focus on your team. I always hear the excuse from leaders "Who has the time for personal development?" We just solved that problem.

After completing these practices each morning, you now have a clear mind and the energy to take on the day.

TIME-OUT: Consuming thought leadership content doesn't need to stop in the morning, but who has time later in the day? I do. So do you. Think of the activities in your day that are routine and consume chunks of time (e.g., commuting to/from work, exercising, walking the dogs). Those are now your content windows to keep working on yourself and leveling up. Never stop learning. Never stop growing.

Take the next two minutes and scroll YouTube for your favorite thought leader or topic. Pick the content you'll listen to and put it on the calendar tomorrow. As an example, I'll listen to the next episode of *Impact Theory* (a personal favorite) by Tom Bilyeu.

JOURNALING: START YOUR DAY WITH WHAT'S RIGHT

If I could select one practice that has centered my mindset most, it would be journaling. I never realized the power of journaling until several years ago when I started to implement it into each morning. The remainder of this chapter will provide you with a suggested framework for journaling, along with some anecdotes to support the impact.

By no means is this the only way to journal. This is simply an outline that has proven to be successful for me.

Each morning, I journal three things:

- **GRATEFUL**: What am I grateful for?
- **GET TO**: What do I *get* to do today (versus *have* to do today)?
- **EXCITED**: What am I excited about today?

We'll unpack each of these in the upcoming sections.

GRATITUDE

Flip on the news, and in many cases, you'll see what's wrong. I choose to start each day with *what's right*.

By answering the question "What are you grateful for?" each morning, it starts your day with a mindset of abundance, a mindset of appreciation, and a mindset of optimism.

Rather than preach about the benefits of gratitude, I thought it might be beneficial to show you a selection of my journal entries from this calendar year 2020. No edits. You are seeing them in their true form.

Of note, this period of roughly four months encompassed the following:

January represented my leap into the entrepreneurial space, launching Purpose Labs midmonth.

March represented the global pandemic/stay-at-home quarantine order. It also became the month I committed to writing this book.

Here are the entries:

- Jan. 24: To make my dad proud. Launching Purpose Labs is in his legacy. I won't let him down, and I KNOW he's proud of me.
- Jan. 25: To have a loving home that is fully supporting me through this massive transition into entrepreneurship.
- Jan. 29: To have a daily opportunity to make my dad proud and to have such a great network to create impact.
- Jan. 30: To have tremendous support around me at a time that I don't have all the answers, but have enough purpose, mission, and energy to fill the world.
- Feb. 2: To be happy, healthy, and honored to have the most amazing tribe in the world.
- Feb. 3: To be able to live my dream and my 'Why.' Everything that matters in the bigger picture is in my control.
- Feb. 6: For my parents and how they raised me to have the character that over the years has been able to build authentic relationships that matter.

- Feb. 11: To have so much potential and opportunity at my fingertips. Now, it's about the decisions and ACTION.
- Feb. 12: To believe in the journey more and more each day.
- Feb. 13: To be back home in LA where I belong, and I'm so glad I stepped away to fully appreciate who and what I have.
- Feb. 14: To spend Valentine's with my best friend, my wife, my partner. Can't wait to spend the rest of my life with her.
- Feb. 22: For friends like Erick to be back in my life.
- Feb. 24: To push through the anxiousness I've had. To be at home speaking and giving back at Cal State LA.
- Feb. 26: To have the opportunity to touch people's lives the way Kyle described yesterday—that was special.
- Feb. 29: For the opportunity to introduce Purpose Labs to the world!!!
- Mar. 1: To receive so much gratitude and appreciation from attendees yesterday.
- Mar. 4: To have the best mom in the world. Happy bday, Mom!!!!!
- Mar. 5: To live my 'Why' today by guiding over 100 people to find theirs. Are you kidding me??? !!!!!!
- Mar. 6: To touch lives the way my dad did. I feel like the luckiest person on the Earth to do what I did yesterday . . . because of 'Why' I did it.
- Mar. 10: To meet my network at the 50. It's awesome to see how new and surprising opportunities continue to emerge.
- PANDEMIC – START OF STAY AT HOME QUARANTINE
- Mar. 13: That my family is safe, healthy, and happy.
- Mar. 14: To have a roof over our heads and be healthy.

- Mar. 15: That my wife is my best friend, and if I had to hunker down with one person in the world, it would be her.
- Mar. 19: For the opportunity to inspire others virtually and stay connected.
- Mar. 24: For the opportunity to put pen to paper on my book outline.
- Mar. 25: For another day of health. The sun keeps coming up as we look forward to normalcy.
- Apr. 2: To have the opportunity to inspire others to author their stories.
- Apr. 4: For the Wolfpack. We're all healthy and staying positive. Love those guys.
- Apr. 5: To be able to reflect back on my life. I wouldn't change a thing.
- Apr. 6: Are you kidding me right now???!!! About to type the 1st words of my book.
- Apr. 8: For the calm storm, where I can focus, think, and do.
- Apr. 10: For each breath.
- Apr. 13: To put pen to paper on the power of purpose.
- Apr. 15: For the opportunity to share *Playing Offense* with the world.
- Apr. 16: To continue to make progress on my book. It ain't pretty, but we're moving.
- Apr. 17: To have found my writing coach.
- Apr. 20: To have a partner willing to push herself and who wants the best for me every day.
- Apr. 21: To have an environment to focus on creating all of this impact and play the long game.
- Apr. 26: For this beautiful walk we're about to go on.
- Apr. 29: To continue the progress and bring my vulnerable message to the world.
- Apr. 30: To coach people to find their 'Why.' I'm the luckiest person on Earth.

- May 5: For my family communicating during these separated and disconnected times. Virtual happy hour was a blast!
- May 7: For the opportunity that is in front of me because of this book.
- May 10: For my mom and all the mothers out there. Happy Mother's Day!!!!
- May 11: For the possibilities. I trust that what is meant to be, will happen.
- May 17: To see the finish line of writing this book.

What I hope you'll see in this sample of journal entries is that we always have something to be grateful for.

On the highest of highs, I was grateful to launch my business. Then I was grateful to put it in action and live my 'Why.' Even after the pandemic, something as simple as the sun coming out and taking a clean breath seemed like a big deal, worth being grateful about. Because of the stay-at-home quarantine, I was able to put my head down for months and grind this book out. Lastly, we all have people in our lives to be grateful for—sometimes, we just need to be reminded of it.

That's the power of a gratitude journal. It's a daily reminder of what's right, even when things are far from perfect.

This daily exercise can unleash the same for you.

HAVE TO VERSUS GET TO

The second item I journal is what I "get to" do today. In contrast, we often think about what we "have to" do today.

Get to do versus *have* to do. Simple words—yet a drastically different mindset. And so is the energy toward the action that follows.

What I do is look at my calendar for the day. I choose an item that feels like a routine element of my job. It can be a meeting, a task, a call . . . the blocking and tackling aspects of our day-to-day work. Prior to journaling this item, I would think of the blocking and tackling as things I "have to" do. Now, I challenge myself to reframe to what I "get to" do.

Here's an example for a conference call. You know, the kind you jump on, say hello, put on mute, then multitask while you listen just enough in case your name is called. Yep, those conference calls.

- **FORMER LIFE:** I "have to" jump on this call.
- **FUTURE LIFE:** I "get to" connect with our partners.

By shifting your mindset from what you have to do to what you get to do, you reframe your energy and your day.

A DAILY DOSE OF EXCITEMENT

As the stay-at-home quarantine during our global pandemic hit, my world, like yours, became virtual overnight.

Zoom instantly became a verb. Much like "Google it," I started to hear "let's Zoom" as others wanted to connect.

While these times certainly had a negative effect on the live events business of speaking and training that I'm in, I took it as an opportunity to evolve with the times—to "the new normal," as everybody started calling it. This led to some of my prior client engagements transitioning to virtual webinars.

In the old normal, when live events were still humming, a webinar may have been a "have to."

Now I was thinking about them as a "get to." My excitement built as I started to craft the experience.

Though I could have used my same content of *Playing Offense* as a plug-and-play solution, I decided to customize and tailor the approach, given the stormy times we were all battling through. My message still touched on purpose, impact, and performance, but it was now equally balanced with grit, resilience, adaptability, and agility. For longer sessions, I took the opportunity to share some best practices and insights around personal and professional development, much of which you're reading in this chapter.

While I would never equate the potential impact of a webinar to a live event, this was the best we could do given the circumstances. Personally, I was inspired and fulfilled to stay connected in such disconnected times. Professionally, I knew that it was the right thing to do, and I felt honored to do it.

Following my initial virtual engagements, I received several notes of thankfulness. The first, from a Dallas Cowboys sales executive, was more in line with what I would have anticipated. Genuine and encouraging.

> *I cannot thank you enough for your time yesterday. It was one of the most beneficial, grounding, and inspiring seminars (or in this case, webinars) that I have had the pleasure of attending. You have given me much to think about and work through.*

The next, an email from a vice president at the MLB club I spoke with, struck me in a unique and unexpected way:

> *Paul—Appreciate you taking the time today with the team. Outstanding content for this unique time. Had my sixteen- and eighteen-year-old sons join the call as well, and it seemed to resonate with them, and they were excited to talk post-call about their purpose.*

It's heartwarming to read any note of appreciation, but this one touched a different nerve and made a lasting impression. Based on the environment of being at home, his sons got to join the call. In typical times, they're at school and this workshop is in person. At an age when many of us aren't taking a moment to think about purpose (I certainly wasn't at sixteen or eighteen), these two young men had the opportunity to hear an inspiring message that resonated. I wish I could have been a fly on the wall for the conversation that was to come, about their purpose, with their dad.

This meant the world to me. I couldn't have scripted the impact. It just happened. If it could impact one life (better yet, two), then it was worth doing.

I feel blessed that I "get to" create experiences like this for a living. I'll never take another webinar for granted.

GENERATE YOUR ENERGY

A power plant doesn't have energy. It generates energy and transmits it.

We are no different. Every day, every activity, and every moment either brings you energy or depletes you of your energy. This applies to what you do and whom you're around. As my friend and fellow author Jon Gordon says, there are "energy vampires" all around us—and they will suck the life out of you, your goals, and your vision, if you let them.

In order to lead at our best, serve others, and show up with our highest levels of energy, we must know how to generate and transmit energy, just like a power plant.

My third and final journaling entry was created for this effect—excitement. When we are excited, we generate energy and it radiates toward others. What if you could be excited every day?

Every morning I journal one thing that I am excited about. I look at my calendar and search for the one thing that will bring me the most juice that day.

But I have a rule, and it's a rule I recommend for you as well.

The Rule of Excitement: If there is nothing that excites me on the calendar today, I move on and leave the journaling space for excitement blank. If the same thing happens the next morning, I will NOT get out of my journaling seat until I put something on that day's calendar that does excite me.

Through this rule, I have guaranteed myself that I will do something that excites me at minimum every other day. In baseball terms, I've created a rule that ensures I bat .500 or better on excitement. Over time, this baseline of .500 has risen to the point I'm now batting 1.000. If you want to have fuel every day of your life, generate it using this journaling rule of excitement.

As a recap, here are the three things to journal each morning:

- **GRATEFUL:** What am I grateful for?
- **GET TO:** What do I *get* to do today (versus *have* to do today)?
- **EXCITED:** What am I excited about today?

As you can see from these pages of my journal, it's nothing fancy. It is, however, powerful. Start your day with this process and watch your energy transform, for yourself and for others.

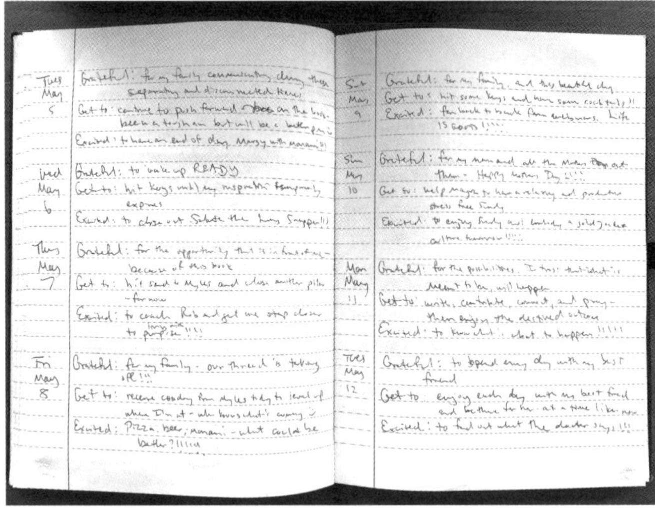

These simple journaling notes ensure I start my day on my terms.

DO WHAT YOU LOVE TO DO

> *"Choose a job you love, and you will never have to work a day in your life."*
>
> **CONFUCIUS**
> Chinese philosopher

Many people read a saying like this from Confucius and think, "That can never be me. Work is work. Work will never be love." to which I would respond with another quote, by Henry Ford: "Whether you think you can or you think you can't—you're right."

If you think you can't find work you love or that work can't become a passion, you're right. For the rest of you, let's dive in to how we can process this journey of discovery.

For starters, let me ease the tension in the room. You have bills to pay. Perhaps a family to care for. Going rogue and following your passion at the sacrifice of a paycheck is not happening!

Cool. That's not my recommendation.

Let's start off by processing your thoughts around this question:

- If you had no limitations in your life—no concerns about money, family obligations, or work requirements—what would you love to spend the rest of your life working toward?

Then, let's go back to the questions in Chapter 8 around discovering your passions (listed below):

- What makes you *feel alive*?
- What are the things you obsess about, daydream about, wish you had more time to put energy into?
- As you were growing up, what did you most love doing?
- What activities make you lose track of time?

Now let's look at the numerous routes you can go based on how you're feeling at this moment—likely one of these four ways:

1. Holy smokes, I just found my passion! Now, how do I turn that into work?
2. I have a strong feeling about what my passion is but still need time to process it.
3. I know there are clues; I see some signs but don't think I've fully put it all together.
4. I'm lost. This is stupid. On to the next section of the book.

Bucket one—sounds like a job search or job craft of your current role may be in order. I'm as excited as you are! Read on for some options on how to navigate next steps. Bucket two or three—read on with bucket one. Bucket four—see you in a few pages.

For starters, this chapter likely won't conclude with you saying, "I quit," then waking up the next day to an email from an HR director regarding your dream job. If it happens, awesome. Otherwise, here's what is more realistic and likely.

Our passions are fueled by the activities that give us the most energy. The answers to the questions you just processed should provide you with some of these energy indicators. Now, let's reintegrate the Ikigai model from Chapter 1.

On the outer ring, your passions are what you love to do. Your strengths and talents (from Chapter 8) are what you're great at. It's time to focus on the other two perimeter areas.

- What does the world need?
- What will the world pay you for?

If you have an idea for the first bullet (what the world needs) and think there's even a small chance that the world will pay you for it, you're in the perfect spot and have already done the deepest thinking. If you're not there yet, stay on this until you have clarity. From there, it's time to put it to work!

This is not your full-time job (yet). For now, it's a hobby, it's a side hustle, it's a weekend gig, or it's you burning the candle in the evenings (after your day job) to get the wheels in motion and create proof of concept, feasibility, and financial viability.

Because of the uniqueness of each person's path, I'll stop here for now. To dive deeper into this process, I would recommend starting by immersing yourself in the Purpose Discovery process, full FAQ available at **WWW.POWEROFPLAYINGOFFENSE.COM**.

From there, spend time with a mentor, trusted friend, or coach who does work like I do who can help you connect your 'Why' and core values to finding your dream job, with the hopes that it blossoms into a flourishing career and potentially a calling. This type of coaching lights me up. I hope it will light you up, too.

WHAT'S MOST IMPORTANT TO YOU

Values are your own judgment of what is most important in your life. They are distinctive to you. There is no right set of values versus wrong. There are no better values versus worse. Values are uniquely you.

When put to use, values can be your most powerful lens for how you see the world, direct your attention, and make meaning of your experiences.

Values can also be your guiding lens toward your daily actions, behaviors, and decisions—in other words, how you show up.

If a lot of this looks and sounds familiar, it's because we've covered values in different sections of the book, with unique applications. Now it's time to bring it all together and hold ourselves accountable to our values—if we want to live and lead with purpose.

INSPECT WHAT YOU EXPECT

Living my values has led to the greatest transformations in my life. My 'Why' opened my eyes and got me started on this path. My values made the impact tangible.

Just like anything else in life, the earlier stages of implementing my values as a lens toward my daily actions, behaviors, and decisions weren't natural at first. It wasn't until I began to measure whether I was living my values that they became habits, which then turned into rituals, and that's when the transformation took off.

As many in the training space say, you have to "inspect what you expect." *This is my ask of you*: to inspect your values if you expect to live a life true to your purpose. It sounds lofty by outcome, so allow me to simplify the initial steps and share a framework that has worked for me to audit my values and hold myself accountable.

Much like journaling happens every morning, think of this as your journal of values, once a week. We'll cover both in this round of applying the playbook.

APPLYING THE PLAYBOOK

CHAPTER 14: PERSONAL AND PROFESSIONAL DEVELOPMENT JOURNALING

Kicking off, as a refresher on your daily journaling, there are three questions to answer each morning.

1. **GRATEFUL:** What am I grateful for?
2. **GET TO:** What do I *get* to do today (versus *have* to do today)?
3. **EXCITED:** What am I excited about today?

DOUBLE DOWN: If you really want to take it up a notch, close your day with a reflective look back at these three questions:

1. How did I serve others/make somebody better today?
2. How did I add value to my organization today?
3. What am I most proud of today?

Choose the questions that you feel most committed to holding yourself accountable to (the more, the merrier), then journal on them each evening. Among all the great leaders I've studied, daily journaling is the most common habit and ritual they practice (with reading being a close second). Once you form your daily journaling routine, let's level up and add weekly journaling to your repertoire.

While many stop at daily journaling, I recommend a form of weekly reflection as well. However, this will be structured around your values, with an endgame of giving you confidence and assurance that you are authentically living your values.

Morning and evening journaling should take no longer than a few minutes. End-of-week values journaling should take ten to fifteen minutes max. That is the time investment in yourself per week.

Time to play offense and make it happen.

STEP ONE

Pick a natural point in the week where you typically reset and flip the page. For some, it's Friday afternoon. For others, it's Saturday morning or Sunday evening. Whichever you choose, this should be the point where you want to close the books on the week that was and start to envision and plan the week ahead.

STEP TWO

Fill out the following sheet with the date and your core values along the left column. The form can be downloaded at **WWW.POWEROFPLAYINGOFFENSE.COM**.

DATE TODAY	This past week, I lived my value of ________ when I ________________.	For the week ahead, I will live my value of ______ by ________________.
VALUE 1		
VALUE 2		
VALUE 3		

STEP THREE

For each value, fill out the second column by answering: This past week, I lived my value of __________ when I _________________________.

In other words, if you were sitting at the dinner table and somebody with knowledge that one of your core values was "impact" asked, "How did you make an impact this past week?" how would you answer?

You can reframe this question for any value. For me, it would be "How did I show up with growth/belief/courage/authenticity/impact?"

For both the question below and the question above, try to focus your answers on actions, behaviors, and decisions. The more specific and action-oriented, the better.

STEP FOUR

For each value, fill out the third column by answering: For the week ahead, I will live my value of ________ by _____________________________.

To help you answer, you can peek ahead at your calendar for the following week so that you have full vision and clarity of where you'll be and who you'll be with, which will allow you to be more specific when answering.

As an example: "For the week ahead, I will live my value of *belief* by pulling each person on my team aside and letting them know that I'm proud of them. This project has been a bear, and they need to know that I'm their partner all the way to the finish line."

Repeat this cycle once a week. The reflection combined with planning will ensure you stay true to your values, so you can show up as your most bold, authentic, and confident self.

This is the value of values—the anchor to living and leading with purpose.

15

LEADERSHIP GETS PERSONAL

By trade, my dad held two jobs as an educator. He taught adult school two nights a week, and his pride and joy was to serve full-time as a continuation high school teacher. In case you're not familiar with continuation high schools, this is typically a kid's last chance. They've been kicked out of traditional school and often come from broken homes. English is a challenge for some, and many have been given up on—some on their way to becoming yet another statistic on the street.

It was on these streets that I had an encounter that has impacted me to this day.

A FATHER'S LEGACY

I was sitting in a barbershop, blocks from the continuation school my dad taught at. In came this bulging seven-foot-tall guy, tattoos on every square inch of his body. If I saw him in a dark alley, I'd run the other way.

We locked eyes, and he was coming right at me, hand starting to rise. I was in total fight-or-flight mode—before I could even react, I closed my eyes and braced for impact.

Instead . . . nothing. I slowly opened my eyes, expecting to see a fist; instead, I saw a finger, pointing right at me.

He asked, "Are you Mr. Epstein's son?"

Still shaken, I couldn't even answer.

He apologized for startling me, then shared why I looked familiar: "I remember you on the side of the stage I graduated from, and just wanted to come over and say *thank you*—for everything your dad did for me."

My tension was easing, and then . . . the moment:

"Your dad was the first person to ever believe in me. I know it may not sound like much, but I've had a job for two consecutive months, and I owe it all to him. He gave me a reason to think that tomorrow was worth it."

This man, who had just scared me to my core, now seemed like an angel delivering a message.

When I heard the words "gave me a reason to think tomorrow was worth it," as if that had been in question, it shook me for some time.

As I reflected back, it became clear. What my dad did was educate. 'Why' he did it was to impact lives. He measured success by the way he touched the lives of people. That was his calling. That was his legacy. And now, his legacy has become my purpose.

FROM THE BARBERSHOP TO THE BEACH

Nearly two decades later, I came across a book of notes my dad's students wrote to my mom and me when they received the news he had passed.

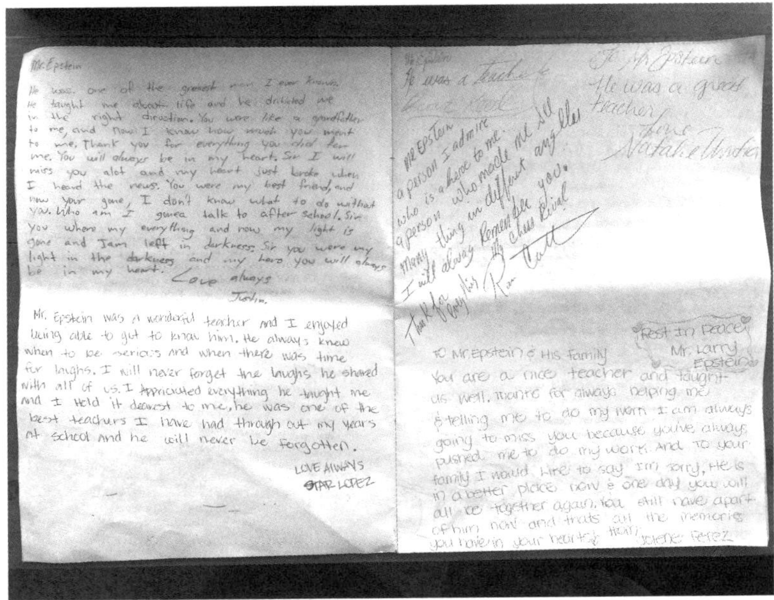

Mr. Epstein

He was one of the greatest man I ever known. He taught me about life and he directed me in the right direction. You were like a grandfather to me, and now I know how much you meant to me. Thank you for everything you did for me. You will always be in my heart. Sir I will miss you alot and my heart just broke when I heard the news. You were my best friend, and now your gone, I don't know what to do without you. Who am I gonna talk to after school. Sir you where my everything and now my light is gone and I am left in darkness. Sir you were my light in the darkness and my hero you will always be in my heart.

Love always
Justin.

Mr. Epstein was a wonderful teacher and I enjoyed being able to get to know him. He always knew when to be serious and when there was time for laughs. I will never forget the laughs he shared with all of us. I appriciated everything he taught me and I Hold it dearest to me, he was one of the best teachers I have had through out my years at school and he will never be forgotten.

LOVE ALWAYS
STAR LOPEZ

Mr. Epstein
He was a teacher [illegible]

To Mr. Epstein
He was a great teacher
Love
Natalie [illegible]

Mr Epstein
a person I admire
who is a hero to me.
a person who made me see
many thing in different angles
I will always Remember you.
Thank for everything
my chess Rival
R[illegible]

Rest In Peace
Mr. Larry Epstein

To Mr. Epstein & His family
You are a nice teacher and taught us well. thanks for always helping me & telling me to do my work I am always going to miss you because you've always pushed me to do my work. And to your family I would like to say I'm sorry, He is in a better place now & one day you will all be together again. You still have apart of him now and thats all the memories you have in your heart of him.
Jolene Perez

These notes from my dad's students bring him back to life every time I read them.

While there were countless mentions of him being a great teacher, there were also comments that pleasantly surprised me, like how much of a jokester he was and how he introduced his students to a game they'd never heard of—a game called Jeopardy—and actually made social studies fun. Countless kids wrote about my dad outside the classroom context, coaching volleyball, which I had no idea he ever did, especially considering his physical limitations and challenges from diabetes. I asked my mom about this after reading all the notes, and she said, "Oh yeah, he loved coaching volleyball. Why do you think we had the VW Vanagon? He bought it just so he could pack it up and take them to the beach to play."

She then explained why he did it: Most of my dad's students had *never* seen the ocean, even though the school was less than twenty miles away from the coast.

Based on their upbringings, they didn't have the childhood experiences that most kids I knew did, so my dad brought the experience to them.

Stories like this illustrated how my dad lived with purpose. How he transformed adversity in these kids' lives into moments of achievement. How he inspired hope in others. And how he embodied Gold Jacket Culture, in and out of the classroom. He left every person he touched better than he had found them. No doubt about it—he was playing offense.

I am honored to live in my dad's legacy—and if I can have one-tenth of the impact he had in this world, then it will be a great life.

PAYING IT FORWARD

Growing up under the guidance of a teacher has its pros and cons. The cons are they're going to watch your grades like a hawk, and they actually know what they're talking about! What was cool was my dad didn't play this part. He handed that role to my mom. She was the hawk!

Since he intentionally wasn't overly hands-on with my schooling, the pro was I got to see him teach others. I'll always remember him tutoring our neighbors or other adult school students at our dinner table on his nights off. He had remarkable patience, never raising his voice, even when the most basic of lessons didn't sink in.

As much as he was a teacher by craft and at heart, I could tell that he was a lifelong student, as well, always curious to learn more, earning three master's degrees in social studies, reading education, and business administration. On the surface he was a student of the topics he taught. Below the surface, he was a student of people. He loved people in such a way that it's now easy to see that the apple didn't fall far from the tree.

LIKE FATHER, LIKE SON

One of the most purposeful perks of getting my MBA had nothing to do with the in-program experience. It was the access that the three letters got me months after, as they presented a door that I'd never imagined.

In 2019 I had a coffee meeting with a good friend and fellow consultant, Santor Nishizaki, who is an expert in the strengths and millennial/gen Z space. Beyond his consulting work, Santor is a professor who teaches a variety of courses, dedicating a significant percentage of his time as an adjunct across a handful of campuses throughout Southern California—one of them being California State University, Los Angeles.

As we talked about a number of business items, somehow, my dad came up in the conversation. I could tell it struck a chord with Santor. He looked up and said, "What would you think of being a professor? You now have the MBA. I'd be happy to introduce you to my department chair. Just let me know."

While it seems like such an obvious connection, I had never thought of it. After envisioning it for a few days, it became a no-brainer. I was in for the process!

And oh boy, was it a process. I quickly learned of the differences between getting hired into education versus corporate—but it was all worth it. I eventually got the green light to serve as an adjunct professor of business at Cal State LA!

All of a sudden, I was a rookie again. It was yet another reinvention of everything I knew. But this became my opportunity to apply what I had learned from my dad.

My top priority was to teach my students about more than the course work (which happened to be marketing); I was going to pour myself into the classroom and teach them about life.

This was the perfect platform and fit as the Cal State LA community is largely first-generation students, many from similar cultural backgrounds, nearly all commuting in while juggling work and family responsibilities.

The autonomy I had from the university and support I had from Santor set me up for success. In the classroom I fell in love with the experience—most importantly, my students. We covered the marketing bases, but we also took a deep dive on leadership and life: From purpose, to values, to knowing who you are, understanding your 'Why,' building your brand, making moral decisions, understanding how to show up at your best in the workplace, and how to be a great teammate. These were lessons outside of the core curriculum, but I hope that they will be the ones that will make an ongoing impact.

While I didn't coach volleyball or play Jeopardy like my dad, I trust that I touched lives in a similar way. Yes, I was the teacher, but I came into it as a student—always learning.

Our last day of class at Cal State LA. These students made me feel "even more alive" every time I saw them.

EVOLVE OR DIE

The reality is we all need to evolve or we get passed by (a figurative death). The only way to evolve is to constantly grow, iterate, experiment, and take action, which will lead to one of two outcomes: success or failure. While we're all after success, I would argue failure is the greater platform to learn from.

Look no further than Jeff Bezos at Amazon for some inspiration in this space. Bear in mind, we associate Amazon with success, and we're reminded of their success every time we see four new Amazon boxes on our front porch. Bezos shares that "it's not an experiment if you know it's going to work," and that "failure and invention are inseparable twins."

How can we evolve if we don't take risks? How can we evolve if we're not willing to fail? Failure is not the wrongdoing; not taking the chance is the wrongdoing.

So, if evolution is the goal, let's frame this as leveling up in business and life. We stack lessons so that we can evolve, grow, develop, and progress.

I believe that we can grow each day by focusing on and stacking three things:

1. Experience
2. Information
3. Relationships

KEEP LEVELING UP

Every day presents us with three opportunities.

1. Each day enables us to pick up incremental *experience*—how much we gain from it is on each individual.
2. Each day provides us with opportunities to gather more *information* based on the work we do, the materials we digest, and the conversations we have.
3. Each day provides us with new potential *relationships*. If we have a blind eye, these relational opportunities pass us by. With intention and focus present, new relationships can be the differentiator needed.

In sum, this covers all bases—what you've done (experience), what you know (information), and whom you know (relationships).

I'm constantly approached by people asking how others achieve success, how others create progress and momentum, and how others perform at peak levels. It always comes back to these essential elements. What I have seen is that those who build momentum to achieve success and peak performance maintain a daily focus on all three fundamentals of personal and professional growth: experience, information, and relationships.

If you feel stuck or aren't happy with where you are, this is a great reminder and barometer to bring you back into a more positive and controllable mindset of adding value:

- Every day, focus on gaining valuable experience.
- Every day, focus on gathering valuable information.
- Every day, focus on building valuable relationships.

If you can't gain the experience in your daily environment, then make it happen in the evenings or on weekends. If you aren't picking up valuable information at work, then get it from a book. If your current network isn't surrounding you with the right types of relationships, then build a new network that aligns with your future goals. This is not the time to make excuses. This is the time to step up and prioritize your development, if you are committed to achieving your highest potential.

Imagine the possibilities when you stack experience, information, and relationships every day, week, and month. These can be the building blocks of transformation.

"One can choose to go back toward safety or forward toward growth. Growth must be chosen again and again; fear must be overcome again and again."

ABRAHAM MASLOW

American psychologist, creator of Maslow's Hierarchy of Needs

COACHES VERSUS MENTORS

Just like professional athletes, musicians, performers, and artists need coaches, so do we.

It amazes me how underserved we are in the business world in terms of the coaches required to consistently level up our leadership performance, skills, and mindset. This is what inspired me to become an executive coach and serve leaders like you. I've seen the power of having coaches in my life—which largely came in recent years. Until then, I only had mentors.

Brilliant thought leader, blogger, and author Seth Godin explains the gap well: "Mentors are not teachers. They were never meant to scale because that would mean too much time taken away from what they do best and remove their value of being a mentor."

Mentors can guide, but there are limitations as they need to stay in the day-to-day game that makes their insights so valuable. On the contrary, coaching is a full-time job. They're not taken away from what they do best by serving. Coaching *is* what they do best.

I wouldn't be where I am without the coaches who have backed me in recent years, starting with my executive MBA coaches, Sue Ann Gonis and Surry Scheerer; in training and facilitation, Matt Whiat and Sara Hannah; on the speaking side, Josh Linkner and his entire team; now, in the writing space, Myles Schrag.

If something is important to you in life, isn't it worth having a coach? I believe so—because I've lived it from both sides. I pour myself into coaching clients to help them live and lead with impact and purpose, just like my coaches have inspired me to live my purpose.

"A coach is someone who tells you what you don't want to hear, who has you see what you don't want to see, so you can be who you have always known you could be."

TOM LANDRY

former NFL coach, Dallas Cowboys; two-time Super Bowl champion

STEPPING UP TO YOUR POTENTIAL

This story takes me back to one of my favorite places in the world—the lobby bar at the Intercontinental Hotel in Century City—no coincidence, the host hotel where my MBA program was held. Shout out to the Wolfpack and the countless good times at the Copper Lounge!

It was at the lounge toward the end of our twenty-one-month residency that I sat down with my career coach, Sue Ann. We were reflecting back on the program; she was asking about my thoughts, career-wise, post-graduation. I shared some of my recent experiences inside of the Leadership Institute and how I loved the consulting and training side, but that there was an itch that I didn't feel I had fully scratched on the speaking side. While the experiences of keynoting organically came about, they were not the focus of our business model. I was determined to get more at-bats.

As soon as Sue Ann heard me talk about speaking, her eyes got even more energized than usual. She probed with more questions, which got my juices flowing about my passion for the speaking space. My passion is based on the impact that I've seen it create, whether I'm on stage or sitting in the audience. Speaking can inspire. Speaking can educate. Speaking can transform.

Sue Ann slowly came to tears and said, "Paul, you have to do this. This is so you. I've never seen you light up the way you just did."

Now she had me teary-eyed!

Then Sue Ann had the mic drop moment where I felt the impact of coaching take over—through the power of belief. This was evidence of that, and then some.

Sue Ann said, "Paul, you can be better than Tony Robbins."

Okay, let that sink in for a moment. For those less familiar with Tony, he is the Michael Jordan of my space. Flattered beyond imagination, I soaked up Sue Ann's words. Whether realistic or not, only time will tell.

But I became an even bigger believer in the mission and vision of what I was after because of the belief that Sue Ann sparked in me. Months later, I pulled the trigger and went ALL IN on this dream. I'm not sure how or when it would have happened without Sue Ann, but I'm glad I'll never have to find out.

Thank you, Sue Ann, for always believing in me and inspiring me to take the leaps toward following my 'Why'—whether growing beyond sports or following my calling to speak. You bring out my best, and I am forever grateful for having you in my life. You have truly been a life changer.

TIME-OUT: Think of the greatest coach in your life. What actions and behaviors made you think of them? Write those actions and behaviors down in the next few minutes. Keep the list visible, and do those exact same things for your team—every day. These microactions are how you will be remembered.

IN LASTING MEMORY

We've talked a lot about our 'Why.' We've also taken a look at our Who: Who we are on our best day. Who we show up as, aligned to our authentic selves. Our Who is our core identity when we look inward.

Now, I'd like to challenge you to look outward for your Who: *Whom will you do it for?*

In my case (as you've read), it's relatively obvious. Everything I do is in memory of my dad. When I'm down, I think of him, and I get right back up. When I'm up, I find a way to connect with him to get even higher. Everything I do is to make him proud.

Thanks, Dad. You're the best.

Now it's your turn.

WHOM WILL YOU DO IT FOR?

Who is the one person that you would do ANYTHING for? The same way I just described my dad, thinking of this person should light you up. They are your rock through the storm, your guide through the forest, your source of strength when needed. They inspire you to no end.

By now you probably have a person in mind. If you can't decide between two, all good. After you apply the playbook, you'll have more clarity on how to move forward.

It's time to interview your 'Who.'

APPLYING THE PLAYBOOK

CHAPTER 15: INTERVIEW YOUR WHO

This one gets deep and personal. Once you do it, you'll never forget it.

Meet me at the 50, and allow me to guide you.

STEP ONE

Identify your 'Who.' It's time to play offense and reach out.

I would suggest not disclosing too many details, other than to say that you'd love to spend some one-on-one time and it's something important. Also, let them know that everything is okay to avoid any worries!

STEP TWO

Set a time in a setting where you are both extremely comfortable and the conversation can be private. Perhaps there is a favorite place you've previously enjoyed and of which you have fond memories (their living room, a lounge in the yard—you'll know exactly where to do this).

STEP THREE

It's game day. Bring a recording device (it can be your phone) and nothing else. You'll want this conversation to be a keepsake for years to come. Perhaps even something passed down between generations.

STEP FOUR

Once you are both settled, here's an example of how I would open up the conversation. Please feel free to make this your own. This is personal. Do and say what feels right.

Mom, I really appreciate you sitting down with me. I've been thinking a lot about the most important people in my life and how grateful I am for everything others have done for me. You were the first person I thought of. I literally wouldn't be who I am or where I am without you. While we're still together (and going strong), I wanted to take some time . . . just to talk. Ask you some questions. Get to hear your thoughts, so that I can hold onto them and listen to them often. I value and cherish our relationship so much, and I'd like for a piece of our relationship to be memorialized. I imagine us listening to this together on Mother's Day or future birthdays, maybe even once your future grandkids are old enough to understand. For these special occasions, I'd like to record this conversation so we can properly remember it. Ready to dive in?

STEP FIVE

Here are twenty sample questions with which to interview your Who. Pick five to ten that resonate most, and keep the others handy if you want to keep the conversation flowing. Again, feel free to make this your own—and remember to enjoy the moment.

> **NOTE:** *I am writing this as if it were to a parent. You can easily modify based on the nature of the relationship.*

1. What have been the proudest days of your life?
2. If you could talk to your younger self, what do you know now that you wish you had known then?
3. If you wrote a book about your life, how would you summarize it?
4. What was your biggest failure? Biggest lesson in life?
5. If they filmed a movie about you, who would play you? Why?
6. What's your favorite childhood memory?

7. If you could have dinner with three people (dead or alive), whom would you invite?
8. What have I done to make you proud?
9. How do you want to be remembered?
10. If the whole world were listening and you could share one thought, what would it be?
11. How did you meet [spouse/partner] and know [he or she] was *the one?*
12. How did you choose your career, and what was your favorite part about it?
13. What made you successful (and feel significant) in life?
14. What do you think the world needs more of right now?
15. What do you believe people want most in life?
16. What are the best (and worst) decisions you've ever made?
17. What are you most excited about in the future?
18. What have you been thinking about lately?
19. What are you most thankful for?
20. What message would you like to share with your family?

STEP SIX

End the recording. Give them a big bear hug. Play it back when you see special opportunities to do so.

EPILOGUE: MEET ME AT THE 50

You, like I, have seen the best and worst sides of leadership. We have learned what to do and what *not* to do. We have seen championship cultures inspired by visionary leaders who backed every word and genuinely put people first in the toughest of times. We have also seen toxic environments we wouldn't wish on our worst enemies.

Going back to our opening question in the preface—"Without title, influence, or authority, would anybody follow?"

Speaking personally, as a leader, on my best day, I need none of those things. On my worst day, I'd be lucky to have a single follower.

I understand the pressures that we as leaders go through. The pressures of winning the short game. Of a results-obsessed mindset. Of end-of-quarter goals or end-of-year reviews. Of a boss who can suck the life out of the room and everybody inside it.

Are there systemic problems to address in business? Absolutely. Are leaders in a tough spot? One-hundred percent. But are leaders also responsible for many of the workplace issues we face today? You bet.

I once heard an executive at a Fortune 500 organization say, "Business is easy; people are hard." Agreed, people can be hard, but often we, as leaders, are the ones making it hard. *The Power of Playing Offense* was written in part to raise awareness of the impact leaders like us have on people, for better or worse. We're often sprinting so fast while chasing the next target that we're blinded to the ripple effects of our behaviors, actions, and decisions on the people in our team.

To make it even more challenging, who's coaching the coaches? Similar to my past experience, you likely are *not* receiving an abundance of leadership development training or support. As if the transition from player to coach wasn't difficult enough, this lack of coaching resources is taking a toll on our cultures, our teams, and the growth of our careers. It's time to stop playing defense.

I challenge you to meet me at the 50 to inspire the leaders of tomorrow through the actions you take today. By applying and implementing the teachings and trainings of this book, you will have more best days and show up as the leader your people deserve. You will be the leader you wish you had, a leader who takes an all-gas-no-brakes mentality into each day, inspired to play offense.

COACHING RESOURCES

You now have the playbook to lead the charge. As you've seen, *The Power of Playing Offense* contains over fifty tools to activate on Monday morning. The complete list of Applying the Playbook exercises, Time-Out activities, and the People360 Blueprint can be found in the upcoming appendix.

To continue the learning online, I have also provided a series of free resources that will support your immediate action steps to implement these practices personally, with your team, and with your organization. All complementary resources can be found at **WWW.POWEROFPLAYINGOFFENSE.COM**.

If you'd like to continue the journey on your own, consider me your biggest cheerleader and fan. You got this.

If you'd like support as a coach, trainer, speaker, or consultant for your team or organization, I would be honored to meet you at the 50.

For more information on how we can partner, visit **WWW.PURPOSELABS.US** or email **CONTACT@PURPOSELABS.US**.

IT'S TIME TO PLAY OFFENSE

This is your time to lead, make a difference, and drive impact. It's your opportunity to transform, personally and professionally.

	Pillar I	Pillar II	Pillar III	Pillar IV	Pillar V	
PAUL EPSTEIN	LIVE WITH CHAMPIONSHIP PURPOSE	BE THE STORM CHASER	SALUTE THE LONG SNAPPER	EMBODY GOLD JACKET CULTURE	LEAVE IT BETTER THAN YOU FOUND IT	PLAYING OFFENSE
			MEET ME AT THE 50			
	PAYCHECK-DRIVEN → PURPOSE-DRIVEN	ADVERSITY → ACHIEVEMENT	DISENGAGED → INSPIRED	CONTROL → CAMARADERIE	SUCCESS → SIGNIFICANCE	
	Leading Self		Leading Others		Leading the Future	

You made it.

Use these five pillars and the transformations within as your guides to keep the momentum going and keep Playing Offense top of mind. You have the tools at your disposal to do just that. The best part is, you're just getting started.

Embrace the journey, knowing I'll be with you in spirit every step of the way.

Meet me at the 50—and let's go play some offense!

50+ WAYS YOU CAN PLAY OFFENSE ON MONDAY MORNING

Consider this your go-to glossary of tools and activities to level up your leadership for years to come. For ease of reference, the page numbers are included next to each exercise. You can also download the complete list at **WWW.POWEROFPLAYINGOFFENSE.COM.**

APPLYING THE PLAYBOOK EXERCISES

TIME-OUTS

PEOPLE360: A BLUEPRINT TO BUILD A PEOPLE-FIRST ORGANIZATION

LISTENING SESSION PROCESS

You're likely joining this exercise after reading about hosting your own listening session in Chapter 9.

Let's dive in.

DO MORE, BETTER, DIFFERENT LISTENING SESSION

As mentioned in Chapter 9, this is an opportunity to engage your team around a candid conversation on what's going right (do more), where things can slightly improve (do better), or where we may have gone off the reservation and a hard U-turn is needed (do different).

SETTING

Ideally this is baked into a larger off-site gathering so the group will feel more comfortable sharing and will open up to a greater extent. See the timeout in Chapter 9 under "Host Listening Sessions" for more details on a full game plan for your next off-site.

The alternative is to host the meeting in office.

TIME NEEDED

Two hours as an off-site exercise, ninety minutes for an on-site listening session.

SET-UP

Flip chart on an easel board with markers (regardless of setting)

MEETING INVITE

If in-office, send an invite to your entire team for ninety minutes. Title the meeting, "Do More, Do Better, Do Different." If off-site, integrate the following into your overall agenda.

MEETING KICK-OFF

You will open by sharing the purpose of why you are all gathered. It should touch on you valuing each member of the team and wanting everybody to have a voice, all to create as inclusive an environment as possible where everybody feels heard. Most importantly, this session is designed to inspire action and positive change. This isn't "feedback for feedback sake." Rather, this is an opportunity for everybody's fingerprints to be on the blueprint—but they have to speak up, if positive change is the outcome you all desire. Lastly, assure them that all comments will be written down with high-level notes so that ideas are captured, and themes can surface as you share out your notes with the team (which will happen in a follow-on session).

The goal is for all attendees to feel safe, valued, and eager to participate.

SIDE NOTES – *While certainly not necessary, I've seen many organizations and teams bring in an outside facilitator for numerous reasons. Anonymity of responses, candid responses, psychological safety, quality of feedback, and/or a professional health assessment being the desired deliverable to learn and improve from—in which case a trained consultant in the organizational culture space can produce one after they lead your listening sessions.*

Unlike the organizational Purpose Discovery Process where I strongly suggest having a professional facilitator with experience lead the exercise, for listening sessions, it is completely subjective as I've seen it work both ways. If you're struggling to decide and budget for a facilitator is not a concern, here would be my recommendation. If your culture is strong (candidly and objectively speaking), you're likely okay to do listening sessions on your own. If your culture has gaps and major opportunities for improvement, perhaps trust has been fractured and thus people may not feel comfortable fully opening up to somebody internally, then an external facilitator may make more sense.

RULES OF ENGAGEMENT / SAMPLE FLOW

Here are the suggested rules of engagement and sample speaking scripts to create your own roadmap. The tone of these scripts will feel general as if they're coming from an outside facilitator. I'd encourage you to customize and tailor the language as much as possible for your specific team.

- The purpose of this meeting is to hear from you and have a candid discussion. The good, the bad, the indifferent. I'm collecting your stories to focus on what's going right and course correct anything that's frustrating in your day-to-day role. This is an opportunity to leverage your experience thus far to inform the future. All organizations and teams talk about culture, but few actually listen to it. That's what we're doing here today.

- As we start the conversation, you'll hear me ask for specific stories. The more specific, the better. This allows us to recreate what's going well and change what needs to be changed. This is your chance to voice directly to me/leadership your experience working here. If you want something to be better, tell me a story about it! An example of a great story is one where you can share the specific situation, a specific behavior, and the specific impact.

- You will see me taking notes. While I won't be writing down any names, I am trying to capture as much detail as possible. If you would like to see what I wrote down, I'm happy to show you. The stuff that we talk about in this room, we would ask the same. Please be respectful to each other and not disclose who said what.

- We'll spend some time on the positive, then we'll transition to the challenges.
- Your comments are all confidential (no names attached to them), but they will be shared anonymously with leadership if helpful for the greater organization.
- Our goal is to listen. We won't be discussing solutions at this stage or looking to agree or disagree.
- I will not jump in other than facilitate everyone's participation and questions. I'm scribing what you say today, that's it.
- Lastly, today is not a venting session. It is purely an opportunity to voice what we can be doing better or different, then formulating ideas and actions around positive change to better our workplace and team culture.

SESSION QUESTIONS

We're going to start by discussing what's going right that we can replicate. (approximately thirty to forty-five minutes)

- Tell me a story about a day that your drove home thinking, "that was a great day." What happened on that day?
- Can you tell me a story about a time when a leader or a coworker felt like they gave a damn about you (as a person, not just at work)?
- *If a Team or Organizational Why is in place—communicate the Why.* Then ask: How are we living up to this?

All great stories. We know any team and organization can get better. We're going to transition to gaps and systems that are frustrating. (approximately forty-five to sixty minutes)

- Tell me a story about a day you drove home thinking, "I wish I didn't have to go back." What happened on that day?

- Tell me a story about a time that you felt just like a number, treated more as your position (sales rep, accountant, etc.) versus an individual?
- Tell me a story about the process/system/structure that frustrates you the most?
- We know that every team/organization can get better. Where are the places we need to get better?
- *If a Team or Organizational Why is in place—communicate the Why.* Then ask: How are we *not* living up to this?

SESSION WRAP UP

- Thank everybody for their time. Then, extend an olive branch that if any comments weren't made today but they'd like to share, they can send you a private and confidential email and/or leave a confidential and anonymous note on your desk.
- Lastly, communicate the next steps. *"Over the coming weeks, I'll be organizing all of your comments and feedback and sourcing themes of where our biggest opportunities for growth and development are. I will present the top themes to the group and we will collectively decide where we can get better, and where we should be doing things differently. From there, we'll put an action plan together so that all of our fingerprints are on the blueprint and you will see your voice turn into action and positive change. Thank you again for leaning in today. I truly appreciate you all."*

ACTION ITEMS

- Get a meeting on the books for two weeks out. This timeline will keep the conversation fresh and hold you accountable to organize their feedback in a timely manner.
- Accumulate all notes (positive and gaps) into one document. The positive themes will be easily apparent. Open your follow-on meeting with

these highlights to set a positive tone, then say, "we need to keep these things going!"

- For the gaps (do better/do different), look for the most frequent themes. Common categories I have seen are leadership, trust, communication, systems/processes, culture, training, career growth/development, work-life balance, and morals/ethics. Populate these sample categories (or other ones that are apparent) and see where the largest quantity of comments come from.
- Cut the list to the top three to five themes. Keep all of the supplemental comments under each, highlight the most powerful comments/words/phrases, and bring this in with you to the follow-up meeting.
- Share out the positives and the gaps (do better/do different) with your team. No discussion needed for the positives. For the gaps, ask the group what opportunities for positive change they see. Notate all of their responses. IMPORTANT—let them speak first. If you share your ideas first, they will not feel fully heard or appreciated and may not even speak their mind because the perception will be that "leadership makes all the decisions, anyway." Don't waste the positive momentum you've built up to this point.
- Once you gather their feedback, call the meeting to a close and select three to five actions that you feel can make a significant change for your team and culture. Organize it in three buckets.
    - » Things you can do immediately
    - » Things you can do in three to six months
    - » Things you can do in one to two years
- Present your final decisions of what will be changing to the group accordingly. My recommendation is to create one to two small wins in the

"immediate" bucket. Then say you will have a conversation with your leader or leadership team regarding the mid to long term items.

Now it's time to bring these early wins to life! Awesome work. Your team will remember you long after your time together for what you've done.

ENDNOTES

CHAPTER 1

1 Hurst, Aaron, "The One Question Your Company Needs to Answer to Survive", *LinkedIn* September 6, 2019, www.linkedin.com/pulse/one-question-your-company-needs-answer-survive-aaron-hurst.

2 "Purpose at Work, 2016 Global Report", LinkedIn and Imperative, 2016, https://business.linkedin.com/content/dam/me/business/en-us/talent-solutions/resources/pdfs/purpose-at-work-global-report.pdf. 2."Purpose at Work, 2016 Global Report", LinkedIn and Imperative, 2016, https://business.linkedin.com/content/dam/me/business/en-us/talent-solutions/resources/pdfs/purpose-at-work-global-report.pdf.

3 Ibid.

4 Ibid.

5 Achor, Shawn, Reece, Andrew, Kellerman, Gabriella Rosen, Robichaux, Alexi, "9 Out of 10 People Are Willing to Earn Less Money to Do More Meaningful Work", *Harvard Business Review*, November 6, 2018, https://hbr.org/2018/11/9-out-of-10-people-are-willing-to-earn-less-money-to-do-more-meaningful-work.

6 Bravery, Kate, "People first: Mercer's 2018 Global Talent Trends Study", *Mercer*, May 28, 2018, https://www.mercer.com/our-thinking/career/voice-on-talent/people-first-mercers-2018-global-talent-trends-study.html.

7 McLeod, Lisa Earle, "Why Purpose Matters: Four Business Reasons Plus One Emotional One", April 8, 2012, https://www.huffpost.com/entry/why-purpose-matters-four-_b_1257295.

8 Malnight, Thomas, Buche, Ivy, Dhanaraj, Charles, "Put Purpose at the Core of Your Strategy", *Harvard Business Review*, September-October 2019 Issue, https://hbr.org/2019/09/put-purpose-at-the-core-of-your-strategy.

9 "2018 Cone/Porter Novelli Purpose Study", *Cone* (A Porter Novelli Company), 2018, https://www.conecomm.com/research-blog/2018-purpose-study.

10 "Purpose 2020: Inspiring Purpose Led Growth", *Kantar Consulting*, 2020, https://kantar.no/globalassets/ekspertiseomrader/merkevarebygging/purpose-2020/p2020-frokostseminar-250418.pdf.

11 Sisodia, Raj, Wolfe, David, Sheth, Jag, *Firms of Endearment*, Pearson Education, 2014, https://www.firmsofendearment.com/.

CHAPTER 3

12 Schreiber, Uschi, Lutz, Karen, Keller, Valerie, Isenegger, Reto, "How Purpose Can Reveal a Path Through Disruption", *EY Beacon Institute*, 2017, https://www.ey.com/Publication/vwLUAssets/ey-how-can-purpose-reveal-a-path-through-uncertainty/$File/ey-how-can-purpose-reveal-a-path-through-uncertainty.pdf.

13 "The Business Case for Purpose", *Harvard Business Review*, 2015, https://hbr.org/resources/pdfs/comm/ey/19392HBRReportEY.pdf."The Business Case for Purpose", Harvard Business Review, 2015, https://hbr.org/resources/pdfs/comm/ey/19392HBRReportEY.pdf.

14 "The Business Case for Purpose", *Harvard Business Review*, 2015, https://hbr.org/resources/pdfs/comm/ey/19392HBRReportEY.pdf.

15 Schreiber, Uschi, Lutz, Karen, Keller, Valerie, Isenegger, Reto, "How Purpose Can Reveal a Path Through Disruption", *EY Beacon Institute*, 2017, https://www.ey.com/Publication/vwLUAssets/ey-how-can-purpose-reveal-a-path-through-uncertainty/$File/ey-how-can-purpose-reveal-a-path-through-uncertainty.pdf.

16 Ibid.

17 Schuyler, Shannon, Brennan, Abigail, "Putting Purpose to Work: A study of purpose in the workplace", *PwC*, June 2016, https://www.pwc.com/us/en/about-us/corporate-responsibility/assets/pwc-putting-purpose-to-work-purpose-survey-report.pdf.

18 "CEO Purpose Report", *Brandpie*, 2019, https://thinking.brandpie.com/ceo-report/.

19 "Purpose 2020 Whitepaper", *Kantar Consulting*, May 19, 2018, https://www.kantar.com/Inspiration/Brands/The-Journey-Towards-Purpose-Led-Growth.

20 Cone, Carol, "The B2B Purpose Paradox", 2020, https://www.carolconeonpurpose.com/b2b-purpose-paradox.

CHAPTER 8

21 Rigoni, Brandon, Asplund, Jim, "Strengths-Based Employee Development: The Business Results", *Gallup*, July 7, 2016, https://www.gallup.com/workplace/236297/strengths-based-employee-development-business-results.aspx.

CHAPTER 9

22 "12 Recruiting Statistics That Will Change the Way You Hire", *Officevibe*, April 27, 2017, https://officevibe.com/blog/12-recruiting-stats.

23 "The Ultimate List of Employer Brand Statistics", *LinkedIn Talent Solutions*, 2016, https://business.linkedin.com/content/dam/business/talent-solutions/global/en_us/c/pdfs/ultimate-list-of-employer-brand-stats.pdf.

24 Spar, Benjamin, Pletenyuk, Ilya, "Global Recruiting Trends", *LinkedIn Talent Solutions*, 2018, https://business.linkedin.com/content/dam/me/business/en-us/talent-solutions/resources/pdfs/linkedin-global-recruiting-trends-report.pdf.

25 Hogan, Maren, "9 Employee Retention Statistics That Will Make You Sit Up and Pay Attention", *TLNT*, November 30, 2015, https://www.tlnt.com/9-employee-retention-statistics-that-will-make-you-sit-up-and-pay-attention/.

26 Ibid.

27 Hirsch, Arlene, "Don't Underestimate the Importance of Good Onboarding", *SHRM*, August 10, 2017, https://www.shrm.org/resourcesandtools/hr-topics/talent-acquisition/pages/dont-underestimate-the-importance-of-effective-onboarding.aspx.

28 Clear Company, "7 Stats the Prove Training Value", *HR Exchange Network*, Stevenson, Mason, https://www.hrexchangenetwork.com/learning/news/7-stats-that-prove-training-value.

29 "Employee Training is Worth the Investment", *go2 Tourism HR Society*, 2020, https://www.go2hr.ca/training-development/employee-training-is-worth-the-investment.

30 Baumann, "The Onboarding New Hire Statistics You Need to Know", *Urbanbound*, 2018, https://www.urbanbound.com/blog/onboarding-infographic-statistics.

31 Rizkalla, Emad, "Not Investing in Employee Training is Risky Business", *The Huffington Post*, August 30, 2014, https://www.huffpost.com/entry/not-investing-in-employee_b_5545222.

32 Everett, Cath, “Survey Shows Employees Want More Workplace Training”, *The Learning Wave*, Training Zone UK, June 29, 2012, https://www.thelearningwave.com/survey-shows-employees-want-more-workplace-training/.

33 Sorenson, Susan, Garman, Keri, “How to Tackle U.S. Employees’ Stagnating Engagement”, *Gallup*, June 11, 2013, https://news.gallup.com/businessjournal/162953/tackle-employees-stagnating-engagement.aspx.

34 “What Your Disaffected Workers Cost”, *The Gallup Organization*, March 15, 2001, https://news.gallup.com/businessjournal/439/what-your-disaffected-workers-cost.aspx.

35 Kim, Rachel, “Gusto Report: Community at work”, *Gusto*, July 21, 2016, https://go.gusto.com/rs/110-WOX-868/images/Framework_Community_at_Work_Survey_final.pdf.

36 Hirsch, Arlene, “Building and Leading High-Performing Teams”, *SHRM*, July 15, 2019, https://www.shrm.org/resourcesandtools/hr-topics/technology/pages/building-leading-high-performing-remote-teams.aspx.

37 Roomtoescape.com, “21 Collaboration Statistics that Show the Power of Teamwork”, *Bit Tech Labs*, https://blog.bit.ai/collaboration-statistics/.

38 Dewhurst, Martin, Guthridge, Matthew, Mohr, Elizabeth, "Motivating People: Getting Behind Money", *McKinsey & Company Research*, November 1, 2009, https://www.mckinsey.com/business-functions/organization/our-insights/motivating-people-getting-beyond-money.

39 Lee, Christina, “Employee Job Satisfaction and Engagement”, *SHRM*, April 2016, https://www.shrm.org/hr-today/trends-and-forecasting/research-and-surveys/Documents/2016-Employee-Job-Satisfaction-and-Engagement-Report.pdf.

40 “Right Management Poll”, *Right Management, ManpowerGroup*, December 18, 2014, https://www.manpowergroup.com/media-center/news-releases/Attention+Managers+4+out+of+5+Employees+Plan+to+Pursue+New+Career+Opportunities+in+2015+According+to+Right+Management+Poll.

41 Dodd, Graham, Rubin, Daniel, “2015 Inside Employees Minds Study: Overview and Implications”, *Mercer*, 2015, https://www.mercer.com/content/dam/mercer/attachments/global/webcasts/new-research-reveals-surprising-views-on-careers-mercer.pdf.

42 Ibid.

43 “Right Management Poll”, *Right Management, ManpowerGroup*, December 18, 2014, https://www.manpowergroup.com/media-center/news-releases/Attention+Man-

agers+4+out+of+5+Employees+Plan+to+Pursue+New+Career+Opportunities+in+2015+According+to+Right+Management+Poll.

44 "2016 Global Management and Rewards and Global Workforce Studies", *Willis Towers Watson*, 2016, https://www.willistowerswatson.com/-/media/WTW/Insights/2016/09/employers-look-to-modernize-the-employee-value-proposition.pdf.

45 Sturt, David, Nordstrom, Todd, "10 Shocking Workplace Stats You Need to Know", *CareerBuilder.com*, March 8, 2018, https://www.forbes.com/sites/davidsturt/2018/03/08/10-shocking-workplace-stats-you-need-to-know/#35e3f112f3af.

46 Rigoni, Brandon, Nelson, Bailey, "Leadership Mistake: Promoting Based on Tenure", *Gallup*, December 21, 2015, https://news.gallup.com/businessjournal/187871/leadership-mistake-promoting-based-tenure.aspx.

47 OC Tanner, Novak, David, "Here's the No. 1 Reason Why Employees Quit Their Jobs", *NBC News*, June 21, 2019, https://www.nbcnews.com/better/lifestyle/here-s-no-1-reason-why-employees-quit-their-jobs-ncna1020031.

48 Mann, Annamarie, Dvorak, Nate, "Employee Recognition: Low Cost, High Impact", *Gallup*, June 28, 2016, https://www.gallup.com/workplace/236441/employee-recognition-low-cost-high-impact.aspx.

49 "SHRM/Globoforce Employee Recognition Survey, Fall 2012 Report", *SHRM, Globoforce*, September 21, 2012, http://go.globoforce.com/rs/globoforce/images/SHRMFALL-2012Survey_web.pdf.

50 Ferrazzi, Keith, "Technology Can Save Onboarding from Itself", *Harvard Business Review*, March 25, 2015, https://hbr.org/2015/03/technology-can-save-onboarding-from-itself.

51 Greenberg, Margaret, *Profit from the Positive*, McGraw-Hill Education, 1st Edition, July 30, 2013.

52 Glassdoor Employee Appreciation Survey, *Glassdoor*, November 13, 2013, https://www.glassdoor.com/about-us/employees-stay-longer-company-bosses-showed-appreciation-glassdoor-survey/.

CHAPTER 10

53 Our Tribe—WD-40 Company, 2020, https://wd40company.com/our-tribe/.

54 Ridge, Garry, "The WD-40 Company Tribe Story: How We Turned a Great Company into a Community of Belonging", *LinkedIn*, July 7, 2018, https://www.linkedin.com/pulse/wd-40-company-tribe-story-how-we-turned-great-community-garry-ridge/.

55 Harter, Jim, "4 Factors Driving Record-High Employee Engagement in U.S.", *Gallup*, February 4, 2020, https://www.gallup.com/workplace/284180/factors-driving-record-high-employee-engagement.aspx.

56 Harter, Jim, Mann, Annamarie, "The Right Culture: Not Just About Employee Satisfaction", *Gallup*, April 12, 2017, https://www.gallup.com/workplace/236366/right-culture-not-employee-satisfaction.aspx.

57 Kruse, Kevin, "Why Employee Engagement", Kenexa: The impact of employee engagement, September 4, 2012, https://www.forbes.com/sites/kevinkruse/2012/09/04/why-employee-engagement/#495816c63aab.

58 Osman, Bulent, "Reversing Low Employee Engagement in Manufacturing", Forbes, April 17, 2018, https://www.forbes.com/sites/forbestechcouncil/2018/04/17/reversing-low-employee-engagement-in-manufacturing/#41a769628f0f.

59 Porges, Maggie, "Dale Carnegie Training Uncovers Major Drivers of Employee Engagement in US Workforce", Dale Carnegie Training – Business Wire, February 11, 2013, https://www.businesswire.com/news/home/20130211005999/en/Dale-Carnegie-Training-Uncovers-Major-Drivers-Employee.

60 Branham, Leigh, *The 7 Hidden Reasons Employees Leave*, AMACOM, 1st Edition, January 3, 2005, https://leadershipbeyondlimits.com/wp-content/uploads/2013/06/WhyPeopleLeave-Branham.pdf.

61 Harter, Jim, Adkins, Amy, "Employees Want a Lot More From Their Managers", *Gallup*, April 8, 2015, https://www.gallup.com/workplace/236570/employees-lot-managers.aspx.

62 Adkins, Amy, "Only 35% of U.S. Managers Are Engaged in Their Jobs", *Gallup*, April 2, 2015, https://www.gallup.com/workplace/236552/managers-engaged-jobs.aspx.

63 Brim, Brian, "Strengths-Based Leadership: The 4 Things Followers Need", *Gallup*, October 9, 2015, https://www.gallup.com/cliftonstrengths/en/251003/strengths-based-leadership-things-followers-need.aspx.

64 Twaronite, Karyn, "A Global Survey on the Ambiguous State of Employee Trust", *Harvard Business Review,* July 22, 2016, https://hbr.org/2016/07/a-global-survey-on-the-ambiguous-state-of-employee-trust.

65 Brim, Brian, "Strengths-Based Leadership: The 4 Things Followers Need", *Gallup,* October 9, 2015, https://www.gallup.com/cliftonstrengths/en/251003/strengths-based-leadership-things-followers-need.aspx.

66 Adkins, Amy, "Only 35% of U.S. Managers Are Engaged in Their Jobs", *Gallup,* April 2, 2015, https://www.gallup.com/workplace/236552/managers-engaged-jobs.aspx.

67 Conway, Joe, "Towers Perrin Study Finds Significant "Engagement Gap" among Global Workforce", Towers Perrin – *Business Wire*, October 22, 2007, https://www.businesswire.com/news/home/20071021005052/en/Towers-Perrin-Study-Finds-Significant-Engagement-Gap.

68 Mikhail, Christine, "The ROI of company culture: Why companies should look at culture's impact on profit", PDR Blog, July 29, 2016, https://www.bdcnetwork.com/blog/roi-company-culture-why-companies-should-look-culture%E2%80%99s-impact-profit.

69 Burrowes, Kevin, "19th Annual Global CEO Survey", PwC, February 2016, https://www.pwc.com/gx/en/ceo-survey/2016/landing-page/pwc-19th-annual-global-ceo-survey.pdf.

70 Dvorak, Nate, Pendell, Ryan, "Culture Wins By Getting the Most Out of People", *Gallup,* July 31, 2018, https://www.gallup.com/workplace/238052/culture-wins-getting-people.aspx.

71 Crabtree, Steve, "Worldwide, 13% of Employees Are Engaged at Work", *Gallup*, October 8, 2013, https://news.gallup.com/poll/165269/worldwide-employees-engaged-work.aspx.

72 "New study shows we work harder when we're happy", March 21, 2014, *University of Warwick*, https://warwick.ac.uk/newsandevents/pressreleases/new_study_shows/

73 "What Your Disaffected Workers Cost", *The Gallup Organization*, March 15, 2001, https://news.gallup.com/businessjournal/439/what-your-disaffected-workers-cost.aspxhttps://news.gallup.com/businessjournal/439/what-your-disaffected-workers-cost.aspx

74 Hastwell, Claire, "8 Ways Great Company Culture Drives Business Success", *Great Place to Work,* November 5, 2019, https://www.greatplacetowork.com/resources/blog/8-ways-great-company-culture-drives-business-success

CHAPTER 12

75 Kuijpers, Dymfke, Simmons, Virgina, van Wamelen, Jasper, "Reviving Grocery Retail: Six Imperatives", *McKinsey & Company,* December 3, 2018, https://www.mckinsey.com/industries/retail/our-insights/reviving-grocery-retail-six-imperatives#.

76 Van Auker, Tracy, Wegmans Press Release, Wegmans, February 18, 2020, https://www.wegmans.com/news-media/press-releases/great-place-to-work-and-fortune-name-wegmans-one-of-the-2020-fortune-100-best-companies-to-work-for-ranking/.

77 Natale, Jo, Wegmans Press Release, Wegmans, November 7, 2019, https://www.wegmans.com/news-media/press-releases/wegmans-ranked-1-on-list-of-the-2019-best-workplaces-in-retail-by-great-place-to-work-and-fortune/.

78 Jonson, Hollis, Taylor, Kate, "Review of the best grocery chain in the US", *Business Insider*, March 6, 2019, https://www.businessinsider.com/review-of-wegmans-the-best-grocery-chain-in-the-us-2017-6.

79 Rohde, David, "The Anti-Walmart: The Secret Sauce of Wegmans is People", *The Atlantic,* March 23, 2012, https://www.theatlantic.com/business/archive/2012/03/the-anti-walmart-the-secret-sauce-of-wegmans-is-people/254994/.

CHAPTER 13

80 Wikipedia: Servant leadership, Wikipedia, https://en.wikipedia.org/wiki/Servant_leadership.

ABOUT THE AUTHOR

Paul Epstein is an expert in leadership and organizational culture with nearly fifteen years of experience as a professional sports executive for multiple NFL and NBA teams, a global sports agency, and the NFL league office. In his role he leads and coaches business teams, most recently the San Francisco 49ers. It was there that Paul had a life-changing transformation—he found his 'Why': to inspire purpose in others so they can play offense in life, a calling he has followed ever since.

As Founder of Purpose Labs, Paul is on a mission to impact millions of lives by sharing his message of Playing Offense as an author, keynote speaker, business coach, and leadership trainer. He has installed the Playing Offense playbook with professional sports organizations, Fortune 500 leadership teams, Chief People Officers, MBAs, and professional athletes—all to live and lead with greater purpose, performance, and impact.

Paul received his MBA from the University of Michigan following his undergraduate degree at USC. He resides in Pasadena, California with his wife, two labradoodles, and their future leader, PJ.